# PERSEPHONE

*He had done what he had to do. All the time he slept she lay there longing acutely for him to go, and when he did she felt the most immense relief and vowed that now she had escaped his presence she would never never put herself in that position again. It was the best thing ever to be free and by herself again.*

Persephone loses her innocence in the Underworld, but finds herself. She is Everywoman, coming through darkness, betrayal and disillusion to discover a new life, a new sense of herself. And she is many women in Jenny Joseph's extraordinary novel, which retells the Greek myth of spring and winter, of good and evil.

Demeter the earth goddess is every worried mother struggling to understand her daughter. Hades is the reckless man, brutal, possessive, but mellowed by the girl he takes for himself, the woman who goes back to him.

In *Persephone*, Jenny Joseph has created a new kind of novel, a story made up of many stories, *our* stories, using poetry, narrative, parody and many other kinds of writing. Like the myth itself, *Persephone* is unforgettable.

*Cover illustrations by Irene Reddish*

# Persephone

## JENNY JOSEPH

*Jenny Joseph*

## BLOODAXE BOOKS

ISBN: 0 906427 77 0 hardback
      0 906427 78 9 paperback

First published 1986 by
Bloodaxe Books Ltd,
P.O. Box 1SN,
Newcastle upon Tyne NE99 1SN.


Bloodaxe Books Ltd acknowledges
the financial assistance of Northern Arts.

Typesetting by True North, Newcastle upon Tyne.

Printed in Great Britain by
Tyneside Free Press Workshop Ltd, Newcastle upon Tyne.

'Who then is Persephone? Is she a moon-goddess? Is she a corn-maiden? Is she a queen of the dead, as she was to her ancient worshippers? She is all these "Goddess and maiden and queen" but she is also an ordinary young woman embodying the actual experience of girlhood . . .'

George Thomson, STUDIES IN ANCIENT GREEK SOCIETY

'Blessed is the mortal man who has seen these things, the rites and mysteries of Demeter, but he who has no share of them in life will never be happy in death when he has descended into the darkness of the grave.'

HYMN TO DEMETER (about 650 B.C.)

# Acknowledgements

Extracts from Part II of *Persephone* were published as a special issue (vol.VII no.1) of the magazine *Argo* in October 1985. Some poems from *Persephone* have previously appeared in the *Bloodaxe Book of Contemporary Women Poets*, edited by Jeni Couzyn (Bloodaxe Books, 1985), in *P.E.N. Broadsheet*, and as a Mandeville Press poem-card.

The cover illustrations and frontispiece are by Irene Reddish (model: Elspeth Penny). The photostory section (pages 234 to 245) was designed and produced by Bloodaxe, with help from the following:

*Photographer:* Moira Conway.
*Prints:* Lisa Mullin.
*Models:* Elspeth Penny (Persephone), Roger Neville (Hades), Farne Conway, Fay Gilder, Thomas Gilder, Marcus Robinson, Diana Taylor and Judith Taylor.
*Locations:* The County Hotel and The Bookhouse, Newcastle upon Tyne.

# PART I

The summer had been ended for some time
If not officially
Before the shock of greyness, blanketing,
Pressed the blind season up against our faces.

Winter, my God, a familiar I had forgotten:
That's all I needed.
The portcullis dropped and locked around our houses.
The long worthwhile campaign to build the town up
Surrounding it with fruitful fields was seen
To have been only a little flourish; frivolous –
The house of straw of the pig before the wolf.

'The dark is back' the eyeless morning said
'The wide white dawns and evenings when the girls
Were out in the meadows gathering at every hour
Are blotted out. They are not beyond the horizon
Waiting their turn to be brought back with all their flowers
When the ball heaves them round, like clock figures
Wheeled to the front when the hour strikes. No horizon
Nothing but a flat plate filled with fog
Jammed in a sphere no breeze can pull apart.'

'So be it, morning of my dearth' I said
Deliberately got back into bed
Gathered all heavy covers I could find
To blot the nothing out, hiding my head
And sank into the nothing in my head.

Then
Close in my ear a blackbird called its song.

*

## Persephone

Exhausted by the festivals
She let herself be led in the afternoon light
Down the field path, the light becoming frail
Non-combatant as these strong spirits passed:
Spirits of night casting shadows backward
Towards the day, operative in their realm.
And with them, spirits of the long night. While the light lasted
She still struggled, still felt she ought to struggle ·
Not to let her companions dance without her
Not to be absent when the man went to plough
Chickens gathering from all sides, looking for seed,
Horses, messengers,
People in and out of houses – the world alert and crowded and she
        there.
But when the dark shut off these active people
Blotting them as if, like a flower drawing in,
They covered their heads with their hands, and crouched in the
        ground
So when the sides of the steep lane became darker
As she drifted lower among umbrellaed beeches
And the sun withdrew, it was easier
Only to move downward, not to twist up to catch
The light on the fields, not to strain to find
A way to the edge where maybe a runnel of gold
Still showed where the open lay.
The strangeness of not wanting the day then silenced her.
'That's better' the shadows said 'you are getting like us.'


## Demeter

Little turrety clouds in an eggshell sky
Like separate skeins of smoke, a charcoal grey
Like bars of black sand under a clear slack-tide;
A sharp outline of roofs, but under this edge

12

The mass of houses sinks in the dark on the ground.
No light-chinks through it yet, no night-time gold
Only the silver cold of the distant sky
Stretching away to the Poles' unpeopled fields.
Workers retired to rest, the harvest done
Gathered under her eye from Pole to Pole.

                *

A woman, her supplies baked, her jams stored
Takes stock of her sleeping domain. Floor swept
Milk set for the cat, oven clean for tomorrow.
She sits for a while surveying, enjoying. This
Has been a good fruitful day as if some kindly
Person had been standing by, fount of energy
Like light from golden hair, encouraging.
The cakes turned out well and the house is all in order.
She thinks of her mother's spirit. When she was young
Her mother would come and straighten everything
Prop up the plants in her bit of garden, mop
The floor in no time with no mess and suddenly
All would be right again.

It has grown late while she sits, too dark to see.
Her skin shudders, head jerks. 'Must be I'm tired'
And suddenly a cat miawls. She shudders again
And gets to bed.

                *

All gathered in and stacked. Men gone to rest.
Demeter, before light fails, throws one full glance
On these far northern harvests, safely gathered.
Now as she travels home, she sees her hearth
Swept clean and ready, the milk bowls set for cheese
Sweet-smelling cooling grasses laid round the fat
Shapeless-bellied marrows by the path.
Everything you could wish for! Such a daughter!
Gift of the God indeed, Persephone.

Powerful, efficient, Demeter is wearied by
The help men need from her, her endless journeys,
To barren pathetic farms to make things grow,
Even good places need her constant attention.
She notices, as she travels, the state of the crops,
But her mind has reached home, there her little nymph
Will have all in order, the blue garb warm from the sun
Fresh and washed for tomorrow. She thinks of her hands
Quick little hands, firm-fingered, always busy
But kind and tender when her mother's tired.
'She will be singing now as she kneads the bread.
She will be patting it into special shapes
Making dolls of it and biscuit men;
Dipping those pearl-nailed fingers into cream
And licking, little cat, with quivering tip
Of moist red tongue.'
She sees her twisting her bright hair into knots
Shiny as corn plaits
The curling bits like vines have strayed on her neck
Downy, like a baby's,
Her eyelashes can blink like a butterfly
When tears shake her body,
And like a vase
Full of good things her slender body stands.
Spry, firm and rounded, best fruit of all her harvests.
And from her toes,
That grip the earth beneath her grass-silk feet
Blue-veined in the delicate instep –
To the crown
Of gold-swathed hair, soft and cool as duck-down
Her body seems to laugh, to sing, to say
'Oh glad and funny and marvellous where I am
And everything is here to entertain me.'

With the smile to greet her daughter on her lips
And the words she'll say already moving them
Nodding and smiling as if to herself, Demeter
Travels the last lap of her journey home.

# 1

Yes, well, of course, you could say it was a nice view.
Where? Oh yes, well, you see Sir, the thing is
The thing is I never look at it. Never go near.
I suppose you *can* see all over London, yes.

Yes, I was glad to move here. There's all the comforts.
Lovely to have a clean place. I keep it clean
That I do do, even if I say so myself.
I like modern and I thought I'd like
To be a bit private. We didn't have no space there.
I thought the block was beautiful when I saw it.
You get some people as'd complain in Heaven.

I use the lift of course when I go out
To get me bits and pieces. I'm not
A big eater. I keep it down
To once or twice a week.
Some people spend their lives queuing in shops
With me it's in and out.
I'm sorry I've not tea, Sir, to offer you
It's early closing you see . . . Yes, I live alone.

Well, when you got a nice place you don't bother
To go out so much do you? What's the point
Trekking into them dirty places when
You can sit more comfortable in your own home? I don't say
I'm lonely now. Maybe before I got –
Here, this may interest you. They say that when
They were building this block of flats, about half way up
They'd got, or maybe putting in winders,
This young lad, first job on the buildings, this boy
He fell from the top to the bottom, down the place
They afterwards put the lift. His first day it was.
I didn't know about that till I'd moved in.
Of course they couldn't really bury him

Too smashed for that he was. I sort of think
He's, like he's buried here.

                    I lost me daughter
Year before I moved here. They thought the move
Would help me, see, help to get over it, like.
I wouldn't go too near that winder Sir.
You think a lot when you're alone, and sometimes
I act like my daughter lived up here with me.
I couldn't think she wasn't anywhere.
I used to think, about the time when kids
Come home from school, I'd hear her feet on the stairs
Well, no, it'd be the lift. Oh, just sixteen,
Sixteen she was when she was took. Oh Sir
You didn't ought to make me talk about it.
Nobody knows. Nobody knows what my Pam meant to me.
Beautiful she was, everyone, not just me, said it,
Beautiful.
And kind and cheerful. I'd come in from work
On Saturdays – I worked in a baker's Saturdays –
'Made you a pie, Mum' she'd say 'you sit down
I'll do the tea.' She was a good good girl.
I sometimes get to think the two of them,
Pam and the lad who fell,
Are somewhere down beneath this tower, – they say it goes down
Down and down; – and I'm not lonely then.
I suppose I think one day I'll meet them there.
I couldn't go on if I didn't think she was somewhere.


*Demeter*

Set in her eye was the jug upon the table
Sun on scrubbed step, the wooden bench, the stool,
The dipper full of milk, the oatcakes cooling
On sanded hearth. And Persephone

16

Persephone with some wreath or pretty thing
Some new little game to please her mother with,
Persephone with berries from the woods
Her daughter with lush cresses from the streams
Persephone who could get a bloom from a stick
And break the gravel into myriad flowers;
So set in her eye that when she saw the room
She thought she saw her daughter standing there
And wondered why she did not answer her.
Then she saw the dwelling wasn't tended
Nothing prepared or orderly, bowls unscoured
Her daughter not there. Well, she would soon come
Her mouth said, while she straightened; but her heart
Went calling everywhere.

As the sun dipped behind a ridge of trees
Demeter ran through the darkening countryside.

The pure pale evening saddened round the trees
Which seemed to have no leaves at close of day
Black on white only; the light went suddenly
And blotted out the earth beneath her feet
Blotted of flowers and fruitage buds and petals
All drawn into the dusk that covered the ground.
Too fearful to go home and have her hope
That Persephone would be waiting there dashed down
Demeter wandered calling through all that night
Hating the dark and the creatures that brushed past her.
Night wailings drove her on – she didn't know where;
And when exhausted she got back, her house
Seemed years untenanted; face drawn, eyes drained
She looked on the fields as the sun rose and saw
The colour was gone out of everything
Sunk with Persephone out of her world.

# 2

She went into the opening in the wood and knew almost at once that someone else was walking there. It was barely a little bosque, and in daylight would have been no more than a cluster of bushes on a common. She was making for the houses on the other side, and thought that taking the path would shorten what was becoming a tedious trudge. It was always more pleasant not to walk along a main road.

Had she not been distracted by the evening with friends and made vague by drinking wine, she might have been alert enough to overrule her instinct not to show fear. She was used to considering it low to presume danger to her person. Other people were after all as entitled as she was to walk through a wood. The long training they say always stands us in good stead took over in this emergency and so she lost the minute when she could easily have gone back to the road.

The man, who can hardly have believed it when he saw her turn off the road of her own accord, very soon caught her arm. Again, the minute when she could have roughly shaken him off or driven her knee into his crotch passed in surprise and a sort of disembodied curiosity. A short panting struggle landed her on her back on the ground among dead leaves for he was tall and stringy. The very little strength left in her from the long weary walk after the meal in an overheated house dissolved as his breath in her mouth and nose sickened her, and the smell of his hand pushing on her face to keep her head down. It was sweetish yet acrid, smelt stale and she tried not to breathe in his exhalations as she would have avoided the caried breath of a dog that has chewed infected meat. But she could not move her head. He had pinioned her with his abdomen and jammed her neck against the bole of the tree with one of his shoulders. She sensed the foetid fumes from his stomach and its functionings being puffed over her face.

He told her he had a knife. She was aware there was something exaggerated in his pose. It was almost as if he was trying to keep up his courage against her because, although she felt it was ridiculous how long a time was passing in which she was doing nothing, in the brief intervals he took his hand off her mouth to undo his trousers she was, in fact, ordering him to stop and not to be so stupid. But it never occurred to her that she could have stopped him and now her right arm, bent back under her, was numb. She tried to push him with her left. 'Give me your watch.' He fumbled at her wrist. At this she too became histrionic. 'You shan't have that. That was given to me,' and when he asked 'Who gave it you – your boyfriend?' she still didn't take advantage of the ridiculousness of this to impose her authority on the situation but heard a melodramatic high voice coming from herself: 'It was my sister's and *She's Dead*,' which, of course, as she had never had a sister, was a total fiction. It crossed her mind that she might be about to lose her life because, from the habit of possessiveness, she refused to have her watch taken, and with that stagey denial her last resistance went.

She really would have preferred not to die in this way because if she were killed she would not be able to keep the incident from her parents. They would be very upset and embarrassed at the sordidity of such a death.

After he had managed to break her knicker-elastic he shoved a somewhat limp bundle of flesh at rather than up her vagina, and suddenly seemed to have attained whatever it was he thought he wanted. His timidity, his feebleness was now apparent. He seemed half apologetic in the slight delaying of his departure. But she was still in her role. As all she wanted was his non-existence she exaggerated her grief to make him run away quicker. She didn't want to have even that amount to do with him that alter- cation and explanation and blame would bring. When he ran off through the wood she went slowly to the road and started limping along it. She had hardly bothered to wipe her face. It was rare in these parts for a woman to be on that road at this hour and a car stopped and drove her to the house where she was staying. The driver was solicitous and urged her to report the incident to the police but all she wanted was to wash everything off, close her mind and not have to do anything.

## Demeter

For nine unsettled days Demeter searched.
You, on the seas sailing – make for home,
Up anchor and run before the sweet South-Easter.
The great glassy calm of the summer sea
Is about to be havocked and torn by such storms
As never on your lives was visited.
Demeter is searching along the shore of the ocean
Has pulled her bewilderment and loss about her.
Wrapped in her unkempt cloak she has withdrawn
From everything but longing for her daughter.
She is calling for Persephone everywhere.
Along the shore and high up on the pass
Where the great boulder marks the wind's boundary
She leans on the rock famished, unwashed, unregardful.
Not famished for food. Her dry throat stabs
But not for water.
'Stone' she beat her palm upon the stone
'Have you not somewhere in you kept an echo,
Some imprint of what travelled through the air?
You have absorbed the weather and what it brings.
Lichen-marked messages are etched into your side.
Have you no message then at least for me?
If you will not give out my daughter's voice
Keep the echo of my cry with you
For all the years you stay here, from age to age:
"Persephone, my daughter. Persephone!"

Mountain winds and freshets by the shore,
Clouds that sail over water in whose surface
Your faces are taken, racing each other to the land,
Have you not seen my daughter, heard no cry?
Perhaps she has slipped on some smooth weedy rock
And her slim ankle swelling and useless, lies wedged
In one of the caves you lap into. Waves,
Have you not seen her as you dance to land
Child hurt and needy far from help from home?'
The chattering white-caps travelled in to the shore

Keeping breast to breast their foamy line.
'We have not seen her' they hissed and travelled on.
The clouds shaped and reformed watching each other
Concerned with the wafts of air that passed between them,
'Not seen' – the faint denial from far up
Drifted down blue spaces to frantic Demeter.

# 3

'What about that storm Friday night, eh? I don't know what the weather's doing these days. Some people say it's all those Sputnik things they're sending up. Stands to reason don't it? I mean, all these currents of air are altered by mountains and so on aren't they? Stands to reason if you've got those bloody great chunks of steel whirling about up there you're going to upset something.'

'Oh, I don't think so. I read somewhere you'd need thousands of tons, not thousands, millions, *millions*, before you could affect the pressure of one square foot of air at sea level. Anyway, it's not Sputniks now. And that's how they tell the weather, from the satellites.'

'Seems daft to me, sending up a whole lot of heavy metal to tell us the weather when it's that that's ruining it. I don't need some scientific marvel costing God knows what to tell me when I'm soaked to the skin and that frost's going to blacken my beans. How'd you like great chunks of stuff bleeping about in your belly, eh? You'd soon get indigestion. Stands to reason. And all that electricity and radar. Bound to affect things. You never know what the Ruskies are up to. Spying's one thing, but mucking about with our weather, that's quite a different thing. I wouldn't wonder if they hadn't planned it on purpose, they're clever enough.'

'But it's American hardware too.'

'Yeh, they're as bad. Bloody cheek, two rich countries fighting cat and dog and mucking up our atmosphere to do it. I mean, we've all got to share the atmosphere, haven't we? Bass is it, George?' He came back with two full glasses. 'Cheers. Well, as I was saying –'

'Ta. Cheers.'

'Whatever caused that freak storm, that's goodbye to my late marrows. They were coming along really nice. Who'd have thought it – beautiful morning, quite clear, not a breath. I noticed it particular 'cause the wife said there was no drying in the wind and she'd get out and take the kiddie to see the sister while the fine weather lasted – Edenbridge she lives. It's lovely down there. Then the next thing I know is I looks up and there's this black fuzzy cloud creeping over the sky. I got me gear away and home on the bike just in time. It was so dark in the house I had to put the lights on. About two it was and then that black rain came sheeting down. Months of work undone in half an hour. And my missus come home drenched. She hadn't took a coat for the kiddie or nothing and there they were, shivering and dripping all over the kitchen.'

'Same thing happened near enough yesterday and this morning – seemed bright and settled enough at first and then the weather completely changed all of a sudden. It didn't seem natural, I must admit. More like the Tropics. But I still don't think you can blame the scientists.

'Mrs Daley? No, I can't say I have seen her this evening, Harriet. Upset about something was she? No, well, I can't recall seeing her in here at lunch-time and I was here till closing time – on account of the rain. Tim'll be in at seven when the staff come. Why don't you ask him?

'She's a gossip all right, that one. The world's worst. Of course if Mrs Daley was upset about something she *would* be on to it. There's never something wrong, from someone twisting their ankle to a funeral, but what she isn't there, sniffing around, putting her oar in and telling you all her family tragedies. When there hasn't been anything specially bad or tragic happening she goes a bit quietish. I never did understand why a decent woman like Mrs Daley put up with her. Now there's a cheery soul. A generous woman. Quite often I've had a pint set down in front of me and I've said to Joan "Where did that come from?" and she indicates Mrs Daley sitting with her bunch; old Harriet, the scrounger, chipping in with "Well it'll have to be on me next time only I'm a bit short this week" blah blah blah. So I lift the glass when I can get her eye and give her a wink of thanks and she smiles and nods back. Must have been a good looker when she was young. Mind you, she still is. She's still got a trim ankle. But a very decent woman, you know. Got a big family, I think. No time for the nonsense some of these old girls'd get up to if they could. I'm sorry if she's got trouble. It ought to have been Harriet something's happened to, then she *would* have something to talk about. Look at her now, over in the saloon, yapping away to old Vera. Bad news, I shouldn't wonder, when she looks that interested.'

. . .

'I felt sorry for her – I really did. You couldn't hardly get a smile out of her, and you know how cheerful she usually is – well, I mean, she's always the one that cheers us up – Mrs Daley I'm talking about, ducks, no I don't think you'd know her. Would Freda know Mrs Daley, Vera?'

'You always feel the better for seeing Mrs Daley. I mean, she likes a drink and a laugh. It's not the same when she's not in. If she's down, there must be something wrong. I've never known her like it before. She don't talk much about herself, do she, Vera?'

'Doesn't get much chance once you get going, Hatty.'

'Oh go on. I'm not like that, am I, Freda? You tell your mother. Mind you she got us a round straight away, same as she always does. She never comes in and sits down and waits but always goes straight to the bar. The first thing you see of her is she's bringing the bottles over. She likes a drop of Guinness herself; I've never seen her drink anything else. Says it's the barley in it that does you good. I thought it was the iron myself. I will say that for Mrs Daley though, she's not behind hand with bringing it forward if you know what I mean –'

'Yes, it'd be a grand place if everyone acted like Mrs Daley there.'

'Well, maybe she can afford it better than some. I wouldn't mind being able to splash it around a bit like that, I don't mind telling you.'

'Is she fairly well off then Harriet? I never heard anything about what her old man used to do – she's a widow, I suppose, like us?'

'Well, I really couldn't say for sure. And that's another thing about Mrs Daley it wouldn't hurt some others to copy – and, Vera, naming no names, you know who I mean –'

'Oh him, Hatty – I wouldn't bother about old George – he ain't got nothing to do but spread gossip since he never went back to work after his operation.'

'Lost his job did he? After all those years there?'

'I think they did try and keep the job open for him. Tried to get someone temporary; but in the end they had to get a man they knew would be there. You couldn't blame them really. Poor old George though. It must've been a blow. He was always on about never missing a day, wet or shine. And to hear him talk you'd have thought he'd gave ruddy birth to Webbers – what with stock control, and the market and industrial security and all. You'd think he was at least one of the scientists there, not just the store-keeper.'

'Is that what he was? Store-keeper? Well I never. Well I never! I can see he didn't want to give that impression.'

'I don't mind saying straight out what *I've* been. Fifty years a waitress, I'm glad to say, and hardly a varicose vein though I have been drawing the pension for longer than anyone else round here. And I don't mind showing anyone to prove it if they doubt it.' She upped her jersey skirt until you could see the roll of orange stocking round her thighs, and the leg elastic of her turquoise satiny drawers coming to meet it – and a still remarkably neat pair of legs they were – and she rolled down the stocking and pointed her foot high in the air.

'Hey, Mum,' whispered Freda, a pale-faced much less energetic woman, fiddling with the stem of a glass with bitter lemon in it. 'The men are looking from across the bar.'

'Let them look,' Vera the erstwhile waitress said loudly. 'Do them good. A look won't hurt you will it boys?' she shouted across to a group of men coated with white dust from a building they had been demolishing. 'If I could drop a few years it'd be more than a look from Vera, you bet.'

'That's right Vera, it's a great life if you don't weaken! If I didn't have to get back home and keep young Geoff here out of trouble, I wouldn't mind coming and doing a bit of demolishing round your side,' a stocky fifty-year-old answered her.

'Come on round, Alan. You mean that great big ball you use, swinging on a chain?' Shrieks of laughter. 'Eh, eh. Tell young Geoff not to mind me. You know old Vera don't mean no harm. I've got grandsons twice his age.'

'Game old thing, Vera,' Alan remarked to Geoff, aged about twenty and whose fair skin had blushed crimson. 'Must be eighty-eight if she's a day. Still does all her washing by hand in her sink. She was very good to my old Mum in her last illness. Never let a day pass without popping in to see if she wanted anything. They ought to get her a ground floor flat, they ought, but she doesn't complain. Says she likes the view. Give her and her mates a drink, Joan, and I'll have another Guinness, and a light and bitter for

Geoff here, and one for yourself.'

'No, no Alan, I'm off. The van'll be in Market Street and it won't wait.'

'Are you sure now? You're welcome.'

'No, no. I've got to be going.'

'Cheers, Alan.'

'Good luck, Vera.'

'He's a good lad, that Alan. His mother was a good woman too. They all lived round here, brothers, sisters, a huge family. Moved to the South Coast when they pulled the cottages down to build the flats, all except Alan and his Mum. Pretty woman, Dora. Eh, they were hard times – ten she had to feed. Her husband was a carpenter but he only had one lung from the war and a skilled man in those days didn't get what a paper-boy gets today. It's better now, much much better, and them who says it isn't don't have very good memories. But we had some fun, I can tell you. Dora, eh. She was a pretty woman, but sweet with it.' Long drink. Long sigh. When she toddled back from the Ladies she said to Harriet:

'What was that about Mrs Daley then? Upset was she?'

'Yes, she was, near frantic. Said she couldn't stop because she'd missed her Patricia down at the bus terminal where she was supposed to meet her. She'd just come in to ask Harry something. Who would Patricia be then, Vera? Her granddaughter?'

'No, it's her brother's daughter I think, and she doesn't half dote on that girl. Mind you she was a beautiful child and she's been nicely brought up – well you can imagine. Mrs Daley's got class. That's what she's got. You never hear foul language from her mouth – not that she's stuck up. If you've worked as a waitress that is something you can recognise when you see it – real class – not la-di-da manners and fur coats – but class. Anyhow, she has this Patricia to stay from time to time. I think there's a bit of bother between the girl's parents or something, and it's peaceful for the girl over here with her aunt; and they're thick as thick; go to the markets, out to the country, come back laden with fruit from farms for bottling. One day they just hopped on a Green Line bus to some bit of a common – we had bramble jelly to last us through the winter. I've never seen such blackberries. Of course, she wouldn't bring her in here. I suppose she still thinks of her as a little girl though she must be seventeen or eighteen by now. Well, left school some time ago, anyway. What was up then?'

'She bought us our drinks and then she had some urgent pow-wow with Harry. I couldn't really gather what it was about but it sounded as if she wanted to know who'd been in this morning. Course, I bin in since twelve and I had noticed a stranger. Tell you the truth what I noticed was he kept on at the girl he was with to have something to eat and wouldn't she like a pie or a salad. And Harry said the salads weren't ready yet but he could make her one as soon as Joan came back from the bank. But she said she wasn't hungry. It's all she did say. She didn't look at all well. He seemed to be concerned about her – very concerned he seemed.'

'And didn't you tell Mrs Daley?'

'No, I did not. She didn't ask *me* did she? Keeping everything very hush hush from us, and when she'd gone Harry wasn't giving anything out either. If it's not meant to be my business then it isn't my business I thought. You never know the background to these things. And if you do tell someone something you think they ought to know, you're only snubbed for being a gossip. Oh no, I've learnt when to keep my mouth shut – least said soonest mended when it comes to that sort of trouble.'

'What sort of trouble?'

'Well, you know, family trouble. Anyway, how was I to know the girl and chap had anything to do with Mrs D.? I wouldn't have minded talking to him – interesting-looking sort of chap, but he was too wrapped up in his own thoughts, you could see that. I did happen to be by them when I went up to the bar and I said "Nice day" just to make them feel at ease. And he said "Oh yes, very" but she said, this was the strange thing, she said "*Nice?*" like that, as though I'd said something daft. Well, I mean if someone says "nice day" it's not meant to mean anything, is it?'

'It's a pity you didn't tell Mrs Daley all that. What the girl look like?'

'I don't really recall her much, the man more, except that she was very pale and kept saying "no" and not much else. She had a hat on, a big wide one, so you couldn't see her face, it was under the shadow of the brim. I remember thinking how unusual it is nowadays to see a young girl in a hat. Pale peeky little thing she looked.'

'That doesn't sound like Patricia.'

## Demeter

Each morning Demeter thought of some new place
To search in. Hopeful from habit she woke
Not believing Persephone could be nowhere. And each new day
Woke clear and beautiful as if to say:
'So translucent the air, so pure the colours
So still the currents like a young girl standing
A gift to the sight before you notice her,
That surely today Persephone will come.
No ruffle, no blearing, clear but unhurtful light;
Sweet air, no burn, no clutch of cold, no bluster.
Surely she must come on such a day.'
And as she trudged on dusty silent roads
Calling and seeking, and getting no trace, no answers
She hurled her grief towards the depths of the sea
She called to the Holder of the Winds and Thunder
'Sky God and Sea God, you who are my brothers
Why are you absent when you see my grief;
Feasting in indifference on the fat of the land
That men I care for bring you? You laugh
And guzzle and tell jokes in your distant hall.
As long as you are feasted, what do you care?
As long as you are flattered, nothing matters.'
Demeter, anguished, driven, is calling Olympus
And goads Poseidon so he turns in his deep
Sleepy autumn cavern; beware, O sailors,
O fishers dreaming in the hazy days,
Such a reversal that shall hit your fleet
As musing by the prow through palmy days
You never thought of; oh many the smashed arm
Raised to protect against the giant wave.
Many the hand crushed with the skull beneath timbers
Slung on remote shores that never till now
Saw signs of shipwreck. The waters
Flung up to the lowering heavens are one great surge
Of boiling rapids and through the dark midday
Go scudding white caps to the end of the world
The furious coursers of the Sky Gods' anger.

# 4

Dear Joan,

Nothing much of interest to relate but the house is so quiet, almost as if it was waiting for something (and of course it is in a way, and soon everything will be in motion with doors banging and feet clattering and voices yelling – as if they didn't know you were in the kitchen!) that I thought I'd drop you a note now while there's a bit of peace. It would be lovely to see you on the 25th and we'll try and get to the beech woods this time.

The only thing that's happened round here is that a lorry sliced a piece off next door's front garden the other day and left a great crater in the pavement – the house on the corner, not the Grays' – and the extraordinary weather. I wonder if it's been like it up your way? We have been having the most beautiful mornings, so delicate and fragile you almost feel the world couldn't last any longer, the leaves all clear colours, yellow and red and translucent, hanging quite still in a sky the colour of sugared almonds. Then there comes a blurring over of the sunlight, a sort of very gradual withdrawal, a sort of dimming; then a slight rain, very warm and quiet and still, and it doesn't clear again. Then sometimes suddenly from nowhere rain pelting down with ragged black clouds whipping along at a great speed behind it and wind dashing about in the streets – every sort of vile weather and as suddenly it's gone. Another day in the evening there was a huge black cloud with a sooty fuzzy edge which looked as if it would spread down and cover everything and blot out all the light in the sky above the roofs. But lo and behold! the black suddenly was gone leaving the sky full of soft colour – lemon, orange, and spear-like streaks of purple cloud, and above them the blue sky widening out with puffy grey balls lit by some far beam.

Sorry to go on so about the weather – my mother used to say I ought to have been a meteorologist (but I gather they hardly look out of the window – just pore over their instruments) but it really has been so dramatic. Which is more than can be said for life in this house – thank goodness, I suppose.

I can hear the approach of the clatter of anything but tiny feet so must close now. We're all looking forward very much to seeing you on the 25th.

Love, Shirley.

# Demeter

For nine terrible days Demeter searched.
'If only I could know' she thought, 'if only I knew
It would not be so bad'; and yet she feared
To turn a corner high up on some pass
In wild and lonely mountains and see the body
Crushed and lacerated on the path before her,
Or swollen floating in some foetid pool.
Hope makes you mad but madness keeps you going.
Not for one instant could she pause or rest
But turned and turned, turning in her tracks again
Often not seeing the traces she peered into
The prints of trotters, leaves torn by the wind:
Everything might signify but nothing led
To any knowledge. Every night the mists
Curled in valleys she had made beautiful.
Her torches lit up the miasmic arches of trees
Dreamlike unstable unreliable.
The world was so full, so crowded, but no one had seen
Or noticed or paid attention or was there
Or prepared to give her news about her daughter.
The world began to seem like a mirage she could not
Touch or make hear, or hear from. She
Stepped through it as through smoke and it closed behind her.
Did the people she asked not see her, not hear her voice
Had they not seen Persephone, not heard her cry?
Were she and her daughter ghosts with no substance, no power?
As in a fever she sometimes heard stray voices.
They neared and receded, they pleaded they wept they begged
Her to take some milk or bread, to eat, to rest.
They brought fresh garments, wanted to bathe her feet
But she could not stop, could not sit, could not manage to swallow
Could not bear their voices, their touch, their clutching.
Their solicitude was for her and their well-being
They did not want to help her find her daughter.
Wrapped in her worry only one tight wire
Throbbed and throbbed through her being, pulsed in her eye
Twitched in the veins in her shaking hand: my daughter.

# 5

It is surprising how there's always someone to notice every little thing you do when you'd as soon keep it to yourself, and that occasionally there's some extremely important event in a well-populated place and not a body seems to have been there or heard or saw anything about it.

It had been a glorious summer that year. We couldn't remember a better harvest. Perhaps that may have had something to do with it – that we were all so busy we let the children roam more than usual. Well, day after day, we'd come in from the fields – I'd come in earlier than the men to get supper ready and see to the hens and Pip (she was christened Janet but her father always called her his little Pippin so she was never anything but Pip) would come in about this time, brown as a berry, covered in mud from the brook where she'd been playing all day – they were building a dam or something to sail their little bark boats in. She was very ingenious and good with her hands, Pip, right from a tiny child, and she'd come along with me to feed the chickens and throw them grain – most of it stuck to her sweaty little hand. She'd squat down in front of the cock, who was a bit of a fierce fellow I remember, that one, and talk solemnly to him as if he understood. 'Naughty, naughty cock,' she'd start, 'now your'e not to eat it all up before the chickens have a chance,' and he cocked his fierce flat head to one side and looked at her with his bright eye, for all the world as if he was waiting for her to give him the word, and then if he came a bit near her hands to which the grain was sticking, ready to dart at it, she'd quickly brush it off and run away. She was a bit frightened of him but she couldn't leave him alone. She was small for her age, very dainty, but strong – you never saw a healthier child. Her hair seemed to ripen with the corn – of course she was out in the sun from morning till dark – until by the autumn it was a sort of reddish dark gold. She was coming up to ten that year.

Goodness, I am rambling on. Shall I fill you up? Help yourself to the scones – they're not long out of the oven.

Well, one evening she didn't come in. As soon as I'd seen to the men's supper and the hens I went down to the stream but she wasn't there. The other children she'd been playing with earlier in the day said she'd gone back over the fields at the usual time and they thought she was going home and they went home soon after. We searched all night. We had our own dogs that she'd grown up with with us, and the next day the police covered the ground again with theirs; we poled the river and we emptied the farm pond. After ten days the official search was called off. They had asked at every house for miles, searched in every barn, sent dogs into every deserted shack – there's a lot of cover in farming country, put out messages on the radio. Not a thing did they find; not a whisper. They couldn't do anything more, but of course I didn't stop looking – couldn't stop. My husband tried to get me to eat, to sit down, to go to bed; and I did try. But no sooner would I get my head down on the pillow than I'd imagine I'd heard something. I suppose it was only the wind or the cries of the small animals being swooped on in the copse, but I'd be up and out in a flash, an old mack over my nightie and my feet stuck into any boots that stood by the door, and with a torch I'd go straight to a particular spot I'd seen so clearly in my mind's eye – maybe a low branch of a tree she was caught in, maybe trapped by a fall of a bank into the stream. But there was nothing and then I'd just roam around for a time until I stumbled back from exhaustion.

Many's the time I woke with a start when the morning light came through the scullery window to find myself in the kitchen chair with muddy boots on and a torch in my lap. And for an instant I'd think it was only the day before we'd missed her and that it was important to hurry out and continue the search; and then I'd realise it was weeks and weeks.

Then the storms came. It was a year of extremes – great heat in the summer and pelting storms in the autumn and the river rose higher than it had done since we remembered. We were very busy making things secure and covering stacks and I just didn't go on my walks for a bit – there was always some emergency where an extra pair of hands was needed. Then when the water receded and everything began to dry out I went for a walk by the stream that runs through our farm to the river, the stream where the children used to build their dams. More to see the level than anything else. And there, thrown up into the grass on the edge along with all the muck was a little square of blue cotton. It was very faded and streaked with slime but it was hers all right. Pip had been given three coloured hankies by her Gran with a little yellow flower embroidered in the corner. The blue one was her favourite and she used to knot it round the strap of her dungarees. Of course I wanted to start them searching all over again, but we still found nothing. And we never have from that day to this.

You wouldn't think it to look at it now, but the farm went downhill after that for a bit. My husband lost heart when I couldn't take any interest in it. I must have been in a sort of coma for months – "depressed" they called it but that's not what I'd call it. I'd call it death – death in life. When I think back to that time I think of it as being entirely without colour – like a negative. It can't be so but I can't remember anything green, any leaves growing on the trees, any colour in the sky – nothing like that – just bleak and wintry. I imagine the North Pole must be like that – except that would be brilliant white, wouldn't it, and this was just dim and blank.

I must've been strong to pull through I suppose. I think I took it so bad because although I'd had other children she was like an only child, being the girl. The boys had all grown up quick – they were strong strapping fellows – good seats for horses, they practically lived for horses. Pip was very near to me. 'Bright little Pippin,' her father used to say, 'there's going to be lovely apples from you one day.' Oh it does seem hard.

Well, what pulled me through was this: apart from the fact that if you don't die you go on living. My sister had a child the next year and she was poorly and the baby sickening and I went to help her. I've always been quite good with babies – animals too. I used to say I can manage anything that grows but doesn't talk. It's not that I'm clever, I suppose it's just from growing up on a farm. You just seem to know when you can keep life going and when you can't. So my sister got stronger and the baby – why, once he was over the first difficulties he was a beautiful healthy child. Never looked back. They asked me to stay on a bit – they realized how empty my own home would be and how attached I'd become to the boy. But that was the trouble. They began to feel I was treating the child as if he was mine – which I suppose I was. So I had to go in the end. It was a long haul, and none too easy between Frank and me at first after I'd been away. But there's always a lot to do on a farm, thank goodness, and I've never been naturally idle. Frank got me those greenhouses you see over there and I cultivate quite a lot for the market. You see things coming up every year, you see new babies and the babies growing up and them getting babies – there's so much of it going on all round you've got to go on with it. I used to long and long to hear something. You know, find another trace of the girl. Sometimes when the mood was on me I'd go walking late into the dusk, but now I wonder whether it isn't better not to know. I've never seen her dead, you see. I think over the years I've got to feeling she's still part of the farm, still part of me. It's funny I should have survived and me being the older one – and she gone under that autumn – we had to presume she did drown. It should be her growing out of my old flesh but it's the other way round with us. She's still part of me but I've gone on.

I've talked more than enough now. Only a very few people have heard the whole story. I don't talk about it. It's part of us, like the air and the seasons coming and going. You know – but you don't comment.

Perhaps you'd like to take some eggs home. And there's a box of tomatoes for you to pop in the back of the van. I've more than enough – there's a limit to the amount you can chutney. We've had a glut this year. And perhaps your wife would like some of my bread. I always bake a few extra. People can't resist my bread as a rule.

## Demeter

Demeter, travelling, saw a scar in a rock
Which, as she neared it, widened to a cave.
She sensed something within, and felt a flicker
And swiftly crouched and sidled and stood there
Holding her torch high up. The basalt walls
Winked and sparkled with hundreds of tiny points
Answering her light;
Riches of darkness, black gold, wealth without fire.

A bundle stirred on dry leaves in a far corner.
'Whoever dazzles my sight with gleams of day,
Creature of the sun, let none come near
Who is not totally on misery bent.
For I am all the sorrows of the world
Condensed into a blackness. Get you gone.'
'You cannot be all sorrows, Hecate,
For I am part of you now, and no one
Will ever picture grief without first thinking
Of wretched Demeter, sorrowing for her daughter.
Woe's harbinger, for once your company suits me.
Have you any sight of Persephone?
She disappeared from home ten days ago.
Lurker in caves, consorter with woe, oh sister
Have you not seen her?'
'Demeter, sorrowing, you are welcome here.
I see your cloak is nearly as dark as mine now
All tattered and bedraggled – but could you not lower
That terrible white light? Alas
I have not seen your daughter.'
Demeter let drop her arm, her muscles unstrung
And sank upon the leaves. 'But I have heard –'
'What? You have heard her? When? What did she say?'
'Wait. Demeter you are entering regions
Where your swift mind and foot must slow their pace
To suit another system. I have heard
A call most eerie, a terrible shriek
That even for me who hoard the desperate's cries
Sent something up my spine like a cold clamp
Suddenly throttling the nerve ends. And a wail so dreary
Drifted over the stifling afternoon air
That the pale ghosts that gaze on Lethe waters
Dazing through eternal mindlessness
Lifted their heads it seemed in sympathy.'
'Was it my daughter? When was this? Where was she?'
'It may have been your daughter. The scream was young.
The moon was at the full.'
                              'O Hecate
You are the first one who has given me hope.'

'How can what I have told you give you hope?'
'Come on, here, bring your torch and come with me.
You are my only friend, my help, my sister,
My other self in sorrow.' Unwillingly
And slowly – oh so slowly for Demeter –
Hecate unbent her painful joints
And hobbled, protesting and grumbling, after Demeter.

# 6

The lorry seemed to appear out of nowhere – it must have been masked by the dip in the ground. The girl was completely unaware of it until it was above her, its huge wheels, white from the quarry, churning above her head. She had a second to fear the studded axle as it rode over her and felt an excruciating jar and crunch where her neck went into her shoulders. Her head was then full of a terrible animal screaming. She did not know it came from her. For her the world was full of this unremitting terrified squeal – there was nothing else – the yelping of hysterically panicked pain and the place it was coming from: the smashed body on the oily road. Her mouth and chest was full of something she wanted to get rid of.

At the inquest only one person mentioned the cry. A nearly blind woman who had been sitting, as she usually did, in a dark little room that looked on to a quiet alleyway at the back of the High Street. People who had been nearer said it was impossible – they had heard nothing above the din of the traffic, she couldn't possibly have. Sitting alone all day she was always imagining she heard things. She said she heard a great crash and rumble of wheels, iron on stone, like the old farm wagons. But the bystanders said that all they remembered was the cloud of dust round the lorry as it disappeared.

*Demeter*

They travelled to the river Cyane
And sat to bathe their feet and take their bearings
Two mourning figures, now much like each other.

The little wavelets bobbed up to the bank
And seemed to linger, seemed to hesitate:
'Demeter we have always worked together.
Sweet wells and springs you need to freshen your earth

And you have always taken pleasure in us.
I have lapped and washed your Persephone's feet
When summer-long she ran among my shallows
And played among my cresses and my willows.
I am glad it is I who can tell you something
Though desolate I had not the power to stop them.
I did what I could. I bring you here her girdle.
When the grim Lord rode in his chariot
Dark beams flashing from the mighty wheels
I tried not to be afraid and hide my face.
I summoned my sisters, my myriads of nymphs
That swim in their thousands in our layers of water.
And in a band we rose, arms linked to arms
To try and make a barrier. What use white arms
Soft raised against that iron? He raised his rod
We had to break up and sink back to our course.
But while he fought to control his startled horses
His attention was distracted from your daughter.
She loosed her girdle and flung it behind her. We caught it
As we sank back. I lay it at your feet.'
The murmur of the water on the stones
Quietened as it receded to its bed
Nudging with a last little ripple the scarf up the bank.

Demeter held the scarf and looked at the water.
She stared at the molten metal that slid down
The curve of the wash as Cyane subsided:
The beams of the sun as it travelled towards the west.
'Terribly bright' Hecate wailed. 'Your daughter
Lost, lost forever.' 'Hecate, be quiet.'
Demeter fingered the scarf and gazed at the water.
'The sun' she said. 'Of course. Helios sees all.'
She looked up. He was far away, far in the west
And moving inexorably down the sky.
'Come on' she said 'Helios will have seen.'
Hecate hunched over and did not stir.
'I cannot come into such withering brightness
It would shrivel me up, any more than the sun
Can come into the regions I inhabit.

Go Demeter and I, your sister spirit,
Will gather my strength and wait for your return.'

Through lashing rain, through dripping gloomy forests
And plains which drizzle and cold mist made seem endless
Through swirls of dead leaves, and sting of squally hail showers
And choking thunderous clouds creeping down hillsides
Demeter pushed her way until she came
Clear of the havoc to the western shore.
Far away Helios spread his hair
(Floating in peace before his boat should shoot
The rapids of the darkness)
Surveying his lands, his islands, his seas, his streams,
Coating the tops of waves, the white cliffs
That lay at this edge of the world, with a cool light.
Embarked among the glowing clouds he looked
All powerful, all benignant, never daunted.
He stayed his progress and the earth lay still
Held in perpetual balance and at peace.
Even as Demeter called from the edge of the zone
He sank and there was nothing. The clouds' arms drew him
Covering him with soft cloaks, laying him down
But still his shaft he sent as a messenger
And like an arrow it went through the upper air
Opening up vistas while the shrubby earth
Condensed and blurred. A stillness settled on it
From the strange busyness high in the sky.
Demeter rested a moment with the quietening earth.
When she raised her head they had separated:
The clear high heavens and the thick mass of the ground.
From the dark woods and plains she left behind,
Ravines and shrub-filled gorges and winding roadways
Sprang little lights now here, now there, now myriad
Yellow and soft, winking among the trees –
Her people setting lamps in cottage windows
To shine through her night and bring her safe return.

# 7

'I'm sorry, Mrs Dumesne,' the man behind the desk said. 'I cannot do anything. It is the magistrates' decision. It is nothing to do with this department. You were in court weren't you? And you heard what the chairman said? I am sure it was explained to you. Well, I'm sorry, but there really is nothing that I can do. That is the law.

'The judge isn't here. He doesn't work here. But Mrs Dumesne, I must warn you that even if you saw him I don't think he could reverse the decision. He can't tamper with the process of the law. He can't just do what he wants with it any more than the rest of us. He doesn't make the law, you know.

'I wish I could help you but really there is nothing I can do if it's got that far. Now please don't get so upset Mrs Dumesne. It may not be all for the bad in the end. She's there for her own good, really she is. And there are people there who will help her, help her get the best out of it. If she's a good girl and tries to co-operate she might benefit from it in later life. You're really not making it any easier by going on like this.'

## Demeter

On the grey rocks bleak as the Graiae she sits
Demeter with her head upon her knees.
'Helios, alas, such regions of the world
I did not know existed; what purpose
Did this serve till I came, matching my grief?
No one can have needed such terrible shores as these.'

'Stored in the corners of the world wrapped
In image, if you like, every landscape
To match the heaving of the heart, or the blank eye
That has looked on horror and become sightless from it.
From vapours and from grit the gods created
All the multiform beauties of the earth

And a cold sigh can rime the grasses, till a forest they stand
Breathtaking in shining glory under my feet
My red-tipped arrows which leap through the frigid air.
These shores, this greyness this flat rippleless mire
Stretches from everlasting to everlastingness
And like the skeleton beneath the skin
Of the goldenest maid or nymph, or like the fibre
Waiting in the peach to wrinkle with age
(The juices once drawn away, only pap left)
This ashen landscape is under every turfed
Springy flower-starred hill with trees aloft
And sprays of water scattered from blossom boughs.
The earth thick with green and growing matter –
Peel back the flesh and grey gum stares at you.
Stare through the turf and slow, miasmic, rises
The total dark that feeds it and engulfs it:
The house of dust where not a beetle can breathe,
Where I am broken off and cannot enter.
You should know it. It is your brother's kingdom.
And desperate for light and cheerful laughter
There he has taken your Persephone
To be his Queen, to stay with him forever.'

# 8

I haven't spoken about this to many people in my life. You know I couldn't touch a woman for a long time after I came back. When I first went overseas I used to think of nothing but. I thought that if I could get that again I'd never want anything. But when I did get back, I was sick the first time I passed my hand over a buttock. It brought it all back to me: the piles of bones. And thinking of the bones brought the smell. It wasn't just that it was bones – I'd seen that before, not a pretty sight, but it stayed as a sight, back of a butcher's. It was that you thought you could tell from the way the bones lay what had happened to them, when they . . . before they . . . when they were more than bones.

And I got the awful thought, and I couldn't get it out of my mind, suppose there was still someone alive in there; an open eye, waiting through all those years for the pile to be moved off its chest – some little child in a coma, kept alive by – God knows what, the warmth generated by that putrefying mass, protection in a great rotting womb. More than anything I was terrified we'd turn over a pile and I'd find a live eye staring at me.

I had nightmares for years. One in particular I didn't seem able to shake off. It doesn't seem so horrific when you tell it. I was in a swimming pool, inside a building, in a basement or something. And the water was warm and very high. And it got warmer gradually and nearer the roof. It was very green, a sort of darkish unpleasant green and I was lifted nearer and nearer the ceiling and I stifled more and more with the warmth increasing and another part of my brain was aware that there was a little boiler, like those cosy stoves – we had one in our back room when I was a child, with a glass front. And I could see the glass front of this small stove let into the wall of the swimming pool under the water where they usually have the grid. Until my shoulder and the top of my head was jammed up against the ceiling and this horrible warm green water was coming slowly up my chin and over my mouth. The details were all very ordinary; it was the atmosphere of that dream that was so indescribably horrible.

You could see the bones hadn't been flung in piles like stripped carcasses of animals; you could see they had been left there to become bones. Someone had just jammed the door on those dying people, too weak to turn their heads, their necks too brittle from long lying, and left them to become a heap of bones. And it must have taken some a long time to die because there were big people – you could tell they must once have been big and heavy, strong as an ox in their day. And these big hulks were the ones on top. The little small bones, the children and small ones, were at the bottom. And there was one large yellow heel bone stuck into a hole in a tiny head. The heel must have ground into the socket of some child's eye as the grown man heaved and urged for air – no more able to stop his propulsion than the unborn child pushing its way, being pushed, into the light of day to gasp for air. You can see I couldn't touch the curve of a woman's hip bone after that; not for a long time. And to this day I bring up if they touch my mouth with theirs.

I know they say once you're dead you're dead, but I don't know. Before that I'd have said the same, that you cease to be human when you die anyway so it doesn't matter much what happens to the remains. But after seeing that – no. I found myself thinking – I don't know what the association was – about a story I'd heard as a child, some fairy tale, well no, it wasn't a fairy tale, some old folk tale or such, about a girl who died walled up in a cave, or bricked up in a wall or something, because she went and buried her brother and he was meant to be left unburied for disgrace – I suppose it was the walling up that reminded me. It had always seemed a pointless story to me – being so heroic over nothing – but after that it seemed to me the most perfect story in the world. For days, for weeks, it seemed the only thing that was important at all – that there had been this girl way back whose only concern was that her brother shouldn't end up like those – those remains.

Turn back
Turn
Back into the shell
Turn
Back down between thin grasses to the earth
Turn away
Turn from such light as there is
And cover your head in a small space
Creep
Creep into the blankets
And sniff, with eyes shut, for the salt and stale smell of the
                bedclothes.
Creep down between the humps of unwashed covers
Heave them above you. Sink beneath the floor
Sink, comatose, shred-winged fly, in the stagnant
Water of the neglected tank
Sodden with cold, inert with slime, airless.
Shrink between cracks in the wall like a woodlouse
There lie curled
The eyeball turned on itself, turned and stuck there.

Turn back
Turn away
Creep inward
Burrow, but not forward, only
Down, in, under
To the dark, to join with the dark
As desperate body clings to unheeding body
Through the black vacuum sinking separate shaking
In a grasp as hopeless as the blank clutch of lust.

# 9

When I went to visit her she was sitting in the same chair. You almost felt she'd been sitting there all the time since last week. She was dressed, but maybe she hadn't bothered to undress since I'd seen her last. She was crouched with cold, but her shawl was off her shoulder, and although her hair obviously worried her she didn't pin it back but occasionally made a futile gesture to push it off her face where it immediately fell back as she didn't alter the angle of her head. I think in my absence she may have groped her way to the yard, clawing a bucket of coal with the arm that now lay in a strange shape, fingers twisted, pulpy tips up to the ceiling, for there was a half-full bucket and there had been a fire in the grate, though the room had that severe cold in it of a long unheated house. Certainly the old man in bed in the back room could not have got the coal. He said he didn't eat, didn't need anything because he could eat nothing, trying to make it sound like a complaint but not bothering to think up a want, but his bed was straight and neat and the room not neglected. A flannel and towel on a rail and a clean glass of water were within his reach. So she must have managed to do for him what he needed. The only sounds came from the occasional heaving turning of the old man and grumbling hawking noises from his throat and innards. She was soundless. It would have been unkind to make her make the effort to bring from such buried depths the spark that makes people speak. It was as if the self that could power the speech was sealed and dropped fathoms under the dark swayless sterile waters of some inner sea, or engulched in the impermeable clay bands in strata far beneath workable soil where things grow.


## Persephone

Those who turn their face to the wall
And cover their heads in blankets at midday
These are mine.

Those who smile and say 'Thank you, that would be nice' and
             never go,
These are mine.
Those who are found, when work has been agreed,
Paint got, gear kept, clothing bought and delivered
Who followed 'I'll be there for sure' with 'Don't fail me now'
And are found sitting in the yard, tools caked, old cans
Cluttered round inert ankles, socks with dead flies
Soaking in week-old wash-water;
Those who make a point
Of asking intently and urgently for help
And when one has struggled through rain to do so
Are nowhere, and the man who has struggled
Is later met with a righteous 'where were you then?'
These are mine.
Those who order all sorts of things through the post
To beautify their homes (to have a home)
And plan to make family trips (to make it a family)
And do not open the parcels and are asleep on Sundays,
Those who take the word for the deed, and sit listless in bars
Miles away from the scene they have suggested
Miles away from the one they suggested it to
Who now sits arranged, ready, and will sit so all evening,
These are mine.
And those who, not winning, stare behind glass
'My limbs not being moved for me, I cannot move them' –
Those who despair in the season for despair,
These, all these, are mine.

Come down with me
Whom I would call my followers
(But following suggests that you could move)
Come down,
You who turn from things,
Into my blank domain where the silence would suit you.

Here only worms and roots grow
Here's unstriving dust
Shells and scabs and the remains of things.

Only worms and roots, husks and cases
And even they
Are colourless and blind.


## Hades

Here is this great black ache, this yawning cavern
Here is so much space, so much longing
Here is such emptiness, such need for filling.
I know the richness of earth, that my sisters, my brothers
Have kingdoms so crowded, so busy, so crawling with life, every
       inch
Is fifty times over sown with seeds, with insects,
Insects that live in stalks, whose stalks have joints
Where thousands of specks of living matter breed –
All that on a tiny turf the size across
Of a little finger's cushion. And the air jostling with pollen
And the sea crammed with fishes. There is hardly room
For a mite to breathe, and yet they breathe, they breed,
They sing, they dissolve, they merge, they float, they rot
And more and more life pushes, bustles up
Taking in air and dancing in the sunshine.

Here in these still cool halls
Where three days' journey greets not a living being
Not a flick of a shoot uncurls, nor a crack burgeons,
Here you could live in peace and rest with me,
And bring some gentle movement to this vacuum;
Break the tamped walls into gleaming shoots
From whose calm sheen and silkiness like your skin
A healthy breath would blow and give me health
And lay the dust and make a rich soft bed
And there I could enjoy you and we would sway,
Laved in sweet breathings coming from the rocks
Bathed in the springing juices of love, seeping
Balmful ichors throughout my dusty kingdom.
And the dark dazzle we would generate

Would better Helios in the thin blue air.
Such riches I would bring out of the soil
If you would join with me and stay with me
As could not be thought of on mean mountain sides
Washed by the enervating ether. Such strengths
I would heave into your smooth curved hips with mine
And give your shining eyes
Such waters of reflection that no one
No one on all Olympus but would say
'The Father of the Gods – he thought her fair
And followed her on earth with sleight and wiles
But Hades' great desire has made her his
And stronger and more powerful than Hades' Queen
There is none.' And there never can be. All
Will come to you, as I now come to you
And lay my dusty black head on your belly
White, small-rounded, silky, to be the filling kernel
Fruit of my great need.

Power over life and death, Persephone,
The hand that stays, the hand that pulls the thread,
Signals the quit-all, gives the ghosts their rest.
Ease me of my restlessness, receive me
And let us sink with our spirits into sleep
Down and down within each other's sleep.

# 10

'When I was a child,' she said, 'if ever I came into the house and it
was empty I was overwhelmed with a helpless feeling. I could not
imagine anyone could feel other than an appalling weight at
having to be the one to do things – get meals, clear the fires, see to
the boiler, open or close windows at the right times, get things into
their proper places, have things ready, turn knobs the correct
distance so that the water-softener didn't go wrong and flood the

bottom passage. I would never have the skill to keep the boiler in. I laboured and spared no effort, and did what I thought the grown-ups did but a thin film of grey ash on damp floors was the result. It was one of the things I was dreadfully certain of – one of the things that made the thought of growing up seem like being tipped in a cold grey flat field with no shelter – that I would never be able to make the place feel right, the fire going, the things that didn't belong in the sitting room not in the sitting room, everything working, things ready, the house functioning. It would not light up and hum properly for me. It would remain black and cold and grimy but I would not be able to go next door to sit in their welcome and warmth and brightness and wait for someone to come and fix everything in my house, because I would be meant to be the one who did that. I would be in it and there was no way I could stop the journey to that desolation of incompetence.'

It is strange, the ideas some people have about themselves. To look at her and her house – both struck me as very efficiently arranged, and pleasant – you'd never think that she would have felt those doubts about her capacities, even as a child.

# 11

It is the saddest thing in the world to hear, on a summer evening, a child say: 'Can I play?' so quietly that the children ignoring him do not need to hear.

This child was stocky with all his clothes on. The ones playing were wild and active. Some had taken off their shirts and their ribs rippled through their close sun-browned skin when they lifted their arms. Their loose hair was flapping with their leaps and dodges. They noticed everything, were quick and alert and full of go. Every now and then when he stood near them, his hands still in his pockets as if to reassure them he would not touch their ball until they permitted it, by some common unspoken consent, or agreement that over there was better, or merely by tossing the ball over there to have him once again on the edge where he could be ignored, they moved away a little, almost like shrugging off a fly. They never once said anything to him, not even a little boy on his own who he went near to, or did anything but look through and round him. Over his head, round his legs, went the ball, never to him, at him, for him, and so did their eyes and words. And in his soft polite nice way he said again 'Can I play?' and positioned himself ever so tactfully where they could throw him the ball if they decided to. But they had decided not to. He drifted out as he had drifted carefully in and circling unobviously came round again and desperately keeping his voice the same, for the same useless sentence, said: 'Can I play?'

# 12

She was such a nice woman – of all people for it to happen to, she didn't deserve it. Very hard-working and loving – she never sat and expected people to wait on her – always stretching herself to save other people trouble. Hard-working and loving and honest. And she wasn't a fool. No, she didn't strike you as a fool, exactly. She was an intelligent woman – a cut above the people she worked with. You'd say she'd travelled a bit – I wouldn't have been surprised if she wasn't part foreign. But a little too honest, perhaps, if you know what I mean. She never thought anyone had anything in their head she wouldn't have had, so if someone told her something she believed it. Exacting, she might have been, if you was near to her. I think she may have made people feel a bit uncomfortable because they expected she'd be easily shocked. They felt they had to live up to her standards. That she expected it. That's what they liked her for. So they lied to her. But I always got on very well with her. I always found her very tolerant. The person she was hardest on was herself I'd say.

Well, either they saw they was on to a good thing, or they thought she could take anything, because more than once she was taken for a ride. And really it was a shame. If you think of the selfish bitches who have husbands at their beck and call, looking after them as if they were china and never a smile or a thank you for it – and a woman like that left in the lurch, it makes you agree it's an unjust world.

The time I'm speaking of she was just beginning to go out again after her husband died. She'd looked after him through a long illness, spent everything on trying to give a bit of comfort while he lay dying – and from all accounts of those who knew him he wasn't particularly grateful. When he had been well she was often on her own. He was a great one for following the gee-gees, and she wouldn't drag the kids among all those crowds when they were young. Besides, when he was on the course he'd look around for his pals – just race-course acquaintance you know but he liked to be recognised from meeting to meeting and not have to think about the company he was with. Then, of course, when he couldn't go out, he didn't like to be alone, and his temper wasn't of the sweetest even before he was stuck in the house all day.

It was nice to see how she was really coming out, quite blossoming in a sense. She was a good dancer – she said she'd done a lot of dancing in her young days; and she was good fun. A good talker. You could have an intelligent conversation with her; and she was game for a little party once she got over her shyness. Never stinted when you went round to her place. She liked a little glass herself once she was persuaded it was all right. But never silly with it. She'd never embarrass anyone, or inconvenience them – she'd rather die than put anyone out – and she very nearly did.

Well, she took up with this – I can only call him a con man. We could all see through him. What she saw in him I never did understand. You could see he laid his plans carefully – studied the form so to speak – and really she wasn't difficult to read. He was nice to her – I mean he was always very pleasant in public and he did look after her in little ways – so he should've. He ended up living off her – well, began by living off her. People like that don't waste much time. He never really put his hand in his pocket – but even over that he was watchful. He'd always buy the barmaid a drink first time he went into a pub and chat a lot with the landlady and landlord and then he'd get included, see, and after that well . . . but he did have a funny way of making women feel regarded and that they were not being taken for a ride even if they were paying. She liked going out – the cinema, for a meal and so on, and she had years of not going out to make up for. And he did look quite presentable in a suit. He was a lady's man. You wouldn't find a man there to say a good word for him. And the funny thing was he wasn't a good looker, on the contrary, a skinny bony fellow with a face a bit like a fox, all muzzle. I do sometimes think women deserve what they get. I can't see what any woman could've seen in a runt like that.

Anyway, we could see what he was up to – and as I say, he seemed practised at worming his way in and had a nose for the weak spots – but she was happy and we thought maybe she knew what she was doing. They did seem to have a good time together, and she of course was one to spread things, so there was quite a little sociable circle. And as I say he was personally attentive. You couldn't fault his manners on the surface.

Well, funny things began coming up and they got more and more frequent. She told us once he had had to hurry up North to see his son who was dangerously ill – and of course the boy didn't know to get a decent doctor so she'd begged him to arrange for his son to see a specialist if it was necessary and he was not to worry about the expense when it was a question of his only son in danger, when for a fact Fred, who doesn't make a mistake about faces – and you couldn't mistake him – had seen him not a hundred miles from here, very red-eyed and totally blotto, but more with gin than sorrow. But he knew where to go for his binges – there were places she'd never have set foot in – never knew existed I'll be bound – and she never came across his drinking pals, nor any of his pals, come to think. And his 'dickey stomach', ruined while serving bravely in the war, accounted for some of the less concealable 'turns'.

I came home from work one day and I saw what I took to be a doddery ill old lady sat at the kitchen table. My wife's very good to lonely old people – I sometimes say she collects them, but I wouldn't have it otherwise. So I think: Doris has found another poor old thing to give tea to, and I come round the table and it's Flo. I had such a shock. Her face was all eyes and nose – big glittering eyes looking fixedly out of these great purple hollows; and she'd gone all bony and starey almost overnight. Her eyes looked as if they were stuck open. She said she hadn't shut them for two nights. I've never seen such a change in a person.

Of course Flo being Flo she tried to summon up a smile and greet me and not keep me from my tea. But the minute she tried to speak the tears poured down her cheeks. I've never seen anything so wretched in my life. This woman, who'd been used to dignity and restraint, never in all the humiliations with her husband had she shown a thing, was sitting there quite openly, all dishevelled in the kitchen with this ghastly attempt at a smile on her face, staring ahead of her with the water trickling down her nose and over her chin, and she beyond even trying to wipe it away.

My wife told me later what had happened, as far as she, or indeed Flo, could piece together.

Apparently he had stayed away from work, not feeling well, and she had hurried off to work as usual before eight – she did some lousy ill-paid job in an exhibition hall, selling sweets at a kiosk or something. Anyway, she'd hurried back in her lunch hour to bring him something special and do any little thing for him, and he wasn't there. The bedclothes were thrown back but quite tidy. Everything was very tidy. There wasn't a note or anything. She was worried stiff and also worried she'd be late back for work. It was quite a way. But nevertheless she went through with preparing the fish she'd bought and leaving a note explaining what to do to cook it etc., in case he'd popped out and was on his way back. She added 'Sorry to miss you. Couldn't wait. Take care ' and ran to the bus stop and worried about being late, and practically out of her mind wondering where he was and what had happened. All afternoon she was on tenter-hooks to get home. But when she called out as she ran up the steps there was no reply and everything was as at lunch time, her note staring up at her.

The first thing she noticed missing, trying to think of what errand he could have gone on, and wondering if he had gone out and collapsed and been taken somewhere, was his coat, that had been on the back of the door. But not just his coat, and this is what gave her a jolt, but the hanger too. It took a long time for her to tell – and over the next couple of weeks she'd mull every little detail trying to find some significance in the scanty bits of knowledge that she had to go on, but the long and the short of it was that he'd scarpered, that he'd taken the money she'd been putting by week by week from that wretched job – denying herself, even walking home sometimes to save bus fares, saving for Christmas; that her suitcase was missing and things like hangers, clothes brush, shoe polish and soap; books of Co-op stamps and her little store of coins for the gas meter – anything without a name to it. Apart from that he'd left with exactly what he'd come with. What he hadn't taken were the things she'd given him – a pottery ornament he'd admired once, books she'd bought him and written 'with love from Flo' in. It was a flit all right. He'd had a couple of dog-eared Reader's Digests and an old *Observer* Colour Supplement with some article he'd been interested in. He prized them enough to take them.

What was more appalling to her than the theft of the money – and later she came to realise he'd been filching here and there all the time – was that he hadn't even left her a coin for the gas or to get to work till payday. She said she couldn't have eaten anyway, and for two days she sat looking at the fish in its dressing of herbs and butter going more and more rotten, as if it represented all the care she'd ever given anyone, all the love she thought she'd had from him. When the bit of gas ran out she had no fire and no hot water and it was bitterly cold. She couldn't go out, she said, in case she missed him if he came back. She found out about the missing things gradually. At first she thought he might come back to get some more things. She said that at every little noise in the street she'd start up and go to the door or window. She couldn't stop herself – but there was nothing. She felt if she could only find out what had happened the burden would be lifted. It was not knowing at all what had happened that made her feel sick with worry. If only she could speak to him all would be clear again. She thought there must be some explanation and that seeing him would clear it up at once.

In the end, she said, she summoned the energy to throw the stinking fish out, and, leaving a note that she had gone round to my wife's, and for him to ring her there, she came round to our house.

# 13

Two men were clearing up in a garage near closing time, one much younger than the other.

'Ain't you meant to be meeting Maureen tonight? If you want to clean up and get going I'll lock up here.'

'I may have been meant to be, but I'm not bothered,' the young man said. 'Let the bitch wait; and if she doesn't want to wait, she can go. I may not even go home that way.'

'Why, Dennis, what's she done to deserve that?'

'Nothing. I'm just not bothered. All cunts are the same in the end. I'll tell you. I was once very particular about punctuality – and I don't think you've found me bad about time here have you? I never kept anyone waiting, and especially not a female, not waiting in a public place where they might feel uncomfortable. Oh, I was very considerate I was, and what did I get for it – sweet fuck-all.'

'Goodness, you're a bit bitter, aren't you? Maureen hasn't let you down, has she? I thought she was devoted.'

'I can't get worked up about Maureen. She knows what I'm like and if she wants to hang around, that's her look-out. I tell you, I had a girl once – I used to knock around a lot on my own and with the boys, and then I got this girl. I thought it was a miracle that she'd come out with me at all at first. There wasn't anything I wouldn't have done for her. I wanted her and I got her and it was like all the sloppy songs say rolled together into one and come true. I was a bit cynical before that but with her it all happened to me and I knew what they meant. I was so happy when we started going out together. The world seemed a different place altogether. Well, it was a different place. She was the sort of girl that everyone turns to look at even if their own girl's not bad. Everyone wanted an excuse just to say a few words to her, just to make her look their way, and people in dance halls or even in a shop or caff, would try and get her attention. Well, I got a day off for her birthday. I worked in a factory then and it wasn't easy, but I did, and we were going to go to the moto-cross rally. She loved anything like that, she liked crowds and excitement and engines roaring, somewhere she could be seen and admired, and it was what I liked too. I borrowed some dough. A lot. We were going to make a real splash. It wasn't as if she didn't want to come. For weeks she'd been talking about it and once when we were walking home after a disco – a pretty crummy place I suppose – we'd passed a really posh place, still serving meals, you could see the people sitting down at tables with candles on them and the women were given a flower as they came in. We saw a couple go in and the waiter gave the woman a flower. That really took Junie's fancy and she said 'You know what I'd like to do one day, Den? I'd like to dress up in all my gear and go and have a meal at ten o'clock at night in a place like that.'

'I'd told her about the moto-cross meeting and she was really excited but the other I was keeping as a surprise – I was going to take her to that restaurant – that very one. A friend of mine who knows his way around told me I ought to book a table, so I did. I don't like telephoning much, so I'd gone in and chosen the table by the window. They were all right in there. 'Special occasion is it, Sir?' and I'd said yes, it was my girl's birthday. I bought some new shoes too, Junie was a great one for style – she wouldn't have been seen dead with someone in last year's gear. And I spent a long time getting ready and went to the bus stop in the High Street where I always met her. Well, she didn't come and she didn't come. You can imagine it wasn't very nice dressed up in all my gear with everyone in their work clothes coming and going, wondering why I didn't get on any bus. And all sorts of horrible ugly people got off those buses and not one had Junie on it. I felt like kicking the sides of the bus each time they drove off. And couples met each other, and I felt like kicking them too. After nearly an hour I went to her house. There wasn't any answer, but the next door people said they thought the whole family had gone off together somewhere. Some relative had arrived from Scotland or somewhere. Every hour I came back, and in between there was nowhere to wait but in a grotty old pub down the road, so the last time I came back I'd drunk a certain amount, to fill the time in. You can't sit in a pub and not drink. It was too late to take her out to dinner by now but I wanted to know what had happened. I was worried about her. Me worried about her! That's a laugh. Anyway, as I was going away for the umpteenth time, this little group comes round the corner, and it's them, the whole family and some others, making a terrific racket, and there she was, singing with her Mum and some stupid oaf's arm round her shoulder. I'd got so worked up thinking what I would say to her and telling her all the things that had been running in my mind and imagining myself asking her what had gone wrong, but when I saw them all so daft like that, quite without a thought that anyone might have been wondering and waiting all night, I didn't want to say a word. All I wanted was for them not to see me. Of course they didn't notice me and I skedaddled and then I really did get drunk. Not in a pub. I bought a bottle of vodka, which I don't like and never drink, and took it home and drank it like it was cups of tea. I was ill for days, and of course I lost my job. I didn't do anything for about three years except hang around and bust things up when there was the opportunity, and when there wasn't I made it. Then Joe asked me to help him, tuning up his racer, and I began to spend more time on cars again. That's why I don't mind doing overtime here: the only thing that doesn't let you down is engines – well, if they do you can find out the trouble and put it right. It's usually someone's ballsed up the last job on it.'

'And didn't you ever ask what had happened?'

'I didn't want to know. I saw with my own eyes, didn't I? Anyway, I've one thing to thank that evening for – it's cured me of bothering where females are concerned. It's funny, isn't it – there's that silly cow Maureen would do anything for me, and the less I'd bother the more she'd do, and there was me and Junie, the same. If you want anyone in your pocket, you just pay no regard to them – treat them a bit roughish and they'll come running. I've proved it over and over.'

# 14

He had three customers all day. One was at 11.40 and he wanted two boiled eggs and bread and butter and a cup of tea, for which he was charged 30p. He left one of the eggs. The other was an old lady in the middle of the afternoon in child's socks with a blue and red band round the top over some very stained stockings, who wanted a cup of tea, but she only had 5p – he usually charged 7p but he said not to worry. She took great quantities of sugar and left a damp patch of urine on the chair she had sat on. The third was a child just before he was due to shut, trying to get money back off coke bottles he had picked up. Derek hadn't had a delivery of coke for a month but he didn't ask the firm he dealt with to come and collect the empty crates because he felt awkward about not ordering any more, although he would have got more from the empties than he'd made in a week. He gave the child some potatoes and some cottage pie since it was obvious that what he had got up at 6 in the morning to prepare for 'lunches 11.30-2.30 – snacks all day' was not going to be eaten, though what the child was angling for was crisps and a fizzy drink. He sat at the counter with the child and did a puzzle in his comic with him. Later when the child had gone he realised he must have laid down his fountain pen on the counter to go into the kitchen and the child had taken it. He stayed with his elbows on the counter looking across the empty café through the window for a long time after the time he usually locked up, not doing anything, not dealing with letters, bills, orders, not clearing the kitchen, not even dreaming, now, that they would start to build on the demolished site across the road and that fifteen navvies with money to spend on food would want gammon and eggs and potatoes every day for 10 o'clock breakfast. He knew he would have to do something soon about shutting properly and clearing out, even if it was only to get a job to earn money to settle the bills for food he hadn't been able to sell. He had clung on, mainly because he didn't like to sack the woman who came in for an hour in the morning to do the vegetables, coming here and going through the motions of preparing for the lunch hour day after day; wasting more and more and, in occasional bursts of fantasy or *folie de grandeur* ordering new things from firms he hadn't dealt with before – like thousands of paper serviettes at a discount on every five hundred; and a sack of loose macaroni.

The health inspector had been round. Before Derek took over the café there had once been lodgers in the rooms above and one had complained in the past to someone about the geyser in the bathroom. That had been months ago – another era – but the inspector looked at it and told Derek he must get a certified gas plumber to put a standard fitting in – this one might blow the house up. It made no difference to the inspector to be told the geyser wasn't used any more. The premises were on his list and the geyser was unsafe. Derek knew that he would not be there when the inspector called to see if it had been done. That would probably not be for some weeks. It was not his most immediate worry. He finally roused himself, cleared the counter and went to wash his hands at the sink. A few potato peelings and the remains of a daddy-long-legs were circling slowly round the plug-hole on cloudy water six inches deep. Derek wiggled with his fingers in the muck and although a little scum joined the floating debris no water went down and the slight movement stopped. He sat at the kitchen table, pushing pans and colanders and an open tin of carrots away so he could put his arms on the greasy edge, dropped his head on to them and started sobbing.

# 15

He'd not been too bad the last twice about getting home in time on Tuesdays for her to get off to Bingo, and that had put her off her guard so that it was all the more aggravating and worrying when the clock hand passed the 12 and started to bend, with no hesitation, towards quarter past 6. Visiting time was strictly from 7-8 and it was the very worst time of day for buses up to that godforsaken dreary long road where the hospital was. And then it was a good seven minutes' walk after you got off the bus.

Surely to goodness he knew about visiting hours, how they rang the bell and you had to go, even if you'd only had five minutes and come from ever such a long way away. But most of all she thought, not of her poor feet hurrying for nothing, nor that she hadn't got any flowers yet and the flower stall by the hospital was so expensive, but of Doreen sitting up in bed waiting for her and thinking she wasn't going to come. She could imagine Doreen's face getting more and more set and the mouth trembling as the other visitors trooped in.

Oh he was a nuisance. It wasn't as if the people he was with weren't the same as he saw every day of his life and would see tomorrow. Why couldn't he come in and let her give him his dinner and go out to the pub later? But no, 'once I'm in I like to stay in,' he'd say, 'it isn't as if I plan to delay. It just sometimes happens. Good gracious, girl, you can't run your whole life by the clock, and you need to slake your thirst and have a sit down after eight hours in that heat. You'd complain more if I did come straight home without a pint to make me sweet. Once you get out you need to forget about time for a bit when you've been watching ruddy dials all day.' It was all very reasonable put like that, but it didn't apply the other way. If she didn't keep account of time once she was out of the house, why, she'd never . . . Why should it always be her who had to rush, just because he didn't want to exert himself to think?

When he saw her face and that she had her hat and coat on he remembered.

'Sorry, love, got a bit held up – but I knew you'd still have time to get to the table you like.' When she didn't answer he added a little less breezily, 'Bingo – your table at Bingo.'

She put his food out. 'Your dinner's on the table and your afters is on the sideboard,' she said.

'For goodness' sake, what's got into you? Aren't you going to say hello and give us a minute to wash my hands?'

'You've had two and a half hours since work to wash your hands. I don't know where you find to go at 4.30 in the afternoon. You know I wanted to get off.'

'Oh we knocked off at 2. They stopped the machines. There was an accident. Upset me it did.'

She opened her mouth and shut it again. Her rage had taken her breath. So he could have been in early. She had less than forty minutes to get to the hospital now and he could've been in hours ago. She slammed the door and her anger gave her a move on so she just caught a bus she would have missed if she had stopped to talk to him. Once she was on the bus her anger dropped with her anxiety and her thoughts turned towards Doreen. She could look forward after all to Doreen's smile when she came in with the other visitors. Relaxed, her mind wandered a little to the girl in the bed opposite Doreen. She did hope there'd been no further turn for the worse, chiefly because she knew it was affecting Doreen, who was very sensitive to other people's unhappiness. Their baby was so beautiful and healthy it made you feel almost guilty when you saw what that poor couple were going through. When the babies were wheeled in for visiting time everyone in the ward came to look at Doreen's baby. He wasn't exactly rosy, more a sort of tawny, like a cox's orange and bright open eyes and a neat downy head. He was so awake for a three-day-old baby, she was sure he took notice when she looked at him and spoke. But of course, Doreen had been a beautiful baby. They were all strong and healthy. When you looked at that pale little husband of the girl opposite, with his thin hair and bad teeth, you could see why things had gone wrong for her. She would say that for her old man, for all his obstinacy he was of healthy stock.

Doreen had told her about the girl opposite.

She'd had a bad time as a girl, apparently; never strong. She'd grown up with a stepfather but he had been all right to her – it was her mother that used to take it out on her. She'd been an unfortunate child, in and out of hospital as a baby, had to wear a brace on her teeth and there'd been something the matter with her leg, so she was used to doctors. Her mother was ashamed of her when she got her new husband – that's what she'd told her anyway, and not just the once. Her mother had had a bad time when she was born and she'd accepted the mother's idea that that was excuse enough for taking it out on her. The older woman had certainly scared her off men good and proper with her stories, and how she'd wanted to die when she saw her daughter for the first time. The girl didn't seem to bear any grudge against the mother, Doreen had said, although everything she'd wanted to do, any job she'd tried to get that would have taken her away from home or given her a chance to get on, the mother had prevented. 'I probably couldn't have managed,' she'd said to Doreen. Of course that had made her Doreen wild. The girl was a mousy obliging creature ever so keen to please and very long-suffering and Doreen said you forgot her personality and what she looked like after you'd got to know her a bit. Her Doreen had been up in arms about her. 'I wouldn't have stood for it,' she'd said when she'd told her all the girl had gone through. Doreen was a great one for not standing for things, but then, the woman thought, she'd never had much to put up with. 'She didn't even think it was wrong her mother behaved like that, telling her what a nuisance she was and how she'd never get her off her hands and then keeping her practically chained up at home. "You've not sense enough to last a day on your own," was her favourite statement, "I'd soon have you running back here with worse problems on my hands." She accepted what her mother said until one day she met someone who seemed as useless and undemanding as herself. He'd been brought up in an orphanage and been brought up to do what he was told. Have you seen him, Mum? He's a weedy specimen to look at, but he's very good to her. Anyway, they were the answer to each other and they wanted to get married. At first the girl accepted that she couldn't because her mother told her she couldn't, but either she got some strength from finding someone who liked her, or the boy had more stamina, but they stuck out and got married.' She was quite capable in the house and good with her needle – she'd had some training as a tailoress and tailoring was his trade, and as neither of them had any expectations for themselves, what would have been a hard and boring life to others was just fine for them, as long as they were together. 'You'd think the mother would have been glad, wouldn't you?' Doreen had said, 'but not a bit of it – wouldn't leave them alone, kept on interfering and complaining, pretending to be advising and helping her inexperienced daughter, of course.' The daughter, with what seemed like great dignity, had told her mother that she was welcome to come and have a meal with them when she wanted to come but she would not go to her mother's house any more. The stepfather had come, Doreen said, but the mother stuck out – she wanted her daughter to come to her. They were very happy and peaceful and then she found she'd fallen for a child. Of course the boy – well she supposed he was a man really but when she had seen him he looked so slight and ungrown up – they were both like children really – well, he, according to Doreen, had been in seventh heaven about the baby. He'd looked after his wife before but he couldn't do enough now. She mustn't lift, she mustn't stand. He bought her food he couldn't afford. He treated her as if she was the queen – and so she was to him. But they hadn't any luck. Things started to go wrong from the start and she'd been in and out of hospital for observation and for a month now they'd kept her in although the baby wasn't due for another month. Of course, she oughtn't to have been in the same ward with the girls that had had their babies but perhaps they thought the company would do her good or probably there wasn't room anywhere else – she was just the sort of person that if there wasn't room for someone it would've been her.

All the girls with their healthy born babies were very concerned about her. Doreen said she was a very kind person and not at all malicious and everyone got in a flutter when she was wheeled off for some examination or when some important doctor had arrived with his students. She confided to Doreen how embarrassed she was at the students – it was bad enough when the doctors examined her, it must've been torture for her. She could hardly bring herself to mention it to Doreen. Doreen said you could tell she'd been crying from shame every time but she put up with it for the sake of the baby and her husband.

When she and Doreen's Dad had visited Doreen on Sunday there'd been some panic the night before – she did hope everything would be all right this time – the bus wasn't doing badly. She'd be there in nice time. They hadn't been able to hear the baby's heart or something but then they had and they went on hoping. It would have been kinder, she thought, to tell her she wouldn't have the child. You only had to look at her to know something was wrong, and when you saw the couple together – why, you couldn't imagine her conceiving, let alone bearing a child. She'd have got through the upset – she was patient and long-suffering enough, but to let her and her little husband go on hoping and go on thinking about baby clothes seemed wrong. Why, she'd even overheard them talking about 'baby' as parents with infants do. They were so simple, real innocents. It crossed her mind they might be trying to keep her going because she was an interesting case, but of course she hadn't mentioned that to Doreen – they were all het up about the girl enough as it was, and they ought to have been quiet and resting having had their babies so recently.

She had quite forgotten about her anger with her husband. She noticed that the girl opposite and her husband were holding hands saying nothing. Occasionally he'd straighten the bedclothes or arrange her flowers. Her Doreen was a bit edgy and she told her mother she was a bit worried about baby's eyes. Her mother reassured her that new babies often looked cross-eyed because they didn't really see at all, couldn't focus, but when she thought Doreen wasn't noticing she took a good look and there did seem something not quite right. Doreen hadn't slept so well, the whole ward seemed to have been on the go all night, she said. They were going to move the girl opposite into a side ward, a cubicle by herself, she said. 'And about time. No one can get any rest with all that going on.'

'Why, Doreen, that's not like you,' her mother said. 'You often have a reaction about the third day. It's just physical. You mustn't get too wrapped up about that girl. She'll be all right. They do marvels these days.'

After the visiting hour she went to get Doreen something from the kiosk in the hall and she passed the young father sitting on a bench in a corridor. He was crying, crying like a child with one arm lifted up to his forehead as if to ward off a blow or keep out the light, and the other clutching a dingy handkerchief between his bitten nails. There was a white-coated man next to him on the bench saying, 'Try not to take it like that Mr Grubb. Come, pull yourself together for your wife's sake. You know, if the baby had been born it wouldn't have been healthy.'

'But what was wrong with it?' he asked very low, sniffing.

'Well, the placenta, you see, couldn't support it. Your wife's physique . . . the placenta was shrinking and couldn't support the foetus.'

'But what was wrong with baby?' he asked again, high-pitched.

The white-coated man, embarrassed at the grief, annoyed perhaps that his medical terms and the common sense of decency not to be too emotional with a doctor, were not working here, drew in a breath and said emphatically: 'The baby had no head, Mr Grubb. It would not have survived parturition. But we did not wish to tell your wife that. We must think about her health now, you know, and get her well.'

# 16

He came in and didn't speak, signalling to his wife to put the cup where he could reach it and thanking her with his eyes and head. He drank it straight off and she filled it up. He had been out from 6 that morning, spraying from the tractor. Earlier in week he'd even considered hiring a 'copter but now he'd decided against it.

'I don't think it's any good,' he said after the second cup. 'I don't think we've got the right stuff. We had the report back from the research station. They don't know what it is. Can't find anything so far. Nothing they can find in the soil they say. And you can practically watch it, whatever "it" is, working through the crop in a day. We had to break off after seven hours to let the men have some lunch and when we came back I could've sworn Hedge Field – which still looked fine this morning – was beginning to go. The shoots seem to go sort of transparent – at first you think it's the light on them and when you get closer you see they're brittle and then they start dying back. By tomorrow Hedge Field'll be gone I daresay. I can't think it was the seed. I got it from the same place I always do. And there's nothing they can find in the soil – and you saw yourself, Dorothy, how good those fields looked earlier in the year. It must be some new disease. They say the hardier they make the grain the hardier some viruses get. You don't just get new strains of wheat – the germs get wily and you get new strains of them.

'It's something overall, anyway, not just on our farm. They've had reports from all over the county, the man at the station told me. And further I think. Of course, it may be starting up independently – same conditions causing it – but I doubt it. And if they think it's a spreading disease – and to see them you do feel the crops are being consumed by something, it's no exaggeration to say it's spreading like wild fire – we'll have to burn the whole crop.

'Day after day for years I've battled here till this farm was a show piece, you could say, a show piece. No finer herd, and no better yield from the grain. And you wouldn't say I was a man to give up easily. But these last two weeks have finished me. I can't fight what I don't know, and this I don't know. I've done everything I know what to do. I've listened, I've taken advice. I've tried this. I've tried that. This is something quite beyond me. It makes you feel ridiculously small and helpless – one small man – what is he but just an animal on his hind legs with his front in the air – against all that – all that dying out there. There's nothing I can do any more. I suppose this must've been what it was like in those plagues of Egypt, only we can't pin it down to locusts. And when you're not used to it, like people over there are, it seems worse somehow.'

# 17

The country was in the grip of extreme cold. The pavements were rutted and then more snow had fallen and it had frozen on top of that. It was perilous getting about and with Nicky and the toddler and the little one in the push-chair a terrible task. But she had to get Nicky to school and there was no one to leave the others with. The two on their feet were not the problem. They were good brave children and didn't complain. But it was difficult keeping the blanket wrapped round the baby and the snow was being blown in his face. Once the blanket got caught in the wheel and this was too much for the battered old push-chair. The cottar pin had come out some time ago and normally the hairpin she used in its stead kept the wheel on. The baby had to get out and stand while she groped for the piece of wire in the snow. People with their heads down nearly stumbled over the little group decanted in the middle of the pavement.

She felt the cold dreadfully herself, but that would not matter if she could get the children into the warm. She had to be cheerful to keep them cheerful so she joked as she fixed the wheel. The worse things got, the more gallant she became, and it was true they were generally fearless and equable children. 'Soon be there, Nicky,' she said as she shoved on across the ruts, to reassure herself as much as him.

Heavenly to be back in the house and to be able to warm Greta up. It looked an idyllic nursery tale as they had come in from the dark buffeting of the grim snow-laden wind; cat and airing clothes round the fender, toys and knitting on the sagging sofa. 'It just shows what you can do by keeping going,' she thought, allowing herself now to remember how awful she'd felt when she got out of bed and how much better in comparison she felt now. She felt a bit queasy and there was an occasional dragging sort of twinge but she knew she could keep it down now. The house and the two children, happy as soon as they were comfortable, rewarded her: she'd overcome feeling ill and she'd ... as she ironed she indulged in her favourite dreaming occupation of making lists: fed the baby at 6, ironed Jack's shirt, cleared the ash and lit the fire, got Jack's sandwiches, made tea, drank some, took Jack some – all that by 7 when he blundered up out of sleep and out of the house to work. When the room was a bit warmed up, given Nicky and Greta their breakfast, made up the fire and, filling the bin, realised how low they were in coal – she'd better buy a bag today although that was an expensive way of buying it, but the coal she'd had on order for a month wasn't likely to come in this weather. She repeated some items and included such trivial things as putting away the children's clothes which she did automatically, and the ironing, which she had not finished – yes, and she'd taken Nicky to school, got bread and milk on the way back and she only had the baby to bath and put down to sleep, the breakfast and sandwich-making things to clear up, and the bathroom to clean, and she and Greta could have a nice hour before she had to wrap them all up and set off to collect Nicky. She remembered she had decided she must get coal. Damn. She really did wish she could leave it, she really was looking forward to the rest of the day, getting ahead without being rushed, and sitting down. But she better not leave it. There was only one greengrocer with any coal left and he was bound to run out soon too. This weather would keep most people in so it was her chance to get some.

When the baby was bathed and asleep she wrapped up Greta, gave the push-chair a threatening look and set off as quickly as she could pretending to Greta it was a game to lift the front wheels. 'Whee,' she said and ran a bit. She was scared at leaving the baby. She never had before but decided that today it was the less dangerous course. She would be much quicker with Greta in the pushchair. There still were bags, she was pleased to see, a pile of them coated with snow. 'My lucky day,' she said to the greengrocer. He was a surly man and she was frightened of his angry manner. The coal was more expensive than she had expected. Still . . . 'I'll take it on the push-chair,' she said, friendly, though he hadn't asked her how she was going to get it home. 'The little girl can sit on top.' He was sitting down on an upturned wooden box in the warm back of his shop with a cup of tea. He gestured. 'They're outside,' he said and didn't move. She supposed everyone went and took one themselves. She pretended to fix Greta's bonnet to stay in the warm a little longer and give him a chance to lift the bag for her without her asking him, and then there was nothing for it but to heave the sack of coal on to the push-chair, lift Greta on top and set off through the snow, which was coming sideways now into their faces. She had to steady Greta with one hand and try and guide the push-chair through the ruts and off and on to curbs with the other hand and the rest of her body. She mistakenly thought it would shorten their way home to go directly across the green.

She got in, filled the coal hod and while she was getting Greta a hot drink the pain came in a great wave through her thighs and across her abdomen and then she started to bleed. She lay down for a bit praying the baby would stay asleep and that she could avoid alarming Greta. There was an hour before she had to collect Nicky. If she could get him and hang on till Jack got home . . . anything to avoid ringing Jack. He was embarrassed if anyone from home rang him at work. She planned to manage and felt better and more confident. This was while she was lying down. But when she got up to put her bloody clothes in cold water and wipe up the blood from the lavatory floor before anyone else got there, she walked straight to the phone and rang the doctor. Thank goodness she had insisted on a phone. The bleeding seemed to ebb a bit. Perhaps the doctor would think her a fraud when he came, getting him to come on these terrible roads. She felt more comfortable when she had washed her clothes and torn up an old towel to soak up the blood so she could put on clean ones. The effort to go across to Mrs Diment would be worth it if she could thus cut out going to collect Nicky and she must go before the bleeding started again. In the rooms on the second floor above the shoe shop Mrs Diment assured her she would collect him when she got James. She was managing everything very well she thought, starting the long trek back to Greta. Two and a half hours later when the doctor called she was vaguely washing up some plates from lunch and trying to peel vegetables to be sure to have Jack's meal ready, in case she should feel worse later. Jack didn't have lunch so he always wanted to eat straight away.

The doctor said she had miscarried and gave her a note to the hospital. 'Don't be too long getting there,' she said. It was not her own doctor but a woman. 'My husband is usually in by six,' she said, thinking the doctor meant her to go when he came in. 'Good gracious woman, you can't wait till your husband comes in. It might be hours. You must get to the hospital at once. Is there anyone you can leave the children with?' She thought and thought and the harder she thought the less did a single face or name or house swim before her mind. There was Mrs Grant at no.12 whom she knew slightly but she hardly thought . . . The doctor picked up the baby and, pushing a teddy bear under Greta's arm, took her other hand and went down the street. She was soon back. 'They're fine. Mrs Grant was only too pleased. She said you were not to worry, she'll be in all day.'

'That is very kind.' she said faintly, 'thank you very much.'

'It is important you get to the hospital straight away,' the doctor reminded her as she turned to finish the washing up.

'Yes, of course, I'll probably get a taxi,' she said and leant against the sink, thinking about buses. The bus stop seemed incredibly far; so even did the phone in the hall.

'I better take you in my car,' the woman doctor said.

After the doctor had left her at the hospital she waited for an hour and a half and went through various office routines and examinations. They had to give her an anaesthetic in order to get the needle into the vein to give her a blood transfusion, they couldn't make the vein protrude enough to get the needle in, she heard them discussing. She felt a crowd round her of overalled and masked figures and wanted to ask them to move away a little so she could breathe and wanted to ask the young Indian woman doctor, whose voice and manner were grating in her head, not to shout, but when she came to, what she had most urgently on her mind was something quite other. She woke with a clear picture of the green she had crossed with Greta perched on top of the coal and remembered how desolate it had looked, and that somewhere beneath her preoccupations with the push-chair wheel, Greta's balance and something unstable inside herself, she had wondered where the men with red noses and bulbous eyes swigging at bottles every now and then had gone. Nothing seemed to move them much. Had they simply not noticed and got buried under the snow as they lay in their stupor or did the cold penetrate even that and drive them to some shelter? But where could they go? She was so glad she was not out on that green now.

'But what about the men on the Green?' she said. 'It's cold in here but it must be much colder out there.'

'Yes, yes, dear, you'll be all right now, just relax and you'll be all right. We'll get you another blanket.' She was annoyed they wouldn't listen to what she was saying and talk about what she was interested in.

'Yes, of course *I'll* be all right. But it is so terribly cold. They won't survive. We're in here, but don't you think you ought to do something about the men on the Green?' They put another blanket on her, but it didn't seem to make the slightest difference to the freezing cold. 'There you are dear, now don't tire yourself with talking.'

'They haven't any blankets and they're outside. What are you going to do about the men on the Green?'

# 18

The woman lay on the surgical bed in the small cubicle and the doctor stood at the feet end turned away from her looking at the notes. He had dark thick hair and was scowling.

She had been brought by ambulance to the hospital some hours before from the greengrocery business that she ran with her husband.

He started to ask her questions, barking up from the file he was holding, not turning to her. 'Name?' 'Address?' There was a sort of whiny twang to his way of speaking she could not place. By the time he was well down in the case saying, 'You are down here as wanting an abortion. That so?' she felt like screaming, 'Surely it's all down there? Surely you don't need to make me go through all that again when I've gone into it time and again every time I've come here. Didn't they write it down so you could read it instead of asking me it all again? Why aren't you asking me other things, saying other things? Don't you know I'm in pain and misery and have been for hours? Aren't I here for you to put an end to that?' But it was an effort to hear him at all and raise enough voice to answer, she was so weak and tired. Through the experience of many interviews with doctors and hospital people to try and get an abortion of this her fifth child, she had learned to limit her words to the barest of sullen replies.

'You were brought here as haemorrhaging, possibility of miscarrying?' She nodded. She supposed he thought she'd brought it on. Perhaps that was why he was talking with such disgust in his voice. How dim could they get? Would she have gone into all that awful business of applying for an abortion if she could have done anything herself? Although on her back she let her head fall to the right, to the wall, away from the light, and tears from her right eye seeped down on to the sheet. It was not from the pain. It was not really from the exhaustion of a day that had begun twelve hours before with receiving deliveries from the market and getting some of the produce ready to put out before she got the children up and gave them their breakfast. It was not regret for this child she would never have, nor for her own life if she did have it. It was a weary sadness so static, so deep, so still, so fixed on her heart, that the only way out was through her leaking eyes: a sadness that she had nothing left to regret, that she had come to this, to be spoken to like this, splayed upon a bench and made to pay in shame and disregard, before this man, in whose power she had carelessly put herself, would let her go, let her turn to the wall privately, with her misery, back to a body that was her own again, to keep her body and her misery from the glare of this light, the hostility of this man. A sadness; and a weariness that there was no end, no joy, no rest.

'Well?' It was he who was well and strong, who ought to be making the effort, not she stretching her mind at such a time. 'Yes,' she said.

She had been brought to the hospital by ambulance but she had not gone out the nearest way through the shop to the front. Oh no, her husband wouldn't want her going through the customers, maybe getting a bit of sympathy. Someone might blame him if they saw. She went out the back and so had to carry her case down the alley and round to the road that way. It had been so nice when she came up to the ambulance and the ambulance man had taken the case from her and put his arm round her shoulders to help her in, that she became positively cheerful with them. Her husband hadn't even thought to occupy the children while she did her disappearing trick so they wouldn't be upset, so she had had to settle them before the telly and pop next door for some sweets to distract them before she slipped out.

When she had begun to bleed in the afternoon a customer had come into the shop. Her husband had gone on a delivery in the van and taken John with him. Whenever possible he took John for company. It must have been for company. Surely a seventeen-stone man could lift boxes of lettuce on his own when she could heave sacks of potatoes? She didn't expect them back early from this particular trip because it was a delivery to a pub and they were always treated there. Her husband loved the privilege of drinking in the pub when it was shut to the public and practically gave the stuff away to the landlord because he treated him generously when he delivered. They would probably still be there at opening time.

She didn't know how to do anything but serve the customer,

who was a fussy one. She was hoping the old man would finish his general complaints about service in shops nowadays before the blood she felt oozing between her thighs began to show. When he had gone she wondered if she had time and strength to bring in the boxes of fruit and veg from outside, but asked the woman in the paper shop next door to keep her eye on them instead, shut the door, and got to the lavatory. Later she laughed at herself thinking 'As if I should care if the whole lot got pinched!'

Apart from the fact that it was extremely awkward just now, she felt immense relief that made the pain unimportant. She wouldn't have to have an abortion after all. Luck had graced her. She hadn't of course been able to be careful about lifting, but she hadn't done anything to bring it on that she didn't have to do. She'd acted no differently in her four other pregnancies, and they'd been all right. She must, she supposed, be very strong. And now she was being rewarded for not doing anything wrong.

She had had to wait till her husband got back before she could call the doctor, because she must be in bed when he came and she couldn't go to bed and leave the shop and the children when they came in from school which would be any minute now. A little before 6 her husband came in well-oiled, to clear and lock the till and lock up, and she told him what had happened, and that they better get the doctor. Her husband didn't show that he'd heard and started being very busy with boxes out the back, which he usually left to her, so she rang the doctor herself. The bleeding lessened and stopped. Her heart sank. Now with a will she heaved the boxes of tomatoes, apples and carrots, heavy Dutch cabbages and trays of bananas from outside. She stretched up to put back the shade. She felt terribly ill, but it was the bleeding that mattered. She got upstairs and started giving the children their tea, looking out for the doctor's car. When she heard him talking to her husband downstairs, she lay down.

The doctor was kind and said they might be able to save the baby if she was very careful. He was an emergency doctor, not one from her surgery. She was to stay quite still till the ambulance came. He patted her hand, interpreting her tears as sorrow at loss. 'Don't worry, my dear. It'll be all right.' These days any tenderness of physical consideration brought tears to her eyes. She thanked him and he went downstairs to phone the ambulance.

Luckily her husband would in no way object if she went against the doctor's orders to rest. So as soon as he had gone she got busy. There was indeed a lot to do, making sure the children had everything for school tomorrow, that she had what she needed for hospital. She spoke to the eldest child explaining as unalarmingly as possible that she had to go into hospital and to tell the other children when she'd gone and stop them worrying. She would probably be ringing from the hospital. If they needed anything they could go next door and ask Mrs Baccolini. She picked up the show bunch of grapes from the top of the box her husband was putting away. 'Where's that going?' he asked. She didn't answer, but took them in to Mrs Baccolini. 'I'm going into hospital,' she explained. 'It will be a heavenly rest,' and laughed. Mrs Baccolini loved fruit. 'You are a good girl, Chrissie,' she said, 'a good girl. Donta you no worry now about the children. I keep an eye.'

She was quite determined that her need not to have the baby, which she had thought was being granted, should not be thwarted now. To give him nothing to complain of, to give him no lever on the situation, she put a plate of food ready for her husband and put it in the oven. He would not have dished it out himself. She was sick at the smell of the food, but managed to get to the lavatory to be so.

So the ambulancemen thought she was a brave and patient woman when she remained cheerful through all the traffic hold-ups and admired her for trying to do what she could for herself. And, she knew, this approval and admiration was sweet to her, as was the solicitude of the doctor who thought she wanted to save her baby.

Her husband had been much worse after she had insisted that he should come with her to the doctor's to discuss the abortion. The only reason she risked his anger to speak to him about it was that the doctor said that he wouldn't consider it, on no account would he consider recommending an abortion, unless he had spoken to the husband.

She had not let the matter drop, as her husband had hoped she would if he made it nearly impossible to talk to him about it, so in the end he had said 'Anything for a quiet life' and let her make the appointment. 'I still don't see why I should come. It's a waste of time. It's your concern, so why don't you do ahead with it. Why don't you tell the doctor I won't come? You know I don't want anything to do with it. What's the point of my going? I haven't the time anyway.'

'Because he won't do anything about it without seeing you,' she almost screamed.

'Good,' he said.

From the moment the husband had realised he had a pressure point, he did what he could to make her life impossible. If he felt in a bad mood he'd bring up the fact that she may have made the appointment for him, but he hadn't, so he didn't have to go, and she hadn't really expected him to go with her to see the quack, had she?

'But I only made the appointment after you'd said to.'

'That was just a little experiment I was carrying out, to test you. *And* I was proved right.'

Another time when he felt a bit frightened of what she might do (she was beginning to be very free with her tongue), he said of course he'd come and he had only been teasing her. Why was she so solemn about everything, couldn't she take a joke?

He had seemed the most reasonable and considerate man in the world at the doctor's, saying that for himself he'd look after as many children as came, he wouldn't wish for one less, he didn't consider them a burden, although he wasn't a rich man, but the family was the most important thing in his life; but that of course, however much a man tried to help, the work of children fell most heavily on the woman, so it really had to be her decision, sad as it made him, and of course he'd back her up in whatever she decided.

'So you want to be free of what you call a burden, do you?' the doctor had at last turned to her. 'I wouldn't have thought bringing up a family with a thoughtful man like your husband here would be so terrible. Of course it may seem hard not to be able to go out just when you please, but a life without responsibilities is really a very dull one in the end. And of course, that's what you marry for, isn't it?'

He was a bigwig in social medicine, she had thought it very lucky to get on his list, and his speeches at conferences were the ones reported in the newspapers, she'd heard, and he had organised a nice new clinic for the borough he had his surgery in. However, every time that she had come to see him he had without fail asked her her name, how many children she had, her age, what her husband's job was, and so on. She began to think this was perhaps intentional. He couldn't surely be that stupid? She had once gone to him about one of the children, and she herself had felt simply dreadful. She looked it too, she knew. She had practically collapsed in the surgery while he examined the child and been barely able to answer his questions, but he had never asked her how she was, and she felt so stunned that he noticed nothing that she said nothing.

Bottled up because her husband had so trapped her and made her seem bad and irresponsible and selfish, something in her snapped and even as she heard her voice giving them a piece of her mind, she regretted it. She was surprised at how well she was talking, but she'd lost her chances now she knew. This man wouldn't stand being answered back.

As her voice rose to repeat that if she had another baby she would not be able to look after the children she had, that she would lose all interest in the entire family, she found a plan ready formed in her mind, already there, like a fruit in a flower. That's what she would do. She no longer didn't know what to do. If they said she had to have that baby she would go, depart, leave. In fact she would go before it came. She would not go back and have another five years tacked on to her obstacle race when she was rounding the bend to enter the last stretch. She would go and find some dark place and stay there until the dark came forever.

She was surprised to find that when she had finished what she considered to have been a horrible melodramatic performance – but the whole talk with the doctor was going hopelessly wrong – the men were deferential, the doctor went to his desk and wrote something and spoke politely to her. When she opened her mouth to thank him and say good morning she found she was crying and couldn't speak.

'Now, now, don't do that. It may have seemed a bit rough to you but you see we have to make quite sure it's genuine for everybody's sake.'

'Of course,' she sniffed, 'I quite understand,' and smiled through her tears, and thought, 'how miserable do these people have to make you before they find out what they need to know? We have to pay because they don't know chalk from cheese.'

Her husband stood apart from her at the bus stop and went straight upstairs ahead of her when the bus came, knowing the stairs and smoke made her sick. She went inside. After that he didn't speak to her except when he couldn't help it, to ask for something he needed, or to complain 'Where's my dinner, then?' when a minute before he'd said he wouldn't be ready for it for an hour. She began to feel this was a relief. Anyway, she'd gained her point.

The harsh voice started up again from the foot of the couch. 'We could try and save this baby, you know,' the doctor almost looked up to say, in a threatening manner. A man like that doesn't really want to save anything she thought. Why did he want to go on at her in this argumentative way all the time? 'Do you still want to go through with this abortion?' Whatever she said would have no effect. She had begun to realise they did not ask her questions because they wanted the answers but for some other reason she couldn't fathom. She thought all these clever men, all this complicated organisation, would be crazy enough to put all efforts and resources (and make her make an effort) to save the baby, only to make her fit for the abortion on the appointed day in three weeks time – by when it would be more dangerous anyway. She didn't answer. If she didn't answer perhaps he would stop badgering her. She closed her eyes, just noticing his very clean white hands, with straggly black hairs getting thicker up the wrist as he held the file. She had won. At last this awful battle would be over.

'I am sorry, child,' she said inside her head, as if she was thinking about one of her born children, 'I had nothing against you. If you had been born I would have loved you and cared for you and you would have given me joy and pleasure and comforted me. It is not your fault that the world is like it is and that I have had to learn to save myself and that you were the only thing weaker than me to go to the wall when I had learnt that. Perhaps what would have been your spirit will find some other place.'

The doctor did indeed say nothing more, not even to warn her when he was going to push his iron hard hand, jabbing with not the slightest care, as forcefully as he could, up her vagina and into her womb. She gasped with the astonishing pain. She would not have done if he had warned her. He moved with such force that her body was drawn down the couch till her legs were hanging over the edge.

'Relax, woman, relax,' he shouted. 'I can't do anything when you're as tense as this.' God, I'm sorry for your wife, you bastard, she thought. Or perhaps you haven't got one, perhaps you can't get one. She knew she must think of something far away, think of something hard. So she thought of something she had not allowed herself to think of for many years.

Just before she had fallen for her third child she had been drawn as irresistibly as a steel pin is to a magnet to a young man who had occasionally come into the shop. There was something absolutely electric between them and for a time they had almost tried, now one suggesting and the other not saying yes, then the other deciding to go forward and the other backing away, to do something about it. They had kissed once, once when he had given her a hand bringing in the boxes on half-day closing. And she had remembered; she had kissed that kiss many many times in her memory over the years. She had often wished in the years since that she had been unfaithful to her husband but the young man was respectful of husbands, and perhaps more than she thought she knew how, she had hidden how much she wanted him. She tried to think of Tom now, of his eyes looking at her with flames in them across the shop, flaring up her blood, that look raking her stomach so that it turned loose with desire and making her heart bang up at the back of her ears and her breath go. She would turn to another customer, carefully not looking at Tom, and her husband or John would serve him and when she looked round he would be gone and she would feel so sick that he had gone without giving her a chance to speak to him. He only had to wait a little but he was so impatient. So she tried to think of Tom, who had been very tall, holding the pit of her back and bending down his head with his sweet soft lips and his cool lank clean floppy hair, with the gentlest of hands although they looked rough and swollen from work. She would think of Tom. He might at least be useful to her at last.

The doctor tugged and a sound shot out of her mouth. She had never in her life, not when she was giving birth, never, felt anything like that. She thought he had pulled away her whole inside, that her flesh was being peeled away inside from her bone cage as you take the skin off coley. That made a sound like rending material, and she thought she could feel the sound of rending and peeling down through her abdomen as he wrenched, and 'curse you, Tom, curse your lips and your body and your desire for pleasure because this is your fault, this is because of you and because I wanted you and you dragged my innards towards you but you never did a thing to help. Oh my God, Tom, Tom.' Her scream for help did not come through her lips but echoed only in her head. This man was tearing out the actual seed of desire. He was tearing her life out. 'He is tearing you out of me, Tom. Ah damn *you*. Oh Tom, *Tom*.'

In extremity, whether the agony of pain or the agony of desire, the breaths exhaled from the depths of the body do not sound, perhaps, so very different from each other. And then she was left and the man had gone and it was finished.

We look at the grass and say, when it is brown,
That is nothing of us, stray wisps,
Flaccid bits not now separable
From the mud they're plastered in.
And even at times when it is green again
There looks no sap, no coolness of life to stroke
The fever off from the skin of the face, no salve
To oil the skin of the hand to growing again
Through crusted sores that metal and hard things caused.

Not without struggle, not without falls and deeps,
Winter has caught us.
Truly a lifeless field under this wind –
This grass never flesh.

*

## Demeter

After a long time Demeter lifted her head.
She pulled her cloak about her and stood up
A tall and grieving figure. 'Helios, I thank you.
I will make even these regions flower,
When I get her back. There will be no place
Where you look down and do not somewhere see
A little plant twinkling, a shining leaf
For you to nourish and reflect your face
And wherever your warmth reaches, through dark
Thickets, through bogs, round cavern mouths, even in clefts
In slate-coloured thunderous mountains, where some of your
       warmth
May be wafted from rocks that absorb you, I will make
The stalks and seeds and mosses come alive
And breathe out goodness. Helios again I thank you
I have only to go and get her now, and we two
Will make the earth shine as it never has
You above a field of green-blade wheat
Watering it like a sea with dancing light
In early morning. All seeds shall sprout
All fruit set, and all women come to term
When I have got her back.' She started at once
To cross again the wastes, the tundra, forests,
Deserts and swamps and rivers, mountains, plains
Full of dust and dry wind, making her way
Back to her home to prepare to fetch her daughter.

'Golden-haired Demeter,' Helios said
As he watched her swift disappearance over rocks
'If you had seen what I have seen you would not . . .
You are concerned with the earth, your eyes are down
Or fixed at most on horizons of the earth.
But I stand in the heavens and I see
Such regions as are never in your purview.
I sail among the oceans of space where the earth
Is a tiny unlikely dot that turns and toils
Slowly in its own time and atmosphere –

And may sink out of sight for all we'd notice.
You and your precious earth and your little ants, men,
That you think the Gods of Olympus care about!
That bit of a speck of green – one little fly
Buzzing about in the blue on a summer's day.
You may need me but I do not need you;
Dust or waving wheat – what do I care or know?
Still, you are welcome to my help when I am there.
Fortune go with you, Demeter, and speed you well
And grace your effort, though you cannot change the law.'


# 19


I don't know whether that last little come-back before she died made it better or worse. Of course it was wonderful to see her open her eyes and recognise us – it was her recognising us that made the difference – and ask for a cup of milk and actually drink it. The wife, poor thing, of course took it that she'd come through, that she was completely cured. But I don't think I did really. I didn't see how that could be. But I can't tell you the difference it made. We could actually talk to her and know she heard and what's more, understood. She was back with us, that's what it was, back in life really, whereas before, we said things and did things and had no idea whether they reached her or not – my wife thought they did. I thought no. I suppose you couldn't call it dead because she moved and breathed, but it wasn't really living. She was muffled, wrapped away. And then it seemed she was going to come back to us after all. I've wondered since what was meant by that little glimpse, when she opened her eyes and asked so normally for a cup of milk, if anything *was* meant. I suppose we've both been out of our minds at times since. Or whether it was an accident, a mistake – I mean whatever it is that decides these things took a rest or slipped up and forgot about her for a while, and the life in her – she was only twelve, remember, and perfectly healthy before

the accident, bursting with it – and her mother's devotion, sort of
pulled her back, and then he, the paralysis I mean, got a grip on
her again and took her down. You can think it's funny to talk like
that. I know what it sounds like, I'm perfectly in my right mind
now, but if you've ever watched a young child die I think you'd
agree that's what it seems like – as if something there is pulling it,
and pulling the child to it, and she doesn't want to go. I wouldn't
have missed that moment when Poppy opened her eyes and asked
for milk. The hospital was very very good, couldn't have been
better. They let us stay there, they did everything they could. My
wife didn't leave the building for six weeks. But I think it was
having her hopes raised so high that crushed the wife.


## Hades

Supplied by torches from the burning fires
Within the earth at Aetna in her island
Demeter came to the threshold of the Dead.
She shivered and drew her tattered cloak about her
She coughed at the dust, and felt her skin crackle and split
She breathed with difficulty. Persephone
Must not be left an instant longer in this.
She shuddered and went on and strange shadows crept
Into the edge of the space her torches made.
She thought she saw the changing wraiths of faces –
Long faces, crumpled ones, heavy-browed, puckered
Ancient skin with redded hair, young ones with roses
That suddenly spread, erupting as blotching fever
And then sank back from sight.

Across a huge hall Hades came to meet her.

She drew herself to her height, normally tall
But knew her strength diminished and lustreless.
'Sister, no one comes here except when they must.
It is long since I have seen you.' 'Brother, I know

You need a Queen. I bear you no ill will. I know that anyone
In this terrible dark place would want a consort.
Even in the nourishing light of day
We do not live if those we love are taken.
We move about and look as if we look
And nod and speak and lift food to our mouth
But we are dead – down here with you in spirit,
Harbinger to real death. I know your need.
But you cannot keep Persephone with you.
Find someone else. Persephone comes with me.
Hades it was a wicked cruel thing
To bring my daughter to this dreadful region.
Now give her back and may no harm have come.
Where is she?' Hades moved or rather
Pulled in some of the dark and pulsing aura
That filled the space round him, his great effect
Blazing darkness, a dazzle so dense you cannot
See with your eyes but all is fired within
With dark unlocated gloom so overpowering
As if the back of the head of an upright person
Is gradually keeled to the ground. Hades receives
All whom the gullet of death has stunned. His kingdom
Has received more beings than sands there are by the sea:
Black specks of grit on the vast shores of Lethe water.

At the far end of the hall upon a throne
Sat a figure so still, a being so pale, Demeter
Thought it one of the place's denizens. She raised
Her torch and stepped forward; the figure stirred
And diamonds clasped about a fragile neck
Reflected Aetna's fire. Demeter shrieked.
'Hush, sister; not down here. We have no horrors
As you up on your earth. Here all is quiet
And orderly and unhysterical. Here is no pain
No desperate striving.' Persephone stretched her arms
And turned her small face up in which the eyes
Were all that spoke, and seemed as if to move
But sank back as the great and powerful shadow
Of Hades spread and strengthened in between them.

'You fool with what you do not know, Demeter.
You are from above. You do not know
The immense power that I can give your daughter.
She will have everything. I will not harm her
For I must have her. She is part of me –
How could I harm her? – and she shall have all mine,
Immeasurably more than you can give her.

'Your sun-dance festivals are in my purview,
The arrangements made, controlled, within my kingdom.
The morning sun's trajectory is planned
To lead him to the sea at evening tide.
The day is his; but only as I wish it.
I hold my hand – and then the ripe fruit falls
Longing for entry into my fructive cellars
As the egg burrows into the ovary wall
And the swathed chrysalis dopes itself with food
And drowses through long winters of its life.
Life is half over when it gets to the light.
The dark is where it starts and where it grows.
Persephone
Is ripe for me now, and when this fruit has fallen
To me, its proper bed, oh then, such riches –
Such riches and such fruit shall we bring forth:
Polydectes, receiver of all, and Perephrata.'

Demeter heard Persephone call her name
So faintly, like the memory of a dream
Persistent and unreachable.
'My daughter, do not heed him. I will go
And tell your father, Zeus, who will make
Him listen to me.' 'Mother' a faint whisper
'I called on Zeus but he did not answer.'
'You fools, you creatures of the daylight both –
Zeus it was who gave her to me. Zeus
Reckoned it was just that I should have her.
My brother and I are in complete agreement.
"Why not?" he said, "I know her what she's worth
You couldn't do better." And he made her mine.'

86

'Why not? Why *not*? You wait till I see him
And *then* you'll know why not. Persephone
I have eaten nothing, nor have I slept
Nor washed nor rested till I found you. Nor will I
Until I get you out of here. My child
My much-changed child, remember the teeming earth
The morning breath on the grass, the chatter of waters
Broken into light by the great warm sun,
Your friends and laughter and animals and flowers
Opening their cool soft petals around your feet
The sweet air like salve that laps around your skin
Flutterings and singing in that sweet air about you,
Succulence of the earth that succoured you
And which we tend. Remember your home, your days.
Hold fast your thoughts against this blackness,
Summon your powers; and I will get you home.'

# 20

'It's no good looking at that newspaper any more, George. You must've wore it out with reading it. It didn't say anything useful – even when it was new and that's nine days ago. She obviously isn't going to answer the appeal. Come on,' the woman said, glancing at the clock which showed 10 o'clock. 'I can't stay in any longer waiting on that phone. She's probably somewhere she can't phone. Get your coat on.'

'She'll get in touch when she wants to. It doesn't do any good interfering, rushing in confronting these young people. She won't thank you for embarrassing her in front of her friends.'

'It's not "these young people". It's Paula. Your daughter Paula. And it's not exactly rushing in, waiting nine days. We should've rushed in. That's just what we should've done. And I don't care whether she's embarrassed or not. What's that to risk when her throat might be being cut? And they're no friends of hers if they're keeping her from getting in touch with her parents. It's not like Paula. I feel it in my bones she's being prevented. Our Paula'd never leave me without some word.'

'You felt it in your bones that she'd been run over, that time you got the police hunting all round the park, remember, and there she was sitting as happy as anything in her friend's house.'

'Better safe than sorry. You want to get your proportions right, George. Nine days. Don't waste time arguing. Get your coat on and bring some cash. You never know what she might not be in need of.'

'If you want to go making a fool of yourself you go; but don't expect me to aid and abet you. You don't know what hornet's nest you mightn't be stirring up that you'll be sorry for. I'm certainly not going to be a party to that.'

'You make me incredibly sick, sitting there with your eye on your pools envelope trotting out all those phrases you get from the newspapers and those discussions you listen to on the telly, just to save you thinking and feeling. And as for making a fool of yourself – you've no fear of that, that's been done for you already. You may seem a clever man George, to your mates who can't fill in forms or write a decent letter, but where your family's concerned, you're a fool.'

When he heard the downstairs door shut, he put the paper down and started to tidy up. He took some money from his wallet and put it in the rent book at the back of the clock to replace the money his wife had taken from it. He stood for some time looking at a photograph of a little gap-toothed girl in a gingham dress holding a teddy bear. There was a polyphoto stuck in the corner of the frame, of an older Paula with a friend, busty in school uniform, pulling funny faces at the camera. He went into the kitchen, washed up and got all the pans shining. Then, taking a plastic carrier bag he went downstairs and knocked on the door of the flat below. A young woman holding a baby answered. The man asked her to listen out for the phone and asked her if she needed any shopping getting.

At 10 that night his wife came back without the suitcase she had set out with.

'There's supper made if you want some,' her husband said. 'I thought you might need something so I made a stew.'

'No, you have some. I couldn't. But you have some.'

'I think I will. I could do with something. I didn't feel like it before. You'll have a cup of tea?'

'Yes, that I will have.'

While he was in the kitchen and occupied he called out 'Well?' so she could start telling him when he brought the tea. She drank a deep gulp, levered off her shoes and closed her eyes. 'You don't know how glad I am to be back here, George. Thank you for . . .' she waved her hand around. 'What a difference it makes to come into a clean place. You've no idea.' He knew she would start telling him soon. She had never resisted the urge to tell him things, so he waited. The grey in her face made her grey hair yellowish. She looked really knocked out. 'I had to do something to fill in the time,' he said. 'I knew you'd be tired when you got back. You have another cup and I'll bring my plate in here – sure you won't change your mind?' He knew she had seen Paula. 'Not just yet thank you dear.'

When he came back in she had her jacket off and was sitting upright again.

'It was dreadful, George, dreadful. I can't tell you how dreadful. I did find her but nothing I could do seemed to get through to her. She refused point blank to come home. Finding her was the easy part really. I went to the place Leila – you know, that tall girl she goes to the disco with – the place Leila works and she said Paula was staying with friends and she told me the name of the road. She didn't know the number but she said I'd know the house because all the others were boarded up and this one was next to a big building that was empty now but had been a garage or something. "Paula's helping some friends do it up, Mrs Freeman," she said – she is a nice polite girl, "so I expect you'll recognise the house. They're all artists so they've done some murals, or wall paintings, or something. It's quite different from the others. I'm sure you'll find it."

Different – I'll say. George – I have never seen such filth. One of these "artists" fancies he's on to a good thing with some old parts of engines from next door so he tinkers around and there's oil and the smell of stale oil, everywhere. He had all these little bits and oily rags spread out on the pavement and I could hardly get up the steps. Didn't seem to put him out – you'd think I was invisible.

He just stayed spread out there – no shoes or anything, and filthy feet, and one of those little transparent crêpe blouses. I don't know whether he expected me to walk over him or what. He didn't move. You couldn't tell what colour he was meant to be he was so dirty, and he had these long straggly strands of greasy matted hair and jewellery, trinkets, dangling from him everywhere. I don't see the point of that, do you, when you haven't even bothered to wash or comb your hair? And the smell! I think he was Arabic or Persian or something. Anyway, when I asked whether a Miss Freeman was staying there he stared past me – I had to ask more than once – and said "Go right in and take a look, lady. Who knows what you might find?" and crawled round the corner of the house *on his hands and knees.*

'You can imagine after that there wasn't anything I didn't expect.

'The worst thing about the place was the smell – there was this funny sickly sweetish smell like old damp blankets that have been shut up in a drawer.

'There wasn't a bell or a knocker or anything – just a big round hole so anyone could put their hand in and open the latch, so that's what I had to do, and inside was just bare floorboards. You could see they were rotten and some of them had gone, either fallen in or been ripped up. The only thing visible was dusty milk bottles along the passage wall, some all curdled with old milk and some with worse in. There were wires hanging down in loops from high up on the wall (the ceilings were very high and there was the remains of what must have been a nice bannister) with some bulbs fitted on to them somehow – it looked terribly dangerous, and everywhere where there should've been light switches, holes in the wall and bare wires showing. I knocked on a few doors but nobody came although I didn't feel the house was empty. It had looked deserted from the outside – cardboard at the windows instead of curtains, and no handles on anything. I didn't know what to do so I opened the first door on the right, very quietly. It was dark in there – boxes stacked against the walls and window, and wires dangling from what must have been an ornamented ceiling once – you know all decorated at the edges like a wedding cake. I should think it must've been a beautiful room once. There was a carved marble mantelpiece in some brown sort of stone with a big mirror between. All sorts of things were pasted on the mirror, or written straight on – the sort of things you see on the walls of public toilets, and a poster of a man with an open shirt and a hairy chest and his fist high in the air and some sort of flag. I was looking around to get some clue and get used to the dark and I suddenly realised – I supposed I'd heard breathing without noticing it – that there was something at my feet. There were people asleep on the floor and I'd practically stepped right on them. They were just on the floor on a mattress with a dirty grey blanket pulled over them and coats on top. The top of a dusty curly head poked out of the blanket right near my foot and next to that just a hump under the blanket. At the other end, wrapped in a shawl made of squares of wool, was a baby. Nobody, not even the baby, stirred. I got out of there pretty quickly I can tell you. And when I was outside the room I thought suppose that hump was Paula. The room next to that, there was nothing at all in, not even floorboards – they'd been ripped up. And then I heard voices and I went down the passage. I was looking for missing floorboards and dangling wires so in the dark I didn't realise that there was a step and I twisted my ankle quite painfully. I knocked loudly this time on the door at the end of the passage, but I couldn't open it. "Push harder – just push, man" a voice yelled and then laughed – quite friendly really. So I pushed and someone inside pulled and I practically fell on top of the biggest black man I've ever seen.

'I suppose it was a good thing I was looking at him because it gave Paula time to realise it was me. Because she was there. Oh yes, although I doubt you'd have recognised her, George. There she was, all done up with this mop of frizzy hair dyed in streaks – and her hair was always so pretty. She had this long trailing skirt that might have been made from a table-cloth and a little skimpy top that showed everything. Slumping around, with nothing on her feet. I've never seen such a change in anyone in so short a time. She's twice as fat and she's really let herself go. If you didn't know her you'd say she was forty, flopping about all over the place. As I said, nothing on her feet and it was a stone floor – these young people don't seem to feel anything – they're either walking around barefoot in the depths of winter on mucky roads or muffled up to the chin in great sheepskin coats when it's hot. And there she was, Paula, who'd never give me a hand in the kitchen and couldn't hardly be bothered to boil herself an egg, chopping and stirring and mixing in a great big wooden bowl, shaking in this and that – goodness knows what went into that food – for a bunch of – well, I don't know what to call them. They were none of them English and they had the most peculiar assortment of clothes on.

'"This is my *mother*," Paula finally said, and went very sulky, but strange to say the black boy by the door was very nice to me. He washed a cup and sat me down with a cup of coffee and talked in a very courteous way.

'The kitchen was quite different from the rest of the house, and there were goodness knows how many people either squatting on the floor against the wall, or sitting at this big table. People seemed to come and go, and a girl with a baby started feeding it and nobody turned a hair and they all introduced whoever came in by name to me and they seemed to like to shake hands. There was a lot of touching all the while. Whoever came in or sat down put his arm round whoever was next to him, man or girl. I didn't mind that, that seemed genuine enough and not at all — you know. Of course Paula was keeping well out of all this friendliness and not saying anything to me. She just fussed over doling out the food. And I must say nobody seemed to get in anybody's way or get impatient or anything.

'Of course I sat on hoping to get the chance to talk to Paula alone. We sat for hours. Nobody was in the slightest hurry to go, or get on with anything and I'm sure that suited Paula, but by about 5 o'clock they started to drift off. None of them seemed to actually live there though no doubt if night came and they found themselves still there they'd crawl on to the nearest mattress. I don't know.'

'Paula must be got out of there as soon as possible, obviously, but from what you say it could be worse. No, let me finish. Look at it this way. You say she's actually cooking and the bit she lives in is clean and nicely kept and those weirdies aren't living there. I suppose she feels it's adventurous to explore the underworld or whatever they belong to. Anybody who's got time to sit around drinking coffee and God knows what else and lay around asleep at 2 in the afternoon must be on to something illegal. But that doesn't mean Paula's necessarily mixed up in it. As you say, they seemed to have girls of their own, and people like that would surely go for someone a bit more experienced than Paula, they'd want one of their own sort. She's probably intrigued by the gypseyish life and what she thinks of as the friendliness of it – after all young people do like company of their own age, and you can be very relaxed if you haven't got to worry about keeping a job and a household. She'll probably get bored with hanging around after a bit – after all she's not been brought up to be idle – she's probably just exploring. I know you've had a dreadful day but maybe it isn't as bad as it seems. At least she's still going to the college and doing her course and she'll soon get in with a crowd there. Our Paula's never been *silly*, Mum.'

'Yes, I thought of all that while we were sitting around talking or not talking – I had to have something to occupy me waiting for them to go. As I say, when they were all sitting around talking, all those darkies and curly-headed Persian boys, with their babies and their friends, I could see the appeal in it to an only child like Paula but when they did go and she had to talk to me I found out what it's really all about and I'm afraid it's much much worse than that.

'The first thing is she is not going to the college any more, although it was someone from the college who first took her to that house – one of the teachers, she said, can you believe that? I must say I didn't really believe that bit.'

'Not going to the college? But she got us to move heaven and earth for her to get in. Of all the –'

'Apparently the people she's fallen in with – oh I don't know George, there was a long rigmarole about never breaking the mould of bourgeois – she said that meant middle-class – values, and how the college was just using people's intellectual energy so they wouldn't be dissatisfied; giving them an interest, a vetted interest –'

'Vested.'

'Yes, in the establishment so that they wouldn't take part in getting rid of it – I don't know, I was practically in tears by the end it was all such nonsense. Of *course* she was satisfied when she got into the college, why shouldn't she be, and we were very proud of her and she liked that – she forgets she liked that. Now she says she never did but just went along to please us but it's no good wasting three years of her life being hypocritical and meanwhile she would be throwing away – oh something about heritage as a truly sensitive human being in society – talk about you trotting out phrases – you ought've heard Paula. Well, I wish you had, really – you might have known how to answer her. I certainly didn't. And all the perfectly simple and important things I'd come to say went out of my mind, or rather I just couldn't get back to saying them with all that lecturing going on. Mind you, I think you could have answered her, because I got the impression that she didn't really know what she was talking about once or twice, when I tried to bring her down to brass tacks. She wasn't a bit like herself. It didn't sound like Paula talking at all. Every now and then she'd get very het up and definite and then she'd just sink back and go quiet and dreamy and almost tearful I thought.

'So I tried to say that she'd known what the college was like before she went there and I thought she wanted to go there to get away from all the things her school friends were being pushed into; to get *into* the middle class, and, yes I do remember this bit, she said I didn't know how blinded you could be by the conditioning of a booj – that word – background and how she realised she would never be fulfilled as a social human being if she went against loyalty to the class she came from. And I said "But Dad and I are working-class, what else?" and what about her loyalty to us? And she said we had just lapped up the bribery of the bosses and weren't in a position to know what the working class, the real working class, was like, or what they wanted any more. And I got annoyed at that remembering how hard we worked to keep her on at school and I said "If you mean Dad was glad to get a decent paid job in the office after years of piece work in the factory, yes he jolly well was, and do you know why? so he could afford to take his holidays and spend time with you and buy you the books you needed to stay on at school and not be too tired when he came home in the evenings to talk to you and take you to things." And, I said, I hadn't noticed she ever soiled her hands much and what was the working class if it wasn't that? Whereupon she said she was working as a waitress. "A waitress?" I said, "what hours?" "Well," she said, she was between jobs now but she was going to help a friend in a café when it was open – they were cleaning it out and painting it up themselves.

'Oh yes, and I said I supposed it wasn't lapping up the bribery of the Borjoosie, or whatever she called it, for her Dad to do the work and she to take the benefits, for where on earth did she think the money came from if not from the bosses? Well, I did manage to get a certain amount off my chest, and I think it did me good after being bottled up for days with all that dreadful worry about where she was and whether she was alive or dead. Oh, I was angry.'

'You shouldn't have been, you know. It's something that a kid like Paula should be trying to put theory into practice. You know, she'll come running back to the comfort of her own home off her own bat if you don't put obstacles in her way.'

'Me put obstacles in her way – I like that. I'm the only one who takes the trouble to find out where she is and what's got into the poor child, and that's putting obstacles is it? But I agree with you. If that was all – that she's trying out some daft ideas she's picked up at the college from people whose parents are rich and can afford to scoff at getting a decent job – then she'd soon see sense. But it isn't all. It never is, is it?'

'Oh.'

'No, of course she wouldn't do all that on her own. Paula hasn't changed all that much, not in that way. There's this man she's taken up with. He's got her completely under his thumb. And I must say when I saw him all hope that we could somehow get through to her went out of me. There's nothing we can do . . .'

'So you saw him? What do you mean, there's nothing we can do? If we know who he is and where he is – no, I don't accept that. Now I know more about the situation I'll go round and have a talk to him.' He saw her looking straight ahead of her as though she saw something in the window pane, so he drew the curtain. 'You needn't come. You've had enough. You were right. We should've done something before –'

'It isn't that, George. This man is thirty-four, has had two wives and I don't know how many children, whom he's left. He's been in prison. And he's completely mad. He reminded me of someone when I saw him, but I still can't put my finger on who. Someone in a film perhaps. He had a completely chalk-white, knife-thin face with spots that he'd obviously picked and lank black hair, and thin as thin he was, but like a wire, strong – he got angry about something while we were talking and he clenched the back of the chair he was leaning on – quite a solid one and his knuckles went quite white and a nerve went in and out in his cheek like a frog's throat when it breathes, and he lifted the chair up over his head as if it had been a pencil, and then the next minute he'd changed tack completely, as relaxed and polite as anything, chatting away, relaxed except for his eyes, and he didn't take them off your face while he was talking not for a minute.'

She didn't tell George, because she didn't know how to, that when Paula was out of the room he'd told her how women older than Paula were really more to his taste, that he was very fond of Paula and intended to look after her but that someone like herself – and he'd switched a look of lust on to her, fixing her with his extraordinary eyes, as she hadn't sustained in years. She did tell George that she'd also seen Paula give him some notes when they were close together in a corner – Paula had been fondling him, behaviour most unlike their Paula's way of going on, she had become quite shameless, and he had put his mouth to her ear in his peculiarly intense way and the notes had passed.

They weren't really part of the household. It was just somewhere Paula had found while one more of Eric's plans to get accommodation had fallen through (he said), and the people of the household had taken to Paula, well, she did fit in fairly easily and did what she could to help, but they didn't like Eric, and Eric was so peculiar about Paula that when he was around people tended to disappear and leave them alone.

'I began to understand the wistful look on her face when they all started to go in the afternoon. I'd thought she didn't want to be alone with me but I think she's afraid of *him*. Oh of course she stood up for him. Eric is God at the moment, but of course a God everyone else is too stupid to recognise and only the loving care and understanding of Paula can bring him into his true inheritance, or whatever. He went off on some urgent business the minute he'd got the money from her – Paula did say he was very restless and they'd go somewhere they'd talked about and planned and no sooner had he sat down than he was fidgetting to be off, talking glowingly about somewhere else. I tried to make her see but it was like trying to talk sense into a baby rabbit that's hypnotised by a snake – there wasn't any bit of her that could listen to me.

96

'She admitted she gave him money but said it was just conventional of me to think the man had to provide the money, why shouldn't it be the person most able to, and women today had broken through that stranglehold and how I wouldn't know, would I, I'd always led such a sheltered life, how loaded society was against a man who'd been in prison – and of course that hadn't been his fault. Eric was doing his utmost to get back on his feet and what he needed was some support and understanding from someone who believed in him.

'"Mostly support," I said.

'"It's that sort of reaction that makes us want to get rid of society as it is now," she said. "Money, money, money is all you ever think of and you always think the worst of anyone who isn't just the same as you. You wouldn't understand someone who doesn't mind about money, or status or getting on." Eric was a free spirit, the sort of person who couldn't be tied up in dreary boojoos rules that killed the imagination, but he wasn't irresponsible. On the contrary, he was deeply responsible to the *person*. He wanted her to go on with her course. He was very keen on her staying on at college and he didn't want her to break with her parents, so where did that leave my theories? and he wanted to marry her and there was nothing he would like more than to be in a position to support her and the children they would have, only he had been so crippled by society that it would take some time, and a lot of protection and understanding, to get him his confidence back.

'I noticed she wasn't wearing her grandmother's ring. I looked at her hand and I looked at Paula and she did stop accusing me of this and that and turned her head away. And I could see a tear going down her cheek. I know how she loved that ring. She's head over heels in what she thinks of as love – pure, unselfish love. It would be better for us all if it wasn't so pure and unselfish. She's been brought up to be trusting and to give, and she has to go and find some really nasty piece of tricky-dicky twice her age to lavish it on.'

'Perhaps if he wants her to go on at college, it is as Paula says. We might not like him but she's right there – you can't go on condemning a man forever for what he's trying to struggle out of. Whatever he did, the man served a sentence and he should be able to start afresh. It's because people won't see that, that people slip back. Good for Paula. You can see how Paula would bring out the best in a man. It would be a terrible thing to condemn a man to the dregs of life forever because we're frightened to do what a nineteen-year-old is doing – to give him a chance. He wants her to go on at college you say and go on seeing us? And he wants to meet me?'

'George. You don't know what you're talking about. I've seen this man and you haven't. There you go with your theories again. You may not believe man is born with evil in him, but whatever he was like when he was born – and you can't imagine him ever being a child – he's evil now. Evil, George. Of course he wants her to go on at college – she gets a grant, doesn't she? and she'll get a good job at the end of it, won't she? – an educated girl, that's what he likes – he told me so. Educated people, he said, he liked to mix with, that's what he liked about Paula, and he wanted to get Paula out from "this scum" – meaning her friends, the people who in fact were keeping him. I must say I wouldn't feel quite so hopeless if it *had* been that coloured chap she was with. I could've got round him I thought. I said as much to Paula and it was the only time I saw her smile.

'"You wouldn't say that, Mum," she said, "if you knew what he was into. Of course he buttered you up, that's his job. He's really crooked. Eric can't do the soft soap routine but he's worth ten of Norman."'

'Well, at least he doesn't want her to break off with us. That's something.'

'In his mad mind he thinks you're Mr Moneybags – part of the decadent feeble Boojoosy who'll always pay to save their face. I kept my eyes and ears open, I tell you, upset though I was. One thing about people thinking you're stupid, they don't hide things. And I heard him say – it was when he was just off after he'd got the money from her, and he'd been very fulsome and personally ingratiating to me as he said goodbye – I was glad of that I suppose. I should think he could be very nasty when he'd a mind to and I wouldn't fancy being at the receiving end of it. She'd gone out into the passage, to kiss him I suppose, which suited him for I heard him say, in a very different voice "Get what you can while she's here. Tell her they're going to cut off the electricity. She's

bound to have some money on her." "But we don't pay elec –"
"No, you cunt, but she doesn't know that and I've got to have
some to get rid of Roger – that's the last one, truly it is, I promise,
and then we'll be free and we can get a place of our own. That's
what you want isn't it?" And then, in a clenched sort of way: "Do
what I tell you. It's me you love.'"

The man and wife talked on into the small hours and the relief
the woman had from getting her experience into words waned,
and the comfort she got from her husband wore out as tiredness
and despair spread through her again. However sweet it was to
talk they were no further forward. She knew that this man who
had got her daughter would never give her up unless her husband
went and threatened him; and that Paula, wrapped in a sort of
haze of physical absorption with the first man who had reached
her sexuality, could do nothing to escape, being totally bound in
the power of his dark spirit.

Does the dog wake thus,
A heavy curtain clinging round his heart
Dust of betrayals lining his memory?

The blanket of the morning shuts the sight
Within the house, and when at last the light
Struggles down brown passages of air
The street, curtailed by winter, hostile, is all that we see there.

But does the dog wake like this, or the crow?

And how does the animal die?
In fear, no doubt, galloping across the field,
Struck in mid-flight, but alive until his death?

The days grow smaller and the freezing night
Tourniquets volition. The day
Returning is impotent to repair
For at our dying, unclenching the hand all that we find there
Is 'Does it matter if we know?'

Heavily the bodies, heavy in sacks, in gowns,
Push their way past tables, past pans on stoves
Knocking papers off desks in their lumpish swaying
Heaviness of the ageing body, slump of winter
Slack breasts, blobbing against dropped stomachs
Twisted blistered toes rigid in slippers.

Limp grass, slack mud, sterile earth.

## Demeter

'We are all banqueting, come Demeter.
Long time since you joined our joys, our festivities.'
'I am not interested in song and feastings,
In tributes and in bonfires of sweet savour.
Mercury, tell Zeus I am here.'
'Zeus is feasting. You know, Demeter, who better?
The best way to get Zeus' ear. Come and dine
And speak to him at table. Everyone
Is glad to have you with us once again
After your rigorous work for the earth's harvests.'
'I am not interested in work, in harvests.
Mercury, soft-tongued, you know my errand.
Hades has taken my daughter and he tells me
It is with Zeus' word he keeps her there.'

Demeter, fresh-gowned, drew herself up to her height.
Golden-haired, she moved and dark gleams
Flashed from her blue gown and from her rain-washed eyes.

She sat in silence among all the chatter
And deep in gloom about Persephone
Munched without thinking from a dish passed to her.
The food made her feel sick but she stared on
Seeing pale on a throne Persephone
Trapped far away from all this roistering crowd.
There was a shout of laughter, and a great shout
Of mirth and power and Zeus yelled across
'Demeter you have been caught in a mortal's trick:
Tantalus' son Pelops was buried in that dish.
With all your knowledge of farms you can't tell the difference
Between the lamb and kid.'
Demeter stood straight up and the laughter stopped.
She threw back her hood, and most cast down their eyes.
'Do you think it makes any difference what I eat
Or that I eat? You and your childish games –
I came here and have waited long enough, Zeus,
To tell you your daughter is in your brother's power.

I see that this means nothing to you. For some game
I suppose, she was the prize, the golden shuttle
To be bandied between you. She is not yours to give
As Tantalus carves his son up in a dish
To be presented and prove he's good at tricks.
You can say I am solemn, that I'm too hard-working
Not good company, and cannot take a joke.
Say what you like. You will not see me again
And the earth will see no shoot, and your flocks no kid
Until Persephone comes back to me.'

She covered her head and no one saw her go.


## Persephone

The streets are buff or grey, the air
Washes about the buildings, scattering
Dust and sounds of a city; there
There are no dogs or children but
On that level not far away
They shout and bark.
The traffic nexus includes the living fields.

The tunnel wind sucks, carrying no seeds.
It pulls the people in, clutching their papers,
Leaving their habitat, still the sunlight's creatures.

Airless and blowy, no light but no peaceful dark
No seasons, no change of weather: why settle a face?
Already the masks of the living are slipping a little
The life where light makes shadows and looks make meaning
Will never come down here to know or disclose us.

The silver lines run underneath the earth
The silver cars run on them through the black.
There are not even worms or crawling roots.
The lights show nothing on the phantom faces.

I have been this one move away from the place
Where eyes smile into others, where lips that move
Shoot a connection to the listening brain:
No hand can lift and reach, here, to stop you falling.

But further still must go where not even
Sterile neon spawns unshadowed crowds
Where no train's roar can simulate destination.
Beneath the silver line only the dust
Can breathe in little pockets, but this dust
Was once compounded of something that knew life
Not earth or worms, but something that touched them.

Deeper, until the memory of that
Is quite beyond retention. I am left
In a region of ash where no fire ever was. The train
Rattles above me and none other passes.
The poor blind ghosts mumble and smear their lips
With ash and grit of tuff that they cram in
Desperate for blood, mindless in their hunger.
This dark is a sterile dark. No riches, no nurture.

You cannot follow, nor your influence.
No shaft of sun nor current flows from where
The sweet world stands in daylight on the stair
That leads to the stars, down to these corridors,
As from an unmoored lightship in an estuary
Drifting, yet signalling continually.
Yet if by some hard stone among the ash
Enduring, I return even to that throng
Of speechless mouths and bodies hurrying
With neither shame, grace nor expectancy
I know that through the lurching and the dark
To lapping light and gurgling flourishing air
I shall be brought because you're waiting there.

*

On the bush emptied by autumn one fiery leaf
Hanging, embalmed; bare dead branches else.
On the bush by the wall one leaf, and one bird;
Who now for the last time calls his cry
Telling some master of the approaching change
Calling to some other kingdom news of withdrawal,
Telling of closure, of sinking, of even that leaf
Fading to sodden earth.
The earth is dun and the last colour going
Yellow leaves in the bush, sparse, sapless
Like the hair of a fading girl.

And for the last time the sun's arrows
Flash in the upper air, tomorrow's promise.
His shafts go speeding through the lofty regions
Searching, and leaving as wake a calm on earth.
Helios is there but not Persephone
And as he passes the dark drops over
The hushed earth, and all bustle ceases. As usual
Tiny patches of dim yellow lights
Spring up through clumps of ground, make darkness visible.
As the long shafts of light shoot away and on
The earth is worn out and still, as worn as Demeter;
And Demeter sleeps as having ended her journey.

# 21

We awoke to a violent storm yesterday. I have time to record this, and it may be the last entry, because communications have been entirely cut off and we have nothing to do but anxiously await the return of one of our party who decided some days ago that we would all perish unless someone could get across the mountains to fetch help. Yesterday it was as if there was some violent disturbance in the sky that didn't touch us – it was all going on high above us, the only effect on the earth being the rapid shadows following each other across the valley and up the slopes like animals chasing each other. Then the sky cleared and all was still, still and rather close and strangely warm. And this was maintained for the first hours of today and then we were aware of the cloud gradually covering the sky because the colour sank out of the objects on the earth. The sharp bright red brick wall with white gables that we found so cheering when we first came here merged with the dun-coloured row of derelict outhouses; the building seemed to step back and exist less, seemed less substantial. And although when we looked up the sun was clear in its patch of sky, this dullness and chill is creeping over the ground where we are.

   We are being overwhelmed and suffocated in a close black cold mist, thin particles of soot seeming to be suspended in this other medium, this mass hovering above, and at one point it suddenly became visible as a shape with defined edges. Then it spread out, interpenetrating everything with an icy embrace you could not fight, every bone cell suffused with icy drops, every muscle tissue lined with it, like a bad breath exhaled over the body like a rot seeping along the stringed nerves an overpowering paralyzing cold until the eyeballs stare out but see nothing I can't see anything any more only this dark dazzle and the absolute antith . . . .

The drowned man rolled in the wave, his eyeballs fixed
Staring for spring in the stars through yards of water;
The fledgeling crushed and cat mauled, the dead sheep
Shuddering for summer in a wall of snow;
The worm making backwards to the warmer regions
Finding dark earth, static, airless, unheaving;
The axle broken and the fixed stars fallen,

The clutch of ice, the blown brain, the spilled heart.

# 22

They had talked to her the night before, her friends, and she had seemed to respond. It was nothing she didn't agree with. Geoffrey was dead and the two years since his death must have convinced her that he would not come alive again. They thought, and she thought, that perhaps this time they had somehow shaken her out of her lassitude and that there was a tiny spark of desire she could fan into life.

When she woke up she got energetically out of bed and looked out of the window. It was a beautiful fresh morning and the sun was running like metal on all the gutters and ridges of the roofs.

She felt cold. She shut the window and all the doors in the flat. Then piling on the shawls crept back into her unmade bed.

The horizon, lethal with cold
Pretty and pink and lethally cold.
The pink dies into brown and disappears
And the cold curls up from the ground, and like a breath
Settles from a low sky, and the afternoon snaps
Off into night.

A slight mist
Like the frosting on cakes coats gates and hedges and roofs;
A sigh full of drops, the cold made visible
As a thin white hoar, is breathed through gaps, across fields
Filling up the air and then our sight –
The shortened sight of a white winter afternoon
And the night drawn down, drawn round, and the black Pole
Utterly still, and no feeling of tomorrow.

A blink of the strained eye and a silent blackbird
Hops across the few feet that is visible world.
I turn and think
Of a winter story of a few years back
But the past and its colours are gone, and only through glass
A face never looking for me swims past and fades,
The voices beyond recall these many years.
This winter night is like a hundred years
None that I have in my mind remembers this past
And this tomorrow lies away from them
White unmarked snowfields they never visit
Terrain I look at but cannot inhabit.

Summer child
Where do you go in the winter when nights are dark
And the ground sodden?

I saw a fly
The sort with long drifting legs, clambering among my ashes
Left from a warm season.

Brown-legged skinny cotton-clad dancer,
And summer drifter –
I had forgotten I had forgotten you
So closed this season.

*

## Demeter

'Beautiful but despairing countryside –
Demeter, shall all be lost?
See how the sun paints the field
Cool on the flank of the hill, and further off
Dappling the stubble; see the little mice
Settling in to accustomed foraging.
The leaves still cling, Demeter, the blue eye
Above the patch of water suggests the nymphs
Would soon return to populate the trees
If they were clothed and whispering again.
Only lift your head and raise your eyes
And the earth will teem and bud and cover itself
In a thick carpet of sustaining growth.
Some fluke, Demeter, may have produced this earth
And set it, green and breathing among rocks
That whirl in aridity in a desert ether,
And given you the power to make it flourish –
A green accident, an unintended marvel.
Surely, chance having given, chance need not therefore
Destroy it – one little wobble
One fault in the crust, one personal mishap
And this unique wonder never again.
                              Nowhere
The streams, flowing with fish that lave the stone
And make spring up the saxifrage and moss;
Nowhere the field where creeps the soft green cover
And herds and lushness and birds feeding around them.
Nowhere insects aerating soil for roots
Of lofty trees swaying about in air
And that air beating with wings to carry
Seed, and pollen.
Nowhere the rain on leaves, and nowhere people
Breathing the sweet smell of your influence.
O let us breathe, and let the seed corn spring
And we will once again lay it all open
And the scent of fires, bramble and cherry wood
Shall rise over your woods, your harvest fields,

Your meadows with their cattle; and from towns
With all their fullness and their jollity
In praise and satisfaction with the gods.
Only raise your head and bring life back.'


'Do you think it is nothing to make the green grass grow?
Raise your head, you say. What do I see?
I see grey tundra coated with deposit of slime
Left by the foetid departing waters, strangled lakes;
I see the cracked earth crawling with stinging creatures
Moving upon each other's back and covering
All the straight tracks with brittle brown bits of wings;
I smell the soil to be sour and disease-ridden,
Such leaves as appear are coated with white mildew;
The animals' soft muzzles are cracked and dried
And froth from their mouths flecks the bony flanks of their
          neighbours,
And the sweet sickly smell of rot under every log
Suppurates from mounds of grass that grows
Only eggs of slugs that eat each other
Leaving a stain and a scum and a blistering rot.
But what you see of the earth when it is dying
Is nothing so awful as where my daughter is.


'Do you think it is nothing? Every intricate snail shell
Beetles and water beetles, every fish, every limpet,
Every little seed in the oak tree bark
That will spring into leaves and translucent white-cheeked berries;
Every breeding fly and every tadpole;
The birds of the air, the eagle and the sparrows
That mob in their thousands round a lump of fat,
The great herds and the swarms that graze the earth
From horizon to horizon – sunrise to sunset;
Everything that grows, every hayseed,
Everything that eats and breathes and breeds
And is eaten of and grows again; the mites
You do not see that dance in the dusty sunbeam
The wingless germs that hatch in the standing pools
Or line the gut of the wallowers of the deep;

111

The green stain left by water on a well wall;
Each little nit that coats the stem
Of sorrel with a black fuzz of eggs; every strange flower
That opens once in twelve years on the desert;
Each tuft of groundsel sprung from a ruined wall,
And rain of leaves sweeping from the willows
To meet the lilies lifting their drifting faces –
This is not done at the raising of my head.
Do you think one speck of this comes without a force
So immense you could not stand its power
Were it no dispersed, not filtered through
The shades, the patterns, the varieties of earth?

'Do you think I can do it with my daughter gone?
The stifling dark I know my daughter lies in
Has choked the conduits of my power – were the earth
Never so blue and gold, never so lovely
Without my daughter it is ash to me.
I cannot move with the light of my day-spring gone.
You see the sun on the land. I know it is there
But in the mind behind my eye that *sees* –
Grey as nadir of the dead time that is coming,
Lightless and airless and a weight upon the heart
So heavy that the whole world has gone numb.
It is not my doing. I would not have stopped.
I have no heart, no strength to lift my arm.
Where do I get the strength to make the earth
Bring to bear, where the immense energy
To fire each grain of matter with desire?
The light of love from my young daughter powered me
Sheen off her skin kindled the forging fires,
The coursing of her blood paced the pump
That kept my engines going. When she opened her arms
And jumped and laughed and looked at me, then love
Opened my heart and over all the land
I saw the fruit in the blossom, the ear in the sheath
And brought it to its harvest. Without her
I am as old and unfruitful as the rocks
That died on the moon five million years ago.'

Desperate they plead beside their sinking cattle:
'The sun is still warm, although the sun is dying.
Call him back Demeter, lift your arms
And he will turn back and straightway climb to his power
And we will be warm again.'
'My daughter has no warmth in Hades' kingdom.'
And from the towns:
'For your own sorrow would you extinguish us all?
You have always had care for men above your own.
Mild and kind Demeter, look here, for example:
A man in a pea-green suit and calf shoes
Bald, balding, thin – give him a bit more summer.
By next winter where will he be? Old,
Past, surely, wearing such suits and walking
Peering down the festive street, padding abaft
The darks, rounds, ripeness of a human harvest.
He has thrown his all upon this summer
Summer and luck he needs, olding; what of him?'
'Summer you ask for? Treats? Festivities?
It is not I who brought about this winter.
Go and complain to him who took the warmth,
The soft sweet breath and touch of my lively daughter,
Who froze the earth to keep Persephone.'


# 23


The washing started tugging as the wind came up in the evening
and swept through the valley. The next day woke to a dark lashing
rain. The plain was deserted. The wind blew all that day and
throughout the night and the next day, and it was seen then that
on the upper slopes that had once been so fertile it had taken every
grain and crumble of soil and only bare rock was left where the
covered earth had been.

# 24

The point at which we decided to turn back came after we had travelled through and grown accustomed to, as we thought, some fairly desolate scenes. In this area the desert had been encroaching for several years and occasionally we saw remains of what had once been settlements on grazing land, outposts certainly but not the pitches of nomadic desert dwellers. Now they were well within the desert. The vegetation line had receded and of course once the desert got a grip there was no remedy to the withering away and desiccation as there might have been had measures been taken at this margin years ago. At this rate the whole world would become a dustbowl before one's eyes. By the time we came to the settlement I am talking of I think we would all have been surprised to think of animals, or plants at all – they were so totally non-existent in our surroundings that we had forgotten we had forgotten about them. Our preoccupations were the wind, the dust and the cold.

At first we interpreted the outer indentation we came across a as wadi, but later decided that, irregular as it was, it had been man-made. It seemed to have been an attempt at an oval and the only thing we could think of was that it had been some pale or other, to mark off or protect an area. We had got used to finding bones, usually in a trail over many miles, the rib cage of a beast, the jaw of a herbivore, cleaned and polished by the wind rolling the sand over it. But what we found here did not seem fortuitous. On this little hillock within the mark, a hillock that could have been swept together by the wind, but again seemed to have that strange intended look of something made by man, were skeletons of browsing animals laid carefully in a circle, as numbers on a clock, skulls towards the centre. By each skull was a skin container of the type used by people in those parts (or used formerly) for containing and carrying goat's milk. Johan scraped the sand away from one and shook it. It rattled. We then found that each contained one or two seeds of durra. We presumed that we had come across the site of what had once been an oasis where they had been used to grow a little grain, and that perhaps the inner indentation round which the beasts had been placed had once been a spring or well, long since choked with sand. The wind, which blew without intermission during the five days of this expedition from Camp Bhati, was already blowing the sand we had scraped away back over what we had found and we knew that very soon there would be nothing to indicate that any living species had been indigenous here.

# PART II

Unease
Wind of March,
Halting
Then upwind from the track the noise of shunting.
Look up, straighten up, see
Swirled branches, swirled clothes in yards
Tugged at, tugging.

Light at strange times, rooflines
Seen in new positions, then sinking;
Echoes sounding from further than yesterday,
Heads lifting.
You find yourself walked two miles from your room
For no reason
Tasting time in unknown parts of the town
Turning this way, that way, stopped before windows
Uncurtained, though still the shut-in season.
Unaccountably women scrub out drawers
Men are late home
And when they come their wives
Are turning things over in high parts of the house
Not crouched in the kitchen.

And suddenly you are reminded there are backs to things
As when the light is switched on behind the gauze
Backdrop that has blanked our sight till then
And the prince goes down through the wood to another exit
Brick wall till then.

A child plays out after dark
First time this year, and you hear:

She is coming
From the paths within the woods
Up the gulleys from the plain
Drumming drumming
Insects building citadels

Bud-sheaths opening with a jerk
All wing-folded creeping things
Heaving up to gasp the air
Thrumming, thrumming
Tricklings, juicings, fattenings, breathings
Sighings, heavings, spreadings, reachings
She is coming; if you listen
Spring is here.

*Oh no, I do not believe*
*As the snow swirls again and the windows*
*Drip from the inside taking the warmth from our breath*
*I do not believe;*
*As the black lines creep back through the newly faced walls*
*I do not believe;*
*Dead letterbox, telephone, eyes down, arch filled*
*Doors shut, blinds down all day, gate locked, lease ended —*
*I do not believe.*

Something is gathering at the edge of the meadow.
Do you not hear
The bird calling across the wet grass
The bird invisible singing from behind thick air
The blackbird's whistle carried by the rain?

*I have heard —*
*Out of the empty season, weary August,*
*When for a stagnant month no call has broken*
*The bronze and heavy sky —*
*I have heard suddenly a blackbird sing*
*And the next thing we knew the year was dead.*
*Crying within walls I have heard the warning,*
*Blackbird's alert, Hades' bird to tell him*
*Prepare his riches.*
                    *So I do not believe*
*Not while this damp and still clings round my head,*
*This heavy emptiness afflates my heart.*

The steam outside is thinning against the stained windows
The houses and trees beyond stand out and come nearer.
Somewhere she is moving, prepare to receive her.

*A cold fury has snatched at the little edges*
*The unfurling of the lime buds, the ragged wave of the elm leaf*
*There are shreds, silk scraps of leaf from the woods on black*
*pavements*
*Purposely pulled apart as when, torn to scraps*
*A page of a book is destroyed.*
*Shoots looking out for air are broken, fronds smashed*
*Harsh whirlwind is up there, black storm clouds with hard edges*
*No vague-sided clouds bringing softness, bringing liquor*
*Balmy for growing, soothing and hushed exhalations,*
*Like velvet nostril quivering, sleeping in hay.*
*Foolish greenery may have arrived out of habit*
*But the pellets of ice are coming, and black rain to cover it*
*Bowing down everything and driving it back to its cave.*

*She is not here. She is nowhere here. I do not believe.*

# 25

'The aim of this inquiry into the order relating to case no. 596, in the charge of Miss P. Sulkins, home visitor in the employ of the Bamborough Area Council for Social Service until last year – the pink file, sir – and transferred from the list covered by the South Midlands (Eastern Section) Administrative Area – the papers in the yellow folder, sir – is to try and establish an order of events that stretch over no little period in time, so that responsibility for the unfortunate outcome of these actions, or as some have chosen to prejudge this enquiry, lack of action, may be apportioned justly between the various bodies responsible under the Act. This has been no small task, Mr Chairman, as a mass of conflicting evidence from a variety of sources has had to be sifted. It has been further complicated by the fact that officers dealing with the case at the beginning of its history have left or been replaced. This, as you know, sir, is a situation that bedevils many areas of the public service but lack of continuity in care for the young can have particularly serious results. It was the not fault of my client, that just as the Visitor seemed to be gaining the trust of the young person who is the subject of this enquiry (she was a child when the case was first brought to their attention as in need of care and protection but is now classed as a young person) she was transferred because of area reorganisation undertaken in response to changes in government policy, and that the officer who took over the case was hospitalised shortly after she assumed her new duties.

'But I think you will also see, sir, as the details unfold, that it is in its nature a far from simple case. The girl comes from a large and extended family and at all times when my client and its officers were trying to obtain information and ascertain the conditions the girl was living in, their task was made more difficult, in some cases very difficult indeed, sir, by the attitude to the authorities of certain members of the girl's family. As this meeting is in camera it is allowable at this stage to point out that certain elements in this family, being of – er – immigrant origin, ah, have a totally different conception of the role of a daughter in a family and of parental rights, and while doing all they could to respect the traditions of minority ethnic groups, and in particular the rather dominant role of the father in such societies, in the last resort it was with the protection of a minor that the Council was concerned according to the law of this country. This family is not a totally foreign family but as I say there were elements of interference that made the task of the County particularly onerous in this case. Also, they come of a class of person frequently on the move from household to household so a great deal of time was wasted by officials seeking to interview relatives who were in fact temporarily with other members of the family in another part of the country, where, of course, the authority I am representing has no jurisdiction.

'I in no way wish you to think that I am suggesting that delays and loss of documents should be treated lightly, but I would like to put forward the view that it was not within the power of my client to remedy the situation they took over from an authority since re-organised under Section 5c of the Reorganisation of Ancillary Services (Domestic) Act. Following the inability to trace records of certain interviews and the fact that other important papers were not presented at previous hearings of this matter, the fire in the building where the former South Midland Area's archives were temporarily housed pending re-organisation was particularly unfortunate and can only be thought of as an unhappy coincidence. As you may recall, Sir, the police did not treat this as a case of arson.

'But I would like to mention that conflicting evidence is not always the result of a social worker being inexperienced and taken in easily by appearances when he or she should obviously have checked with an independent source. As I have pointed out, sir, independent sources are very hard to come by in these sort of areas. As I think you will agree when you have looked at all the evidence it may well not have been quite so simple in this case to determine what was the best for the girl, as we, looking back on events from this point in time, may think. It was, I agree, unfortunate that my client could not have stepped in earlier. It has been suggested that early alarms were ignored but I would like to emphasize that we are greatly curtailed as to actions a public body can take based only on hearsay and rumour. I am sure you will agree that it is in the best interests of the traditions of our society that there should be these circumspect checks and controls on what a public authority is permitted to do to interfere in the private lives of individuals, but at the same time it does make it difficult to act promptly and, in certain cases, and this must be one of them, one can only regret the outcome.'

'Thank you, Mr Pettit. Now I will just briefly run through what I have here to make sure we are agreed. The subject of this care and protection order, then a minor, was found to be living, as man and wife, with her uncle –'

'Yes, her uncle on her mother's side – her mother's brother.'

'With her mother's brother, a man obviously considerably older than she. When questioned they admitted that this state of affairs had been going on for some time. Have we the report of that interview?'

'Document A, sir.'

'Document A. That the man, who was belligerent on several occasions at first, threatening the social worker called in by the Visitor, said it was no business of theirs as it was a family matter and that the girl's father, his own brother, had given his consent, and what more could you want, and there was no higher authority than that, and no wonder there was so much crime on the streets if the government took away the father's power, and why didn't they do something about crime on the streets instead of invading people's homes. He challenged the social worker to find that the girl lacked anything. He was in a far better postion financially to help her than her own parents who had a lot of children and responsibilities, whereas he had no children and everything he had would go to her. When the subject of education was brought up and it was pointed out that the girl had not been going to school he said that she was not learning anything at school anyway, that she was much safer here than at the school she had been to, where she had been threatened with knives in the play-ground and that she could learn all a wife needed to know better at home. It became obvious to the social worker that the man was quite beyond the reach of modern opinions about the education of girls. Later he became less abusive and rather pathetically said that he kept himself to himself, that the girl was not roaming the streets getting into trouble like the girls who went to school, that he had no one else to care for him, that to deprive him of her company now would be cruel and shameful to an old man who had provided her with a home, protected her and looked after her in every way. That tallies so far?'

'Yes, sir.'

'He mentions his brother – but I thought you said he was brother to the girl's mother?'

'That is so, Mr Chairman, but I gather that there is a very strong bond among these people between brothers-in-law and that they regard them as we do blood brothers. But in addition there was apparently some connection between their grand-parents so they may have been cousins also. It is a very complicated family tree, sir, which we could not pursue beyond two generations.'

'Ah yes, I begin to see some of your difficulties. Now, as to the girl. When interviewed she agreed she was not ill-treated. She said she had wanted to go home at first but had got used to it at her uncle's house now. She stayed in mostly looking after the house and cooking and seeing to his clothes. She said she sometimes longed to go out, to a disco or an amusement arcade and be with other girls, but her uncle was strict and didn't like her going to those places, and although she was sometimes lonely she couldn't stand the thought of going back to that school, especially now she had been away from it for so long because anyway her friends wouldn't be there any more and she would be treated like a little girl and the things they had to do would seem more stupid than ever because in her uncle's house she was treated like a grown-up, which she was anyway, and she ran the house. That tally?'

'In fact, sir, by the time of this interview she was mature in, well, in every way, sir, and struck the Visitor as a very competent housewife. The house was well-kept and clean and even the garden looked well-kept, which her uncle said had been an awful mess before she came. She was quite mature in her answers, and as you will see from Document A, sir, the Visitor got the impression – we have to rely on their experience in this sort of judgement – that she was more or less in command of the situation and had gained poise and experience from it and that a second traumatic removal from what in fact was a secure home for her would at this stage do more harm than good, especially as the relationship between the girl and her father was not good. The only complaint – and she was not really complaining against her uncle, perhaps I should rather say the cause for depression – was that from time to time she was very homesick and longed to see her mother and girls of her own age.'

'The next step was that the parents of the girl were visited?'

'Yes, sir, after some delay due to circumstances already referred to.'

'Quite. By and large they bore out what the girl's uncle claimed – that it was with their consent, or even connivance, that the girl had gone to live with her uncle in the first place. Report of that?'

'Yes, sir, Document B, and I should here direct your attention to Document B1 which is a report of an interview with the girl's mother submitted on her behalf by the latest Visitor to have taken over the case. She apparently told her, contrary to the impression given in the former interview covered by Document B, that she never condoned her daughter's going away – which she referred to rather dramatically as a "kidnap" – that she did everything she could to bring the matter to the authorities at the time, but "was prevented", that she had certainly never agreed to her daughter living with her brother, that her daughter's health had suffered alarmingly, and that she never told any social worker that she had agreed. It was all a plot to distort what she said, a plot between her husband and brother to take her daughter away from her, and her daughter had never got into any trouble while she was with her, and that she ought to be with other girls of her own age and with her own mother. I might just interpolate here, Mr Chairman, that the school report, Document C, confirms what the mother said about the girl never being in trouble when she was at school. The woman went on to say that the social worker had written down what her husband had told her to because she was frightened of him, and because she was a young nit-wit from college no more capable of understanding the wily ways of men like her husband than she could fly. As you can see, sir, this lady is quite a redoubtable lady and it was with great difficulty that we persuaded her to await the outcome of this enquiry before insisting on seeing you personally, sir.'

'But what I don't understand is why she said none of this before. No record of such an interview was presented at any of the previous hearings, it seems. The mother-instinct of this "redoubtable" lady seems to have developed rather late in the day.'

'It is true none of this came out earlier. Miss Winkelmann, the worker who presented this report, Document B1, is present, sir, if you should wish to question her on it.'

'Can you give us any clue, Miss Winkelmann, as to why this protest came so late, and can you give us some indication of the form of these attempts she mentions to get her daughter back? I think it is quite important to establish whether in fact the County had information at their disposal which would have enabled them to act sooner in this case.'

'I shall ask your indulgence of a rather long exposition, Mr Chairman. The case is a complicated one. On the day of which we are speaking, the mother came home from work and was surprised to find her daughter not yet in from school. She usually got in before her mother. After two hours she no longer believed that ordinary delays were keeping her daughter, who, according to her mother, was usually very punctilious about telling her if she was going to be late and where she was going as she knew her mother worried. There was a very strong bond between mother and daughter. The mother first went to the school which was by now shut, but she found the caretaker who said there had been no event that might have kept anyone late at school that day. He had not noticed her daughter, either in the stream of girls pouring out of the school gates, or leaving after them. She next went to the houses of friends of her daughter. According to them she had been at school that day and came out with them at the usual time and, as far as they knew, had gone the usual way home. After this she returned to the house hoping against hope that in the interval her daughter might have returned, but there was no sign of her. She then set out to her sister's, some considerable journey away on the other side of the town. At this time her husband was in fact not at home. He had businesses in the North and used regularly at this time of year at the end of the summer sales, to go the rounds of his shops, take stock, examine the books, and so on. When she got to her sister's it was late and she was worn out so she decided to stay the night.

'She wanted to ring the school the next day but her sister told

127

her you could get into trouble if your child was not attending school. It was, however, through this sister that she eventually found out where her daughter was. The uncle had apparently come to the school gates at the end of school and when the girl was a little way on her way home had caught up with her and taken her to his house. When the girl's mother and aunt came round to his house to take her back he became so violent and threatening that they decided they might be endangering the girl's life by staying and arguing. Each time the mother tried to contact the girl's father by phone she got some evasive reply from premises she thought he might have reached – either he had left the day before, or was busy with the accountant, so the poor woman set off herself to track him down. Another brother they tried to contact was worse than useless apparently. The men of the family always formed a very solid front to the outside world, and at times to their womenfolk, and as it had been the custom among their people for children to be looked after by the men on the mother's side of the family, especially if a brother had no issue of his own, they didn't see why the sisters were making such a fuss. It really is very difficult to convey, sir, the immense difficulties this woman was up against, trying to give her daughter the benefits of a modern education but bound herself by a family subscribing to a quite different system of "mores".

'For this same reason once she had caught up with her husband (and been sent quickly home as being very undutiful and immoral travelling about alone and not remaining in her place at home against his return) it would have been inconceivable for her to go to the police. The police are very unwilling to interfere in family matters and apparently when she threatened to go to the police whatever he told her he would say to them if she did report her daughter missing convinced her it would be useless for her to take such action. She tried various tactics with her husband and brothers to no avail. She most certainly at no time condoned what had happened to her daughter. It was only when she ceased her household duties, refused to cook and clean, refused herself to eat, and went and sat day after day in the park, never changing her clothes, and wandering about with plastic bags full of old newspapers, that anyone took notice. She began to be what is termed "a public nuisance" going up to strangers, not begging under the terms of the act but importuning them to help her get her daughter back. She was a good deal teased by children playing in the parks, according to one park-keeper who was sorry for her and tried to help her, and once had her bags snatched by a gang of youths. Finally someone spoke to a policeman about her, saying he thought it was disgraceful that such a person should be allowed to lurk about near to a play-park for the under-fives, and that "nutty beggar-women" should be kept out of the parks. After a lot of confusion at the police station I was brought in. I later found out that the school had enquired at the house after the girl's continued absence and been given some plausible excuse for it by the father.

'When his wife began to make life difficult for him the father ordered his brother-in-law to send back his daughter. You can see how completely unconcerned this brutal man was about the feelings of the members of his family. The brother-in-law, the girl's uncle, did not contest the father's authority but he had had the girl's company long enough for him to feel he couldn't bear his house without her. He became very gloomy and depressed and according to the girl it was only then that he interfered physically with her. He took her out to a restaurant one evening, a farewell dinner, he said, as she was going to go back and live with her mother, and he gave her a lot to eat and drink and later that night came into her room and raped her. He knew that among his people no respectable girl would expect anyone to marry her after that and that the parents would be only too glad for him to keep her. He had reckoned without the mother, however, who started behaving very violently, plunging the house into darkness one night trying to electrocute herself, and threatening to wreck the warehouse where her husband kept his stocks. She has had treatment in hospital for depression and is under sedation at the present time.

'I have nearly come to the end of what I have to say but there is one final complication if I may impose on your patience a little longer. I hope, Mr Chairman, that when deciding on this appalling case you will take the following into consideration. The girl herself, whether having imbibed the traditions of her family, or through the physical bond created by cohabiting, through no fault of her own, with this man, has become attached to her uncle, and while longing to be with her mother considers herself in some sense bound to him by family arrangements as if she were indeed married to him. After what has happened I do not think this girl will be able easily to adjust to a normal teenage existence for some time and I think any order forbidding her to see this man again would not only be unrealistic, but would place an intolerable burden on a young girl who, it seems to me, has had quite enough strain already. She has a very strong sense of duty and a great capacity for making relationships, and so far, by some miracle, perhaps because of the very close bond between her and her mother, her experience does not seem to have coarsened her or made her cynical. I think the mother would soon regain her health if she had her daughter back again to live with her, at least for a period. The mother at no time neglected the child. It was only when she was deprived of her and was frantic with worry that she started behaving in an irresponsible way towards society. I would further recommend that a strong warning be issued to the father, pointing out to him that if he should continue to molest his wife and daughter the law allows an injunction to be brought against him, forbidding him access to the marital home.

## Hades

He took her to the exit slowly
Sadly and long, looking his last at her
And when they had reached the place where the mine widened
Into a chamber, and she pausing to breathe
The unaccustomed air of the realms above –
Too sharp, too rich a mixture for her shrunk lungs –
He stopped and said 'One last thing I must show you.
You never have seen this room in all your time
As Queen of the kingdom, and yet it is the heart
The still eye of the power that should be yours,
Power over life and death, power that through death
Can make rise up anew. Persephone
All the time you have dwelt with me you have mourned
And looked with horror on these territories

And so they seemed obnoxious, blank and weary
And you an exile
Infinitely trapped in an airless narrow place
Dry field of dust, no gleam or warmth of day.
I will give you some ease before you go
And make you think less sickeningly of this kingdom.
I will bring you home.'

He took her into a little recess aside
At the hub of many passages, many roadways.
A high wide bed with a dark red cover
Pillows banked at one end, and wooden posts.
A silken-patterned carpet, and carved wood chest
On which stood a jar of poppies, autumn picked.
A soft fur coverlet draped on the foot of the bed.
He laid her down and held her head against him
And stroked her neck until she lay against him
Her hair a pale spread cover on his robe.
She saw the silken flash of the sheen of petals
A black hypnotic centre held them together
A soft warm air pressed on her eyes and closed them.
All was so still she could hear the tick of a beetle
Miles away chawing in Hades' hall.
Here they were safe and still, none here to stir
Flittering worrying ghosts across their path.
The stillness was the music of the earth.
Hades came over her and wrapped her close
Within his blazing darkness, spread and melted
Around her with a dark dazzle. He moved
And a flash that shuddered up her spine to the back of her head
Then, as if fire was liquid, burst down her limbs –
Stars falling through the night –
Diffused through all her being
And became a warmth, a safeness; loosening, healing.
She lay in Hades as the bear in his skin:
Mingled, fitting, inextricable.
They slept and the earth hushed, and all paused
Who on their deathward journey were taking their way
And waited on the thresholds of their passing.

131

Later he fed her on fruit and smoothed her body
And took her again and again, took her down with him
Further each time into the dark of his power;
And eased some knot
That had been choking him this long time gone.
Persephone woke in the quiet dark, and peaceful
He lay there, peaceful the air about them,
Breathing, calm and easy; and a great joy
Stirred in her veins that had been sad so long,
And with a spurt of strength she turned towards him.

## Persephone

She awoke sheltered by dreams
Tall trees at the edge of the wood
The arms of the night criss-crossing to shield the air;
She kept still to hold the shadows close, like a coat
But the day swallowed them, leaving her
In an open field and no trace of the place she had been.

# 26

When I first came out of hospital I didn't feel like going out. While
I had been in there there'd been a day or two of beautiful weather
which we didn't know much about inside, although there was one
big window where we used to go and sit and have a smoke – the
ones who were getting better – and you could see a big tree from
there, so you sort of felt it must be nice outside, and the people
who came in from outside weren't so muffled up.

But then the weather changed and although things were green
and flowering it was cold and windy and it seemed strange there
should be all that blossom, wrong like, as if it had made a mistake
and popped up at the wrong time – that was because I had felt the

warmth of those few nice days. So I stayed in and felt shivery although after you get used to being out of hospital you do feel better for breathing real air – without all that disinfectant stuff I mean. But I did feel cold and I tired easily.

Then one day I had to go to the Post Office for something – one of them forms I daresay – so I thought I better wrap up, I better take care, you're very vulnerable after a long illness you know, and I put my old long mack on and one of the kids' mack hats and Wellingtons and I went out in the rain, feeling, in a depressed sort of way, 'Well, if I get ill again, what can I do? I'm meant to be well now and it's not much cop.'

Then, after I'd walked about a bit and done my errands I suddenly felt much better. It seemed a warm sort of rain, not a harsh wind you know. And I felt very glad I'd come out and I lifted up my head a bit and let the rain come on to my face and I thought 'rainwater's good for the skin anyway'. And I looked at people I passed a bit more, and all of a sudden they did seem nice and smiled back. And I felt like I remember sometimes feeling as a child when I was doing something a bit difficult, a bit daring. I felt 'Ooh, what an adventure!' Silly, wasn't it, when all I was doing was going down the road to the Post Office? But it was a little achievement, going out in the rain that day when there seemed nothing on earth to want to get better for, and feeling better all of a sudden. And I had a funny thought – I suppose part of the excitement of getting out again after so long, all that oxygen – here, this is silly, you'll laugh at this. I did, I know. I thought: 'If I was a plant I'd feel like growing.'

It begins to be light
When the child comes home from school now
Lingering in puddles, satchel banging knee.
The fir tree stands still behind him
The moon and the sun stand still in the light blue sky
The moon pale, its edge mouse-eaten like cheese.
The sky is pale, like crystal, without heat
Indeterminate, like a girl waking.

The earth turns
Carrying its slugs and singing birds and light,
Bringing to the surface all its buds and shoots
Its fledgelings in new nests and baby mice.
The softened warmer side comes uppermost
Hard black clay and icy silent waters
Tilt underneath, waiting another year.

The earth turns.
It brings the twittering children, and the birds,
Busy brown creatures, chattering freckled waters.
The infant stretches to the strengthening sun
The infant stretches, sensate, wakening
And, widening with the flowers his star black eyes,
Turns with the earth out to the year that opens.

# 27

She was frightened but she wanted to please him. She knew it was the thing she mustn't do, mustn't let herself be persuaded into, that it was death, the end, that there was no going back, you could never get back to the same position. It was the most irrevocable step you took in your life; but she didn't want to lose him.

All the time she was with him she longed for him to put his arm round her shoulder. When they stood at the curb to cross the road her back ached for the support of his hand in its pit. Everything of his she liked to touch. If his hair swayed into her face as they settled in the bus she wanted to hold it, to rub her cheek on it, to put it to her lips, and she thought there would be no pleasure in the world like giving in to him, which she had been anticipating with impatience but anxiety for so long. Surely then he would do anything for her, everything, always. He had said as much. So that it was a terrible let down to her to find it so distasteful. This wasn't like love at all, this wasn't what she felt when they kissed, or when he put his mouth behind her ear, or rubbed his hands over her stomach, or when, alone in her own bed she had imagined he was there with her. Now he was here it was horrible and uncomfortable and nasty and there were no lovely feelings of love. And he was quite different. It was really frightening how different he was. She would never have let someone like that come home with her. His mouth was open and drooling and his tongue lolling between his lips and his eyes staring as if he didn't see her and everything about him red, and his hands bruised her skin where he tugged at her to move her where he wanted her, and he was making awful noises and pushing at her and pushing at her without the slightest gentleness almost as if he didn't realise it was her.

And was it for this awfulness that she had taken the great jump that would divide her from the rest of her life, that she could never go back to, for this she had put herself beyond the pale and ruined her life?

She felt rubbed and sore and hurt all over and she only wanted him to stop, only to stop because she was sure he was damaging her somewhere up inside her. And he didn't take any notice of what she was asking or saying and he didn't take any notice of her at all. And she really began to hate him with such little strength as she had left. She wanted him not there, but at least if he would just stop, just for a minute, and say something to her. And then suddenly he did stop and she was all sticky and messy and she thought he would speak to her now and comfort her or beg her in his whisper to kiss him, as he had done under the bridge the other nights they'd met. But he lay quite dead to her and only made an irritated noise and shoved her when she started stroking his arm, for he had got what he wanted. He had done what he had to do.

All the time he slept she lay there longing acutely for him to go, and when he did she felt the most immense relief and vowed that now she had escaped his presence she would never never put herself in that position again. It was the best thing ever to be free and by herself again. He had looked ridiculous blundering into his trousers. So she washed and then slept.

And when she woke she turned with such longing to where he had lain and called his name and thought she would do anything for him, anything at all he wanted, because she loved him, she loved him, she loved him.

Put one foot before the other
Slowly
Press on the joints and lever up the hill
Carefully
Hand on rail and pause before the corner
Wait until the road is clear
Creeping
At even pace to the other wall again
And so
Haul you slowly to strength, to light of day
Until you stand, unpropped, in feeding sunshine,
Lungs aching less as air is accommodated
Dizziness passing, all your strength returning.

*

## Persephone

After a day of rain, towards the evening
Just in time to show before the dark
Drew another sort of curtain over the air,
The rain stopped. The sky cleared and moved back
And tiny wisps detached and movement began
A distant exchange of paces, high above
High above and far other than our world
The currents, stars, and pathways of the wind.
And at this time appeared on the edge of the field
A group of figures, huddled, in the centre
Pale and slow the one whom they were leading.

And far across the land their coming was felt
As a pathway of light like a finger moved.


## Hades

As the rain falls on the earth
As the sky lowers over the dust and soothes the hard-packed clay
As the moist air leaning on it softens it, opens it,
For the tips of the threads from seeds not to be broken,
For the liquor to carry the seed to its nourishing bed,
So my dark covering has made this great fruition.
I send you fertile back into the daylight.

*

Shut all day was the house, shut against rain
But somewhere beyond this rain the sky is lightening,
And out of the day's ending into the sleeping rooms
Out of this quiet afternoon, through the still house
Matching the unexpected sun on the wood of the stairs,
A sudden blackbird raised his head and sang.

## Persephone

So through the days her influence was felt
Creeping from the margin of the wood
Where last the light had died when she had gone.

Is it the shadow on the wall
Is it the paint
Light-shaded on the east side of the house?
The day strengthens like a woman drawing breath
The master-work of sunshine hardens now
In patterns through the pear tree on the fence.
Even when the shadow dies, the upper air
Is tightening to the pitch, and when the haze –
The sighs and exhalations of earth's night –
Is breathed away, the long stop of the held note
Will be released in the sky, and the tympany
Clash into spring. The flash of the cymbals
Is like the sheen on swaying hair
Tossed in joyful running down the hill;
A thickening and blurring of the twigs on trees
Has opened into lime-and-lemon leaves
Earth-green, water green, gold-green of the old wheat stalk
Persephone's hair in glimpses everywhere
The blur and fuzz of spring.
Rush green, an acid green, almost the green
That gleams on rotting fish; not dark green
From the moss viridian, not emerald
But army green, dung, green of the mud
As it changes into grass and becomes clothed
Gold-green of rushes and water-roots.

Look at a bare field. Blink, and the splash of sunlight
Is in fact a hidden bud of primrose.
We blink, the sun has dimmed, the tree stands there
But she is about, and likely to appear
In strange flashes, in corners of drab fields
A trickle of leaves, a shadow on a wall –
Dandelion against a garage – and soon oh soon

Hand to soft mouth she will call, from river banks,
From the cold clay clamped round last year's corpses,
From the blank eye of winter's malsain winds,
All her attendants; who will rise at the toll
Of a far bell carried on the sweet south air –
Her accoutrements the gay dense cover of earth.

# 28

They had at last somehow got together in bed in a house momentarily empty of other people, neither of them expected (momentarily) elsewhere. They were old friends whose support of each other over the years in the trials and tribulations of love affairs, marriages, jobs, lonelinesses, had become far more important to each than any possible physical flutter. All that turbulence went on elsewhere for each and this third circle linking two others was its own territory. It was an open and strong relationship. Each liked and was comfortable with the other's spouse. The family life of each was satisfactory. It was like brother and sister, with a tinge added, and more courteous.

And at once they had to acknowledge what probably they had known but not wished to push before the other – that physical flutter had been their bond, certainly at first, though by now there were other more convenient linkages; for they found each other very beautiful, very desirable.

They had had a pleasant walk and an easy supper. It was relaxing for each not to have to strain for approval in the parade of love.

The early evening had been fine and then it darkened over with thundercloud and got warmer. The house was hot when they got back into it and they walked around with nothing on in the dark rooms with windows and doors open.

'It is like summer,' she said, 'being able to leave everything open and not being cold.'

But they could not make love. The darker skin of his thin muscled slightly furry thigh lay hard and firm on the pearly white sheen of the round of her hip, and his desire was stronger than before, but his cock was nowhere. He eased her as he could.

'Perhaps I shouldn't have talked about Margaret,' she said, trying to comfort him. 'What beautiful legs you've got,' as he stood up to dress.

'Well,' he kissed her goodbye, 'I will take my beautiful legs and my useless member away and let you sleep.' They both knew that nothing between them was diminished, their affection could stand the disappointment of their hoped-for treat. Greedy children, safely back on ordinary fare.

She slept as the wind got up and he drove with leaves whirled against his windscreen. Suddenly she was wide awake. There was a lot of commotion. Something was happening.

It was raining. It was raining in gushes, sweet soft noisy rain over all the gardens and dusty earth, sluicing the stained pavements, dampening crusty brittle walls, running down the windows. All the gutters were full and busy, everything in the night active with the rain.

To her ears the pattering and shshing of the water gurgling in drains sounded like a sort of singing every now and then, an aural counterpart to her inward calling his name, calling him to her. At one point nearing home in the very dark country lane overhung with soughing branches, he thought there was a tree down across the way. It was an illusion of tired eyes, but before he got back in the car he stood, his collar open, looking up at the sky where there was nothing to see but black, and let the water splash down on his open face, his wet shirt clinging to the skin of his chest and belly. And she felt, though comfortable in bed, as if she were standing with the rain sluicing all over her, streaming soothing over her breasts and down her thighs, warm and comforting and she hoped that he was not in difficulties on the road and that he was thinking about the rain. It would be a fine day tomorrow, she knew. And after that miraculous drenching, she really did sleep.

## Demeter

Demeter travelled swiftly to meet her daughter
And everywhere she stepped, after she'd gone
Little stars of flowers began to grow.
Passing she looked at the flanks of the fields with interest
And as her eyes moved on, a yellow-green haze
Disturbed the hard line of the smooth brown surface,
Soft down on a young chin, imperceptible
Except to those that love them.

## Persephone

See, the earth is garlanded for you –
The brown bare outlines thickened and gone vague,
Gaps filled up with fronds; and little shoots
Exploring over ditches twine around
All spare pared dead wood they can clamber on
Venturing forth as all things do this season.
The tendril of the vine waves in the morning
To greet the sun and as the light looks over
Earth's edge, sparkling the grass, the sappy stems
Show all their workings, vulnerable, pale, pellucid.
The earth is garlanded and wine jugs cooling
Everything swept and everything decked for welcome
Open doors, open arms, open faces, eyes raised, eyes looking,
Young men in clean shirts, laughing; laughing in doorways
Waiting for something to ride to; waiting, expecting
Ready for your return.

\*

You see this rain
Slanting out of a copper sky
Falling from the middle of the air
Not higher than the trees or buildings
Immense light still bright behind the edges
And the woman in a sunhat running out to save the washing,
And you hear it, how it soothes with its gentle patter
The crinkled earth:
Big soft drops you can separately hear, splashing;
A black rag flaps across the corner of the eye –
Blackbird homing from green –
And this rain is trickling down gulleys, into the splits
Of hard old tracks, stamped hard with sorrowing feet
Cracking with weariness and desiccation.
And if a seed, pushed by the winter wind
And rotted as a useless wisp of hay
Is licked into the light and rained upon
There stands your wheat.
Rain, you are loosening something in my bones
Soft fingers draw back coverings in my head.

Something undoes with a little lurch, rose
Of blood opening in the body
Body that pumps these rivers of the world –
Torrents of love to make the grass grow,
Persephone's moist breath in the rising corn.


*

I hope no one is miserable on this day.
The sun sparkles and the fresh earth tingles
And the air wafts in great gulps of fragrant verdure.
The dance of the motes at midday is like stringed music
Vibrant and perky, gay and sweet to the ear.
It falls and it lifts and it lilts and is never still
But runs on with just rhythm and clear notes, and as counterpart
The brooklet over stones
So cleaned, so rounded, runs on with it too.

High above the sea a speck hovers,
And far below the creaming dash of water –
So far, it looks like lace lazing around
Rocks that, this high, lose their jaggedness.
So high you do not hear the crash, only the wind
Sighing in thrift and grasses that lean out
Against the sky.
And as the buzzard travels, and the lark lifts
Higher and higher its eternal bubble
Of piercing sound that never breaks, until
The sky is one blue
Except for dancing points when you stare up,
Whose heart does not leap and travel as far,
And who has not felt the strength that love of the world
Would give to one who leapt out into its air?
And could we shout with the lark or crash with the sea
Who would not shout across the bulks of the hills
And up the inland valleys clothed and quiet
That she has come back into our world again:
Fruitbearer, bringing riches, Persephone.

I hope no one is miserable on her day.


*

## Persephone

Come into the fields, wife
Now that the night has fallen;.
Let us look at the stalks
And see if they soon will be ready,
Ready for the grain in the flower
The gift of the Goddess, nestling.
The stars I shoot into you
That burst and fall in your rivers
Will float in a shower on the land
And the flower will burst on the stem.


## Demeter

'Demeter, see, the corn at last is sprouting
And the old ewe that three times has miscarried
Delivered of a healthy lamb last night.
Demeter, praise be, this benison is yours
Demeter, life renewer, great Goddess.'

'The valley is beautiful: Persephone makes it so
Your fruit will set, but only by her doing.
The liquors and the fibres of my body
Can only be revivified by hers.
Her comely flesh and growing bones it is
Conveying health to your stock and to your seed.
The firstling, the milk teeth, the forming corn
Are hers. And when she has gathered all her tribute
She brings it to me, and from this comes my strength.
The spring and its doings are hers. But she is mine.
See in the milky kernel of the wheat grain
Her shining teeth
In the sheathed silky bud of the white hedge rose
Her firm and tender little pointed breasts
Tight holding their hard fruit
And like a twisty flower where insects seek honey

Are the convolutes of her ears
Whose drum of skin receives the breezes' whisper
As shells do the sea's murmur.'


*

O tiger, O leaping animal
Skin that the sun reverberates on,
Green lancing sticks whirling the air that lies
Bright white about your points
O repetition
Of birds for the first time ever heard,
Persephone out of the house of darkness:
Sun, voices, spring.

# 29

Thank you, Mr Chairman, for that most generous introduction. It made me a little uneasy. I looked around for this other speaker, this eminent historian who had been right in the middle of the action, this acute analyst who assembled with such thoroughness the material I too had worked on, who had packed it into enlightening and readable volumes. And then I realised it was meant to be me.

But I come here to address you, in all humility, because I am very interested in the subject of your conference; and with the vanity of an old man I would like to take part, not as an outsider addressing budding scientists – a bit of "general studies" thrown in for relaxation between the serious business – but as a fellow enquirer into the workings of the brain.

I see from the programme, that you have ahead of you Professor Dorrf's report of current work at Bell, also presentation of material on recordal systems, and many other gifts straight from the horses' mouths. I would not, if I could, trespass on these pastures. But the brain and questions of its function, and the part "memory" (and I put it in quotes) or rather, a consideration of memory, can play in furthering our understanding of this function, belongs of course to everyone as a human being, from the stupidest person who cannot read or write to the top people in biochemical research.

So my talk is going to be a personal one. I see that the title is down as *Historical Memory*, but I would prefer to call it, if it must have a title, *Memory of History*.

The tricks the memory plays can be extremely annoying. As an historian I know how valuable a commodity – and I mean valuable in terms of hard cash – it ought to be in these days when the whole of life, our own present as well as the past, seems to reach us pre-packaged in the form of interviews and telly-probe. But I am thinking back to the days before the war – the '39-45 war in Europe, that is – when a reporter was actually expected to know the place he was writing about.

I was in Europe for those crucial years – the Mediterranean, the Balkans, and then of course the Polish Corridor, Berlin. And I was there again, briefly, as the war drew to its close.

I knew what was going on, all right. I wasn't stupid and nor was the highly efficient organisation whose representative in Europe I was. But in those rare flashes when one can shed the present self and all it is in command of I realise that there were really only two occasions when I did personally feel the times on my pulse in such a way that I remember *them*, and not what I have since reconstructed of them. It is those two occasions I am going to tell you about.

Here I think I am probably going to disappoint you. It was not, alas, I who had been inadvertently left alone for two minutes in an antechamber where by chance lay the plan of the Althaus plumbing system – to prove, as so much that is missing does, the crucial piece of evidence when, later, people were trying to fit together the events that fired the conflagration of the civilised world. Nor was I the innocent bystander taking his lunchtime beer in his local, to whom Shmekov slipped the information, two hours before the police grabbed him, that altered the Alliance's whole strategy towards the opposing powers in the Southern Apex.

I am going to tell you of two glimpses that have retained their clarity for me over the years while important and famous things have faded. Both were on railway stations, the first in a town in Eastern Germany.

I was drawn, by the figure of a woman looking at it, to a child's face at the window of a train that was beginning to move. The little girl seemed to be with a group, the carriage was dense with bulky figures, and I had the impression someone was trying to get her away from the window. She seemed to cling to the surface of the glass with her poor little face. It was quite white and her eyes, two great black lamps, fixed on the woman. The child's face moved not a muscle. The mouth was shut. The woman was very tall and straight. She was wrapped from head to foot in an old-fashioned opera cloak, of blue velvet. It was autumn and the air was beginning to nip. She struck me as prosperous and gave the impression of being a celebrity – an actress or a singer I supposed. Suddenly she flung out her hands towards the window and her face up so that the hood fell back from her head and the cloak streamed behind, held only by a brooch at her throat. A mass of thick brown hair tumbled down. 'Klara,' she screamed, 'Klara, wink mir doch zu, mein Kind, wink mir doch zu (wave to me, my child, only wave).' The child's face remained frozen at the window and was slowly carried sideways down the wooden platform. Then the carriage came to a curve in the track and the window could be seen no more.

The other memory is of a suburban station in the South of England. It was spring and the war in Europe was drawing to a close. I was travelling up from the English coast on my way to London to arrange the final leg of my journey home. I had originally crossed the Atlantic thinking I would be away a few months, but the brief tour had stretched into years.

The only other person in the carriage was a young woman. Few people travelled at that time who didn't have to. She had pale hair pulled back severely, and a black beret. Her coat, old and worn but once good, was also black. She was very thin and sat quite still in a corner. She looked out of the window but hardly seemed to register what she saw. She shuddered every now and then and pulled the coat lapel across her neck, although it seemed to me quite a warm day.

The train was slow and stopped several times for no reason we knew of and with no apparent likelihood of continuing. I offered her a cigarette and a drink of coffee from a flask I had. You young people have no idea what it was like for people in Europe then to be offered a cigarette or a piece of chocolate or something like real coffee. She looked at these objects in my hands for some time and then raised her eyes to my face. As she did so the sunlight that was splashing through the trees along the track, caught that part of her hair that was not covered and, ill as she obviously was, it shone like pale gold, as if it was a source not reflection, of light. From my experiences in the Occupied Countries I could tell she was starved. Very haltingly she began to respond to my conversation.

She had been caught in the South of France at the outbreak of war. She had been visiting relatives there. She had worked for the Underground movement, involved in forging passports and papers for people trying to escape across the Channel; had been discovered but saved from death by a German, who had raped her and kept her as his own prisoner. Finally, he had to hide her in a cellar. Her life had become inextricably involved with him. She had grown to womanhood through him. He was the only man she had ever known and now the only human being she saw. The last few months she didn't see the light of day at all. 'I shall never be able to forget him. He saved me and fed me when he could, and cared for me. He had had an English half-sister, much older than him. He said I reminded him of her. Of course he had to leave when they retreated.' She had stayed in the cellar for what she thought was about three days and then realised that she hadn't felt the vibration of gunfire for some time, perhaps a day and a night. She decided to risk going out; she would soon be too weak to move. She expected to be shot the instant she emerged. But there was no one there. She walked through miles of deserted rubble and there wasn't a soul. She thought the strange light must be due to her dizziness but then she realised it was spring and the sun was shining. Later she worked out that she had been kept underground for four months.

Luckily she had walked, or tottered, in the right direction, and after days which she could no longer recall, sleeping in barns and eating raw eggs when she could find them, she woke up in a Red Cross Hospital. These clothes she had on had once belonged to some Duchess, she said. She had shared a blanket with her in a cave in the Marais. She laughed, and it was the laugh still of a young girl. 'You meet all sorts in the Underground, you know.' The Duchess had been shot at the time she herself was captured. I felt she wore these dark garments in some sense to keep the spirit of her friend alive. She was now at last returning home. Her mother had been informed and would probably be at the station.

She lapsed into a deep silence which I did not try to disturb. The effort of talking after those months in silence and darkness must have taken the little strength she had. She was obviously delighted with all the green of the fields and copses of Kent, the railway banks seemed to be opening in flower under our very eyes as the train went through the sunshine. The twigs on the brakes were all beaded and bulging as with countless white droplets but it was not frost or rain but the swelling of buds.

Our carriage was at the front of the train so that when she got out she was right at the end of the platform beyond the canopy with its wooden fretwork coping, in the middle of fields. You have to imagine something very bare. There were no notices, no signs, nothing that could indicate where he was to a traveller, so that the clean worn wood of the country platform and the solid unadorned brick of the little building seemed very much a part of the wooded slope at the back of it.

This was one of the places where the train seemed to feel no reason for going on. The driver got down from the cab and walked slowly down the platform and disappeared through a solid wooden door. It was very quiet and the noises from the wood became distinguishable, as if the wood itself had suddenly moved down nearer the track. There had been little birdsong in the devastated places I had come from and I think it was the striking on my ear of the calling of a blackbird, so meaningful somehow as it sounded out clearly from the delicious chatter in those trees, that made me feel the war was over. I looked at a block of sun on the platform where the light came through some missing roofing. I listened to the birds singing and watched a curl of grey-blue smoke rising into the sky from the station's brick chimney, and winter and the war seemed unbelievable. This place must have stood here like this for all those years, and I imagined it retaining always this season, a pocket of perpetual spring – almost a source of spring from which the frozen bare earth in other places could be revivified, as those old maps depict in each corner a Wind holding in his bursting cheeks the force of the wind everywhere. Of course it only gradually came to mean all this to me through the succeeding years, through my memory of it. At the time I was worn out, still reacting no doubt from living for years on end in fear and dread. I just sat, looking at the lovely day, glad the train was in no hurry.

The girl moved a few slow paces down the empty platform – she had asked me not to get out and help her – and then she stopped. Her straight little black-clothed back looked very distinct and lonely in all that green and blue and sunlight. I followed her gaze down the long empty platform and there at the other end stood a tall figure. There was no one else. It seemed a long moment while they remained thus immobile and then the young woman put her head and shoulders down and rushed like an eight-year-old, knees doubling up and arms pounding. At the same time the woman moved, incredibly quickly – she seemed to glide quite upright, and they met just beyond the platform roof in the sunlight. As the girl tilted her face up to her tall mother her hat fell off and, the mother's fingers clasping the head, the hair came loose and fell down the black coat like a cascade of shining water, as soft-looking as a swathe of new mown grass.

Now you will forgive an old man for indulging in his memories.

Your chairman was kind enough – before he let me loose on this most patient audience – to say that my attitude, for an historian, was very unhistorical and I took it that that was meant as praise. Some of my former colleagues would agree that my recent work is unhistorical but on the contrary condemn it for this – or rather they would condemn it did they not resort to the easier course of dismissing it as the gutterings of a senile mind. But I think that in this company I can dare to make a few observations without being thought altogether gaga. Perhaps this is where eighteen and eighty are in accord – for at eighty it is more important to be interesting, whereas no doubt at sixty it is necessary to be right.

Now, what I want to say before we partake of some refreshment is this. It may seem sentimental to wish to see in this return of the young woman to her mother, in a spring in England half a life-time ago, the restoration to her agonized parent of that child snatched in a darker place, a darker time. This is the fabrication of fiction, you will say. Of course our historical mind forbids this comfort. Whatever lucky chances there were and miraculous escapes, all through history there have been despoilations, deprivations, tearings asunder, deaths and devastations, and among those to whom nothing is restored must be people around us, people we see. But memory, you see, is not just a recorder, it is a pattern-maker. You are all familiar with the theories that pattern-making is not a characteristic of the brain but is the way it works, its very nature. This is certainly so of memory and it is so of art. So I would like to leave you with this suggestion that art, better than a scientifically-constructed computer, is a useful analogy for the brain, and that the more that can be found out about the workings of memory, the more usefully shall we be able to understand the links between them.

# 30

*The scene is laid first in the Leewood Arms, a pub with a garden in an unspecified part of W.11 in London, and later in Pete and Ellie's flat one block away from the former pad of the Leewood Road (Demolition Protest) Commune.*

DRAMATIS PERSONAE:

Pete and Ellie, members of the commune now living together as a couple.
John, a visitor from the past

*Pete is a bony Londoner with a sallow but healthy skin and clean floppy fair hair, Ellie an attractive girl in her early twenties, her light greenish hazel almond-shaped eyes showing her to be of mixed blood. John, an older man, reveals his unease by his rather fast speech punctuated by a high-pitched too-frequent laugh.*

SCENE 1: *In the Leewood Arms. John speaks first.*

JOHN.    No Ellie?

PETE.    She said she hopes to see you later, round at the flat.

JOHN.    Party?

PETE.    No, but she wants me to bring you back for a meal. She said she'd get on with the cooking better if I came down here on my own.

JOHN.    Ellie cooking? What's happened, man? I've never known Ellie voluntairily stop home to cook when all of us been sitting around in the boozer chewin' the fat. What you done to her, Pete man? Chained her up? Why, don't you remember that 'casion in the Compasses when Ellie –

PETE.    I do remember. No, well, listen John. I couldn't really tell you much on the phone, and anyway we can talk now. It's not that she wouldn't have liked to come, but we've got a baby now. A live one this time.

JOHN.     Gee, that's great, man, great. Great-great-great. But she could've brought it. I see plenty of females has their little bubbies wiz'em. See round. That's what the Garden's for.

PETE.     She'd rather not. She says the smoke in the pub's not good for it.

JOHN.     Smoke? You given up smoking then?

PETE.     *(Sliding back momentarily into their old way of talking to put John at ease.)* No, man, course not. But we don't, like, smoke, like, where the baby sleeps. Anyway, like I said, she wants to make you some food, man.

JOHN.     Well, I don't know 'bout that. I wouldn't want to put Ellie out. Why don't you and me go some place, see who's out and about down the Grove? Don't worry, man. I got dough. Let's go and rouse a little action, huh? See who's home. Get it together, huh?

PETE.     I don't think you'd find many of the old lot. Most of them have moved off since they broke the squat.

JOHN.     Joe?

PETE.     Joe went back to Ireland. His mother's got a place there. Ben got busted so Pru took the kids to Glasgow to live with her Mum. I saw her once or twice since, before the Coconut closed, but not for ages now. Hein – you knew he was a qualified dentist? He said he only needed to do two or three locums at these school clinics to see him round the other half of the world and he went off. You heard about Anna.

JOHN.     No.

PETE.     No? Oh. *(Pete goes to the bar to get more drinks. It is noticeable that John does not.)*

    *Long pause.*

JOHN.     Thanks, pal. Well.

PETE.     Well. Well, there was an accident. Nobody really knew what happened. You know how rotten that house was. Apparently someone had taken a piece of wood for the fire. It seems the piece they took was holding up a window sash. Anna had been mixing it, and she felt sick, so she went to put her head out of the window. The whole frame gave and part of the wall crashed down as well. It was after that we got moved.

JOHN.    Sad, man, sad. Sad-sad-sad. You want a draw? *(John draws deeply on his joint and seems to be gathering his strength for an onslaught. He takes a breath and then:)* Those lousy beaks. Those lackeys. Breaking up life, killing innocent people, that's what they do. All the time I was away what kept me going was thinking of you here, a real live community, people really living, people really loving. We created something here, something live and good and untrammelled by the *rigor mortis* of this dying, stinking society clinging with its preying claws so hard to its privileges because it knows it's dying, only it wants to kill everything else too, only able to say Thou Shalt Not because it's envious, because it's cold and impotent – they only have to sniff a little bit of genius, of freedom, of life, and they're on to it with the lackey hounds tearing it up, and for why? *(As his speech progresses the Amero-West Indian is dropped and a Scottish hectoring sharpness enters the vowels and consonants.)* Because they're frightened we will reveal their rottenness to the people, they're frightened that we will reveal the truth to the people, and once the truth is revealed to the people they won't be able to cow them and keep them from making a free society, a society of human beings. Killjoys. Robbers.

PETE.    John, I'm not a public meeting.

JOHN.    *(More natural.)* But you know I'm right. You agreed with me. What's happened to you? It was through me you read Fanon. It was me put you all on to the Om prayer. It was me who warned you of the Fascist element infiltrating at Danino's. You were all political innocents, a dupe for the Pigs and the Pigs' masters before I joined you. It was me who gave those Scottish kids, hounded by the bourgeois religious repression of their homes, a shelter from the hounds of persecution.

PETE.    Those Scottish boys are in detention.

JOHN. There you are. On your own you couldn't even protect innocent children left in your care from the Fascist thugs. The Pig police take innocent children and let the real criminals, sitting in Westminster, sitting in board rooms, go free.

PETE. Five of those innocent children knocked down an old woman of 79. When she was found they reckoned she'd been lying there for three hours. They could not get the strap she was clinging to out of her hand. Presumably it had once been attached to her bag. One of the boys said later there had only been a tin of cat food and a bus pass and an old purse with a pound and a key in it anyway, and that they wouldn't have had to hit her if she hadn't clung so hard to her handbag. They threw it away. She was hardly a capitalist.

JOHN. Unfortunately the innocents get hurt, never the criminals behind the scenes. Revolution is built on the sacrifice of the innocents.

PETE. *(Remorselessly.)* Before they left the house the boys also urinated all over the murals of Kamala and the Wheel you painted in the top room and smashed the player Ron had built, slashing the recorder with a knife.

JOHN. Oh.

PETE. *(Gentle.)* John, we were so pleased when you rang, man. Ellie wants to see you. Please come home and we'll have the meal she's doing and if you've nowhere to go you're very welcome to stay. Things have changed, as you see, but we haven't joined the ranks of the bourgeoisie exactly. We make do with the dole and Ellie's going in with a friend who's just started a café which'll help with the food. Ellie's seen her Mum once or twice. She's been very good. She sent clothes for the baby. But we haven't changed our way of thinking.

JOHN. *(Very nasty.)* Well, well, well. Who'd've thought little Pete and Ellie would be turn-coats. Little Pete and Ellie who used to hang on the very words of Uncle John. We may have been poor and ignorant in Glasgow but ratting on our friends was something we left to the narks, the narks and the prosperous classes. And there *were* friends in those days. *(The switch to the Scottish accent*

158

*is sudden.*) Not just each of for himsel' and the divil tak the hin'most. Low and poor as we were we knew the value of brotherhood. There was very little else we did have in those days. Och, weil. That's this rrotten worrld I suppose.

PETE.    We haven't ratted on our friends. I've just said, you're welcome to stay.

JOHN.    If I've nowhere to go. Well, maybe I have and maybe I haven't. That's no slur when there's thousands homeless through the crimes of the property dealers. Now that the little spot of reality I'd made in this mean city has been so lightly abandoned by those I'd thought it would be safe with – but you won't catch me compromising with the lackeys. You know perfectly well that under the present system someone who sticks to his principles and speaks out against injustice isn't going to get a job or a council flat.

PETE.    You seem to forget it was you who left the Road not us, John.

JOHN.    *(Shifting.)* Well, I'd heard someone had told the police where I was hanging out.

PETE.    The police knew we were there. It was an open squat.

JOHN.    Yes, well, when one has spoken out for freedom against dictatorship there are other people gunning for one. They don't forget so easily where I come from. The forces of oppression in Glasgow had their eyes even on schoolchildren then.

PETE.    The police didn't say it was for public speaking.

JOHN.    They came? What did they say? Who squealed to them?

PETE.    When did we ever take any notice of what the fuzz said? Come on, John. I said to Ellie I'd be back, with you in tow, by 8. It's nearly 9 now. Let's go.

SCENE 2: *Pete and Ellie's flat. Ellie comes to the door. She has a clean apron round her neat waist and her hair smoothed back. She holds out both her hands to John.*

ELLIE.    Come on in. Jo-ohn!

JOHN.   E-ellie! You're looking great, just great.

ELLIE.   It's great to see you, John. (*She brings in the food*.) Sit down. Grab a spoon. I'm starving. I thought you'd spirited Pete off somewhere.

JOHN.   (*Eating hungrily*.) This's good, man. *Vair* good. (*After some minutes*.) My, that was good, man. Best meal I've had in weeks.

ELLIE.   Have some more.

JOHN.   Well, just a wee scoopfu' mebbee.

*Later*.

PETE.   Ellie, go slow with that booze.

ELLIE.   I'm all right. I waited an hour for you to come, and, from the look of it, I've got quite a bit to catch up on. I'm tired you know, Pete. I'm entitled to a drink. The place doesn't get cleaned up and Jonquil put to sleep and a meal ready just by sitting on your arse in a pub.

PETE.   I do know, Ellie. But take it easy all the same.

JOHN.   You've got it real nice, here, real nice, I must say. Matches? Ta. You going to join me or you passed up that too?

ELLIE.   Here, give.

PETE.   Ellie.

ELLIE.   Oh stow it, Pete.

JOHN.   (*As he gets drunker he gets nastier*.) Yes, real nice, haven't you? I see they didn't smash up your discs and equipment Pete. Amazing what influence can do. You've really got what it takes – or sumpin' like that. What you tell the fuzz to get them to leave you alone?

ELLIE.   What do you mean?

PETE.   Here, Ellie. Have a drag.

ELLIE.   I want to know what he means by that remark.

JOHN.   Anything more in that bottle?

160

PETE. I'm afraid not, John.

ELLIE. And it's not much good keeking in the kitchen. There's only dirty pans there.

PETE. Ellie! Don't!

*John goes into the kitchen.*

ELLIE. Well, you know what he's like, always on the cadge. He could've brought something.

PETE. I wouldn't have wanted him to.

ELLIE. Pete, where's he really from? He's changed his accent again.

PETE. *(Relieved at her friendliness he hugs her.)* Oh Ellie, *love* you. His father was English and his mother Scottish. They went to live in Glasgow when he was three and his father, who was a solicitor, got taken into his father-in-law's firm and became a partner when the old man got past it. He said his mother died when he was away at school in the South of England when he was ten.

ELLIE. Oh, poor old John.

PETE. Sh. Don't let on you know any of that. *(To John.)* Find anything?

JOHN. Tell you what, you dear folks. I'll go and get a bottle of something down the road.

ELLIE. No really, don't do that. We don't want any more, do we Pete?

PETE. Oh I don't know. If you feel like it John, that'd be nice. *(Aside to Ellie.)* Let him, Ellie, let him. A breath of air might help.

*Later.*

PETE. Whisky! John – you shouldn't have.

JOHN. I thought Ellie here needed a little pepping up. It's so quiet here, I suppose you usually go beddy-byes at 10 and Pete does the washing up while little wifey puts her feet up. Cheers, Ellie, you've quite domesticated him.

ELLIE.    Yes, Pete did do the washing up while you were out – we wouldn't have expected you to do it. And, unlike you, John, we're not married.

JOHN.    Me, *murr*id?

ELLIE.    Well, she said she was your wife, the woman who came to the squat, and that since the payments for the children had stopped she was –

JOHN.    Ah the bitches, the bloody bourgeois bitches, once they get their claws into a man and draw blood they nae mair let go, ye ken. I suppose the Pigs put her on to me.

ELLIE.    No, the Pigs were on to something about some holiday fund that disappeared – some scheme for sending kids in Homes on a holiday that people in a pub had contributed to – fraud, they called it. I suppose you'd call it 'Glorious theft for the sake of the Revolution'.

JOHN.    You're all the same, you women; that bitch was nae mair ma wif than –

ELLIE.    Have you ever seen a dead baby, John?

PETE.    Ellie, please. What on earth has that got to do with it? Why bring it up now? You shouldn't drink whisky. You're tired.

ELLIE.    I fucking am tired. Anyway, I'm asking John, not you. Have you?

JOHN.    Why, ye ken in the tenements of Glasgow every mither had watched one or two, or mebbee three of her bairns die. The infant mortality rate in 1936 in Glasgow in that part of the city was 3/5 of the births.

ELLIE.    And where were you born, John?

JOHN.    Me, why? I don't see what you're driving at. What's that got to do wi' it?

ELLIE.    Don't you know?

PETE.    *El*lie!

JOHN.    Yes of course I know. I was born in a place called Denham.

162

ELLIE. In Scotland?

JOHN. In Buckinghamshire. But my mother was a Scot and it was true of the Glasgow of her time.

ELLIE. So you've never seen a baby die?

JOHN. No.

ELLIE. No, I thought not.

PETE. There's no merit in it you know, Ellie.

ELLIE. I know that, Pete. God I'm not claiming merit. If anyone knows about lack of merit it's me. But if he hasn't seen that he can't go round preaching to other people about their morals. Excuse me. *(She tries to get past them.)*

JOHN. Now, now Ellie man, calm down. I'm sorry if I've upset you. Here, have a swig of this. *(She pushes the bottle away. He is so alarmed he gets his accents muddled.)* I tek your pint. I quite tek yer point. I know you had a terrible time and the last thing I meant to do was to upset you. I've a great admiration for you, you know Ellie, a great admiration. *(She leaves the room.)* I'd best be going Pete.

PETE. You won't stay? She'll calm down soon. She's tired and she's not used to whisky now.

JOHN. No, no, I'll be going. Thanks for the offer . . . I wouldn't exactly fit in here I can see.

PETE. Take what's left of the whisky then.

JOHN. Yes, ta. Say goodbye to Ellie for me and thanks for the food.

PETE. She'll be back in a minute.

JOHN. I won't stop now. But Pete, I may be a bit of a shit mysel' and not exactly a paragon of virtues, and mebbee I'm not what I made people think I was, but that doesn't mean that it isn't true – the greed of the bourgeoisie, the oppression, the need to show it up for what it is. You know that. You see how easily these people win. But that's the trouble with women, their thinking's never separate from what they feel in their belly. That's why I had to

163

leave, man, that's why I had to get free. No ideas, only feelings. The minute a bitch has that burden in her belly, bang goes your chance of pure thought, of civilisation. But I wouldn't have thought it of Ellie.

PETE.     You wouldn't get much of a civilisation without it, though.

*Ellie returns.*

JOHN.     Ah Ellie. I'm off now. Thank you for the meal. I'm sorry if I was offensive. It was a bit of a shock, you see, coming back and finding everyone had moved out, the happiest time of your life just a pile of rubble.

ELLIE.     Would you like to see the baby on the way out? She won't wake if you're quiet.

PETE.     As long as you don't breathe near her.

ELLIE.     Oh Pete, I'm not that fussy am I? She's quite strong now.

JOHN.     How old's the wee bairn?

ELLIE.     She's four months.


*The three grown people stand looking down on the sleeping infant whose soft breathing seems to have spread the tawny bloom over its ivory skin. It sleeps on, oblivious of everything but the source of life within it that is strengthening it daily. They kiss and John departs.*


# CURTAIN

# 31

She had gone to bed early thinking of the luxury of a long night's rest but woke from sleep unwell. It was more a feeling of alarm than pain. It wasn't like any other sickening or illness she had known. She thought separately of her head, her chest, her shoulders and arms, her belly, her thighs. There was no pain and yet there seemed something the matter with each part. There was something wrong everywhere. It was as if the blood had been drained from her, leaving no strength, but it wasn't a peaceful emptiness. Something definitely was going wrong, as if life was draining out secretly through her body and all the parts, empty of blood and strength now, were being gradually drawn down, away from their station and function. She was deadly weary but could not rest. She was too frightened to rest though she kept still. She was very frightened and felt she was dying, irreversibly something was happening, there was a sort of imminence but she could not pinpoint it. There was just this immense dread in her chest and belly. She felt very cold.

She got up carefully. Her head was dull but not unbearable. She was a bit shaky but she got the children's breakfast and cleared up Bob's. He had gone early because he was going on a surveying job. It wasn't a warm day though it was meant to be spring, and she felt colder thinking of him standing about in the mud of a building site. He later told her he began to feel unwell at about 8 and at 10 doubled over with what he thought was a stitch. He knew it was 10 because the brickies had gone for their breakfast and he smelt bacon.

She lay down after she'd got the children to school. Nothing had gone wrong with the first two pregnancies. Perhaps this was just a new form of indigestion. Indigestion made you feel funny things. The sickness lightened a little and her spirits rose, but when she got up she felt sticky warmth between her thighs. She put her finger to the soaked nylon mesh. It was blood trickling down her leg.

She managed to ring her doctor but felt there was little point as she was convinced she had lost the baby.

They put a red blanket over her in the ambulance and it was soft to her touch but then the pain did come, up in the wall of her back as if something was being pulled away like the backing from sticking plaster. She was very aware of her dirty jacket smelling of cooking, her blood-soaked trousers and her uncleaned shoes.

She woke up some hours later and everything was clean and white and she was clean and was lying in a fresh cotton garment between stiff sheets. She supposed she had lost the baby but she herself felt reasonably comfortable apart from a plastic pipe stuck into the back of her hand which was sore and meant she couldn't move. She did not put her other hand down to feel her body. She didn't want to come against the flat slack flesh. She did not ring for a nurse because she didn't want to have to seem cheerful and she remembered from the two births of her live children, which had gone well, that this was a rule in hospitals. However, one came in soon and asked her how she felt. 'Not too bad,' she said. 'How long will I have to have that?' 'Not long, luv. We're just putting back some of the blood you lost. You're certainly looking a lot better than when they brought you in. You're a lucky girl, you know.' 'Am I?' she said. 'I suppose so.' Did the nurse mean that she had nearly died herself? 'Come on, cheer up. We can't have you down in the dumps like this. That wouldn't be good for the baby, would it? If we hadn't got you up here pretty quick you could've lost it, you know.'

'You mean, I didn't lose the baby? The baby's still there?' Her right hand shot down to feel her bulge and she cried out with the pain of the needle pulling. and then laughed at what she'd done. The nurse came to the bed to fix it and as she bent her head down the woman threw her left hand round the warm brown neck and pulled it to her.

'Oh, thank you, thank you,' she said as the tears rushed down her face into the nurse's hair.

# 32

It was not only because he wanted no extra work that the husband had tried to persuade his wife she had enough on her plate without insisting on a birthday party for their four-year-old.

'It's too much for you Ciss; you know the baby will need feeding in the middle of it and he'll get all upset and really Jo-Jo would be quite happy if you just filled the bread bin with sponge fingers and sat her in front of it. A party at that age is ridiculous.'

'Just because the children are easy to please, why shouldn't I make a bit of effort? It's as much for the older children as for Jo-Jo. Being unsociable can be very catching. I don't want them growing up like the Hales. I must say, they *are* a gloomy lot, aren't they? Now, if you could just pop down to Paine's and get three or four bottles of orange squash, that would save me tomorrow. They'll still be open.'

When he came back she had cleared away the supper things and was pressing out biscuit fish with her eldest child's toy cooking set. As they put the presents at the bottom of the sleeping child's bed she said anxiously: 'Are you sure you think the umbrella's a good idea? It might be a danger.'

'No, of course not. She'll love it. She won't be able to get it up on her own anyway. She'll just have it when she goes out with you.'

The four healthy children lay sound asleep, their breaths coming and going almost visibly in the light from the street lamp that came through the flowered cotton curtains. It was a warm night and Jo-Jo, wakeful and excited earlier, had kicked the bedclothes off with her feet, and one leg had slid over the edge of the bed until her toes touched the floor. The baby had just begun sleeping all through the night so had joined his siblings.

'What a nestful. Don't they smell nice? Come *on*, Ciss. You must get some sleep.'

'Only because they've been bathed.' She left the room reluctantly.

They sank immediately into deep sleep.

Four hours later, before it was yet light, the wife heard a

movement from the children's room. The baby wasn't crying. She heard stealthy steps. As the door to the parents' room opened, she held her breath. She was so tired these days she was prone to strange fears. Their bed had a wooden footboard and she saw a flicker of movement behind it in the half-light. It was a peculiar bobbing movement travelling irregularly along the top of the board. As this thing got near the end obviously making for her side, away from the door, she realised what the round blob was — it was the nub of the umbrella they had bought their daughter. She came round the corner, this tiny thing who did not reach to the top of the bed board even with the extension of the umbrella. She came along sedately in the middle of the night in complete confidence, the umbrella raised and perfect, with a look of absolute bliss on her face to show her mother what she had got for a present.

## Demeter

And so Demeter in the lengthening days,
Demeter and her daughter
Went through the land; and even far in the hills,
Mewed in town alleys, or closed in wooded cliffs
Men felt their passing, and tired heads lifted up,
A sniff in the air, a gleam of sky, a lightening
A strengthening in their fibre, and back to work
They urged now, opening barns, turning mould
Urging and expecting, looking up
Unscrewing windows, lifting shutters, lingering
To see which way the wind blew, looking
Outward, seeing the world;
And all to do, and wanting to.
Coats looosened, straight standing, welcoming the time:
Hoping, expecting, never mind for what —
Just busy in it.

Demeter and her daughter covered the land
Steadily without hurry, all complete
Staying sometimes in places where the mother
Had rested in her sorrow, and their people
Found themselves rewarded, and the land
Returning swiftly to health; and they knew
Their Goddess present, life instinct in the core:
The bare tree crowning, the cold bare sky hazed over
With leaf, with birds, with shiftings, with light pouring
Over hard edges, filling life in the bowl
Of their fields, of their homes, of their bones, and into their children.

# 33

He did not hear the usual 'Yoo hoo' as he came in. Wherever she was, upstairs, in the garden, in the quiet little back room over-looking the hedged side-patch of grass, she always seemed aware of his entry and made a point of leaving what she was doing to greet him.

But he heard a clattering from the kitchen and there she was, on her haunches on the floor. There was nowhere for him to put his feet. Grids, bits of oven, bowls of scummy water, soap, scrubbing brush, lay all around her. He picked up a rubber glove whose open end was sucking in brown greasy water. There was steam and a smell of cleaning powder.

'What on earth are you up to, Janet? Darling, that can't be good for you. I thought you were meant to be watching your blood pressure.'

She swivelled round, one arm rubbing away in the oven. 'But it's very good for the oven. I haven't forgotten your dinner. It's all laid out in the back room. Cold, I'm afraid, but you could heat some soup if you want – the top's done. Carry on and eat. I'll have something later when I've finished this.'

'Sweetie, you know I said if there was anything heavy that needed doing you were to wait until I got in and I'd do it. Surely we could have managed with the oven as it was? What else have you been up to?'

'Now, Tom, do go and have your meal if you want it so I can get cleared up. I want to be in that room soon and I shall need the table.' She clattered with the grids, rather excessively he thought, twisting round to reach for them beyond the bowl of soapy water.

'*Don't* stretch like that. You'll rupture something. Why didn't you ask me to pass it?'

'Tom, dear, by the time I've asked you to pass something, and you've said what and where is it and didn't I mean the other one, I can get this oven done and the baby born I should think.'

She worked all the while, each hand doing something and no move wasted, as if she was in an obstacle race.

He supposed she was doing it because she wanted to.

'Have a break. At least come and eat something.'

'I'll come in a minute.'

As he was finishing, exerting himself not to feel guilty, she came in drying her hands.

'Well, that's done, and the kettle's on. Oof!'

He went to make the tea. Everything was back in place, cloths wrung out, sink shining.

'Come on now, feet up.'

'No, don't make me too comfortable. I've got a lot to do. While I'm down here I'll do out these cupboards. I tell you what, while you're on your feet, get me the cutlery drawer out and the metal polish. I can do that while I sit and have my tea.' She opened a cupboard to get some rag, and plastic bags rolled out, so, on her knees, both arms working, she at once emptied the shelves.

'Bring a damp cloth when you come, Tom.'

'Hang on, I'm looking for the metal polish. And have we any more sugar? I can never find anything when you've had a sort out.'

So she got the cloth herself. 'Damn, I forgot to get sugar. I did so much shopping I just didn't feel like carrying any more – I've cooked for days so I can concentrate here.'

'And so you needn't use your clean oven.'

'Well, of course, that too. Now, sweetie, get me a bit of newspaper from the box, and dump all the silver on it, and while I'm at it, you might get the vase and candlestick from the sitting room, and I'll do your trophy if you like.'

'Janet, what is all this? You're supposed to be taking things easy, and I come home after a day's work and a beastly journey hoping for some restoration and some intelligent company. You let everything go for weeks and weeks and obviously find just getting a meal tiring enough and you know I don't want you to do anything that's too much for you. Honestly, the house is fine as it is. Then suddenly you want to do everything at once – things you don't touch all year must be done *now*. You'll be wanting me to scrape out the gutters next.'

'I hadn't thought of it, but it would be a good idea to clear them before we get more rain. This patch of dry weather won't last forever.'

She got the newspaper herself. 'Come and talk to me while I do the silver.'

'You haven't asked anyone in tomorrow, have you?'

'No, I have not – I'm far too busy. That's just it, Tom. You'll have to forgive me, and I promise I won't do anything to harm the baby. I was getting so fed up, week after week and not doing a thing, not feeling like doing a thing. I think it was that perpetual low cloud, it seemed to creep right into the house, and then those terrible winds. I felt I could hardly lift my arm to comb my hair it was such an effort; but most of all I got so depressed knowing everything was piling up and I wasn't doing anything about it, and soon I wouldn't be able to.

'So when I woke up this morning, early for a change, and the sun was actually shining, I suddenly felt lighter. I found myself just doing things without even thinking about them – my fingers seemed to work away on their own. And it was heavenly to feel active again. As if I'd only been half awake before so no wonder I couldn't do anything.'

'And you've been on the go, no doubt, ever since.'

'Oh, I have. I've got a lot done. And I feel so much better for it. Honestly, I think I *would* have damaged something inside me if I had sat still. I've had a marvellous clear out – got every single shirt on to the line – and when you take that off you could put it in the bucket so I can get it out tomorrow.'

He noticed there were no lampshades on the lights, and that the mantelpiece was bare and the cushions without covers.

'Are you coming up? Call it a day now, for goodness' sake.' But the parabola of her impetus was not yet come to rest. 'I'll be up soon. Go and warm the bed for me.'

Now he had gone up she needn't modify her actions to spare his feelings. She knew he thought she was putting it on, showing off – well, perhaps she was, but to herself not to him.

She cleaned the paintwork in the little dining-room and wiping and fondling each one put back her ornaments: a thick blue French glass bowl, a round-bellied wine bottle with a candle in it, the clock, a school photograph of her two born children in a silver frame. It did look nice polished. The little one was podgy with puppy fat and a front tooth missing and a ravishing smile and hair all over the place. The older one more solemn and neat, hand carefully on younger brother's shoulder. That must have been Pete's first year at school. And a card 'Happy Easter to My Mum' with a by now much bedraggled feather stuck on a drawing of, she supposed, an egg, that Clarissa had done at Nursery School; and a hyacinth in a pot that Tom had got for Mother's Day. She took a deep sniff of it. Heavenly! What a marvellous flower it was, so fresh, so luscious, and such a smell.

She ironed the covers and as she sat sewing them up round the cushions she felt her energy ebb and realised she was very chilly, and oh how the flesh above her knees ached! Quickly she stowed the silver away, put up the lampshade and left the others on the table. The kitchen floor was all splodged with greasy soapy splashes, so she used the last of the hot water to wash it. What a boon really hot water was. How quietly gleaming the kitchen was. No noise, nothing out of place, nothing left dirty. How nice to come down tomorrow and open the door to the same calm welcoming atmosphere, the floor all sweet and clean and ungritty. She heard a car go up the road and then still heard it as it travelled some way along the road at the top, and realised the wind must be coming from the south for the sound to come to her so distinctly. A barking broke out for a bit and then was still. It must be late, there was an eerie splash of light, a bar across the taps and the edge of the table – the moon had moved to the gap between the two houses opposite, to a position where a finger of light came through the kitchen window.

It seemed almost to speak to her. It had appeared, it would

move on, but for this moment it was there for her – almost as if it had waited for her to be alone. Just filling out to the half, it looked strangely unfinished.

All was straight, her house, all was ready. Like an x-ray her mind went through walls to every room and every cupboard and felt everything clean and orderly and done within them. And a great relaxation rippled through her brain to her muscles and nerves. She would sit down for one minute and then she would go and warm herself beside Tom. How comfortable it would be up against his warm back. She sat bent over with her arms held under her womb, supporting the weight of it a little. And then she straightened up, a bit shivery but not with cold, and opened her blouse and unwrapped her skirt, and pushed her belly and breasts forward into the shaft of the moon so that the light lay across her. Oh, it would be a wonderful baby. She felt marvellously well.

# 34

Ah, this is the life, this is the life. Steam of pouring coffee. Inhalation gulp ah delicious. Vigour. They had cleared up yesterday, thank goodness. A slant of sun on large clean table, dancing barley-sugar splashes through the marmalade jar. Dig of knife scoop on to crusty toast. Nothing better, not zabaglione, not boeuf flamande or praline paté from Switzerland or bifstek au poivre in Dieppe, not the most exquisite ten-hour long preparing meal and succulence in restaurants, or home-made lemon mousse, no délices, *nothing* like good fresh bread lightly toasted, cool with butter juicy with chunky marmalade, and coffee on the nose on the palate down the throat gulp. Ah, oh, sigh, gorgeous.

Everybody gone, house quiet, free day, stretching, stretch of limbs to the day, stretch after night, day ahead, exciting.

Special article on Latin America, read that later, perhaps little wandel down to pub garden at lunch carrying the paper, treat outing ½ pint and seeing the world, back to nice clean house still one's own no interruptions. Go out to get not let it come in.

173

Eight o'clock now, everyone gone, everything cleared up, pile of brown envelopes already in pillar box, reading this quite dense exceptionally good book on cities before 8.30 in the morning, get those seeds in today, but now vigorous black letters on smooth white page, really getting down to it; all in gear, everything clicking in evenly going round, peace and activity suspended in an active stillness like a basket on a wave, Moses rocking in the rippling bullrushes all that coiled sleeping force.

Ah, this is the life, no doubt, another cup while the coffee's hot and fresh, toast some more. -'mm.

# 35

The telephone rang at last at 9.30.

'I expected you in at 5 for your tea. (Yes it is.) I was just telling your Dad it was you. I said I was just . . . What? Where are you? We were worried. (No, Fred, nothing wrong. Give me a chance to find out for goodness' sake. I can't hear a word the child's saying with you going on.) Where are you? There seems a lot of noise. Oh, Julie's. I can't hear you very well.'

'Hang on, I'll turn the radio down.'

And then the child's voice came loud and clear:

'Mum, can I stay at Julie's? Because I'm going to help her with her paper round tomorrow so she can get it done early – the people don't come before 7 and we've got to be at the bus terminus by 8.30; because that's when we've arranged to meet – meet our friends of course and so if I help her with her round she can get it done in time. We're all going swimming – Julie's lending me a costume. She's got two, well, actually, one's her sister's but she doesn't use it any more and Mum – we went to the fair. Julie's big brother gave us the money. It was terrific. I went in one of them cage things and I got it over – well, you have to push with your legs and you sort of pull with your arms and nobody else could do it. But I did. Julie couldn't and she's bigger than me. Julie's frightened of the high things. She screamed and felt sick.

But I like the scary ones. Well, of *course* you go over with it, you're inside it, see. It was terrific, Mum; and we're going again tonight. I mean, can I? Because there are more people there on Saturday and all the people we know will be there and it's more fun when there's a crowd. Please, Mum, I'm not tired. Anyway, I thought if I stayed at Julie's we could have an early night and I'd be here in the morning. And Mum, Mum. I wan a coconut. Yes, I mean I won one. We haven't eaten it I'm bringing it for you. No, you didn't have to knock it off you had to choose thingies on a card. It was good at the fair, Mum. And Mum, if Dave and Anna call round for me tomorrow morning can you tell them we've gone to the Prince Charles baths and to come there, and Mum, I went to the shoemender's to collect my sandals, but they were shut and I need them for tomorrow evening because – Oh, thanks Mum. Yes, yes I will. Of course I will, Mum. See you tomorrow when you come in from work. And Mum: Mum, thanks for letting me go to the fair.'

# 36

'Oughtn't you to be fetching Lisa – she's been there since 3 and if they're having a party tonight they'd probably like to get her off their hands.'

David Carlson didn't really like his daughter staying for hours at the Davis's. The house was very mucky and rotting food spilled in the side alley next to it which attracted the most bleary-eyed flea-ridden dogs. He always noticed pools of oil and empty coke cans round the house if ever he passed that way. The whole street's youth seemed to tend their motor cycles outside it.

But also he had imbibed long years of his wife's punctuality and orderliness. She was most welcoming and wanted their children to have their friends in, she was a neighbourly woman, but if those children were still what she called 'hanging around' by the time dinner was ready and she was held up in the business of getting the evening meal dealt with, it put her out. She liked everybody to be busy at something. She liked them to come, but she liked them to go.

'Oh, they're not like that. There's always someone to keep an eye on the kids, and it doesn't seem to bother them having children round and up till all hours. I don't think the children go to bed till the adults do. I never see fewer than six or seven young men sitting around in the kitchen when I go in there, I've never worked out who's a brother or a cousin or what. They sit around waiting for Daryl. I don't know how Mrs Davis does it. She just lets them hang around, they never seem to give her a hand. I don't know how she can ever get on with anything. Of course, she's got no life of her own. She just lives through her children.'

The Davises had originally come from Grenada and the Carlsons had got to to know them because their eldest child and Daryl had been friends at school. When Lisa, a late addition, had come along, it had been very helpful to have such a friendly place to leave her occasionally. She loved it because there were children of her own age, of every age, and they adored her because she was such a pretty baby to spoil.

When Mrs Carlson went round she had a glass of something, excused herself from a chicken leg saying they had just eaten dinner. There were great pots of food steaming on the stove and dishes piled with fruit on the sideboard – pineapples, bananas, strange plum-looking fruit, and fruits she didn't know the names of. As soon as she could, without appearing rude, she said she'd better take Lisa home. Daryl, a very tall thin young man with a neatly-trimmed beard, with a red knitted stocking tammy buffon'd up on his hair, with thin features and a beautiful skin, more black than brown (his mother's face was a shiny cinnamon) black and pointed like the African in pictures of the three kings, came down the steps into the kitchen with this tiny fair mite at the bottom of his long arm holding his hand. She was also clutching his knee and he was swinging her up on his foot at every step and she was screaming and laughing.

When they came into the light her mother saw the child's face covered in blood and felt faint.

Lisa ran to her mother holding out a brilliant sticky red ball.

'Daryl's give me a pomganny for his birthday,' she said, shoving it at her mother's mouth for her to taste.

Mrs Davis wiped the juice from the child's face and hands.

'That was for you to take home,' Daryl said, 'you weren't meant to eat it now.' He swung her up so she was on his upper arm, patting his face quite hard and pulling at his beard. 'Aiee, Lisa don't do that man. That doesn't come off, that's fixed on that is.'

'Come along Lisa, you must come now. Thank you ever so much Mrs Davis. Say goodbye now, Lisa. Daddy's waiting.'

'Bye, darling,come again soon.'

# 37

He had chosen not to go with his parents to buy plants. This was a day to do something on, a day to use. The sun splashed and faded on the bath as he lay in hot water. The hair of his bush floated and he made a swell in the water with his hand to make it ride up and down like seaweed over waves. You could understand the connection made between hair and being manly but when you came to think of it, it wasn't really true. There was Pete in his class who really needed to shave twice a day, who had a deep voice and a very hairy chest, and he was a known bender; and there was Stuart, who couldn't look at a cloud or a diagram in TD lessons or even sometimes a house without seeing a version of the female anatomy, and he was as smooth as a babe.

'Seen any good houses lately, Stu?' he would ask when he saw him. Giggling at his own hilarious wit he heaved himself out of the bath. He padded about in his freedom with a towel knotted round his waist and put some toast to grill. On his way to mop up the bathroom he stood before a mirror admiring his Egyptian slimness of hip. It was a zig-zag orange and blue striped towel, and it should have been dazzling white cotton, with a gold bracelet on his lean bronzed strong-muscled forearm. He ripped his muscles, bent his arm, pulled a scowling face lovingly at himself and said 'Dig that crazy muscle, baby. Never mind the bath water, feel the rinse.' 'Hey, Stu,' he heard himself say, 'thought of a good one today as I reclined in my boudoir.' God – sniff – he dashed down and burnt his fingers yanking the smoking toast from under the grill.

If only there was someone here to tell these brilliant things to. He was noticing everything, the way the light played on a broken brick in the wall opposite and sometimes it looked hollow and sometimes it looked a bulge, which proved that you couldn't say that what you saw, however carefully, scientifically, you analysed it, was a scientific fact. But if what you saw was an illusion then how could you use the fact of that, to prove it was an illusion? Oh, that was brill. He'd dumbfound Stu with that. Illusion and reality, that was real philosophy, real thought. That was deep, man, deep; the meaning of life. He put some more toast on and watched this time.

The sun faded. The brick wall outside the window looked dark and gloomy. He tried to grasp what he had been rehearsing but he seemed to have lost it. The sunlight and cloud came and went, rode over and away on, just as possibilities of what he would do next did. One minute he was full of longing to get on with the things that swam into his mind: sorting his stamps, cleaning his sports gear, starting his diary, writing his play. The next it was unbearably sad to think about any of them. He went into his room and put on a record while he decided what to do and for a time became lost in the music. He clicked and jolted his head funky-chicken fashion and pushed out his lower abdomen in syncopated spastic jerks. 'Na, na, na, baby' ducking his head down and shaking it, his elbows bent up and his clicking fingers held high behind his ears, while he footed round the room. 'Na, na, na. Tha's not my way, baby, Tha's not my way.' 'Yao-hoo' he let out as the record ended.

With an ache that almost made him bend over, he longed for the hours before evening to be done.

He had told them he had things to do at home, had saved up the day for solitude. Now he felt he would burst if he couldn't impart all that was going on in his mind. It wasn't real till it was let out and tried on the air and approved. That was another discovery. 'You know, Cookie,' he heard himself saying, 'until you say a thing . . . .'

He went out and got the potatoes for his mother, bought a doughnut and put the kettle on when he came in. It was lovely out.

He'd settle down now. He did a crossword while the tea brewed. He'd forgotten the stamp hinges. He'd go and get them. It had really been wonderful out, soft on the face with a little breeze moving things about a bit, the streets busy, everyone moving around, cyclists swerving in loops – no hands. He should have gone out earlier.

Then it clouded over, purply and menacing. A few large splashes fell and then a lot. That was the end of that then. Shit. The house darkened. He poured another cup of tea and sat in dejection in the kitchen. He reversed his decision not to ring Stuart. There was no reply. Of course, he had said he was going to help out at MacDowell's Dad's wallpaper shop. That was that then. The rain sheeted down and there was nothing whatever to do. All the happening was going on for other people miles away. Here no one would call, no letter come, no ring startle the weight of quiet. His parents were probably having coffee and pastries in a place among people; Stu would be laughing and larking about with his mates at the wallpaper shop. The boss brought in cans of lager for their break. Cookie would be coining it at the green-grocer's stall, munching fruit and putting on the courtesy act to old ladies. Marie – he couldn't imagine what a girl would be doing in the morning. He had a picture of her sitting permanently on the edge of a table at Dubal's swinging one leg and looking out at him from the group she was with. He could only imagine girls in the evening when they all walked along and Marie stopped in front of a shop window to see that her clothes and hair were as she wanted and they all came up behind her and did the same so they were like a group photograph on a record sleeve, wiggling their fingers and poking out their tongues and saying 'Yoo-hoo' to their reflections. That had been a great evening.

He wanted to be where something was happening.

He heaved himself up, out of his day-dreaming as he had out of the bath, and took out his stamps. It was a long time since he'd looked at them. He hadn't concentrated on one thing for years now as he had when he'd started collecting stamps at the age of nine, so careful, so worried, so never leaving anything for a minute that could be done straight away by him. An hour passed while he ordered pages and laid damp stamps on blotting paper with tweezers.

He was much more content now, though melancholy about himself and what he'd come to. He'd keep it in good order from now on. Buy a new book with a padded leather cover. Keep them to show his sons.

The telephone rang. He ran. It was Stu.

'What's the old recluse up to, then?'

'Didn't you go to the shop, then?'

'Yep, I'm there now. We're all going to the Bird and Baby. MacDowell's got a load to deliver and he wants a hand so we'll do it in the lunch hour; new headquarters of the respected firm of MacDowell and Co: ye esteemed Eagle and Child public house to be found (if it be not removed by ye demolition men) at the corner of – you feel like coming then? Or are we deep in mystic thought, O sage?'

'Mystic thought can wait, you bet. Eagle and Child it is. Or rather would be, Stu boy, but we-*ell*, the thing is, y'know, there's a little thing called money, cash, geld, spondooliks, like, whereof which I have not got.'

'Oh never mind, come on. MacDowell'll pay.'

'Boy, have I mighty thoughts to tell thee, O Stewpot. Great, great. See you in half an hour.'

He pushed everything dirty in the kitchen into the sink. He prinked himself before the glass where formerly he had gazed. He patted his hair to the right state of fluffiness, turned his trousers up the right amount of cuff, gave a quick loving look. He was all right now. And how he was all right! He'd put his stamps away later. He intended, as he hurried out, to be back in time to clear up before his Mum got back. There were probably as good as two hours ahead when he would be among company, among conversation, in the throng, the best time of day to be out and about and in a pub, in the middle of it all, all going on, him with it.

The spring rain soaked him but it was warm and he licked it as it trickled down his lip. With a whoop he leapt over a huge spreading puddle where a drain was blocked with litter. He was in good nick, in good shape. He could jump the road, never mind the puddle. He could jump the traffic blocked in the downpour. Nothing would stop him.

# 38

'He's just taking advantage of you. You can see that, can't you?'

'Oh yes. But if there was no advantage for him he wouldn't come.'

'But that's totally undignified. He treats you abominably and you never say a thing because, you say, he doesn't like women who complain. And then the minute he wants something – which is only ever one thing – you're all over him, making it easy for him and when he's got what he want he says "Thank you very much. That was nice. See you soon." And you don't hear a squeak from him for months and months. And you never say you'd like to be taken out for a change, or ring him up when *you* want a bit of company?'

'I did ring him up once. He'd come round and it had been so nice, and we seemed to be so comfortable with each other, not just in bed you know, and it didn't occur to me we wouldn't do things together and see each other. And I felt so happy and excited so I did ring him up.'

'And?'

'Well, he was busy at the time, you see. I think he had people with him. It wasn't convenient to talk.'

'Not convenient! Not convenient to *him*, but he expects you to be available the minute he wants. Do you ever say it isn't convenient for you? It can't have been very convenient for you that time he rang up in the middle of the night drunk after someone else's party.'

'I did ask him why he hadn't let me know on his way there that he would be coming later. I should have liked to be able to look forward to seeing him, but he said he didn't know how the evening would turn out.'

'You mean he couldn't pick up anyone grander, so he fell back on you.'

'I suppose so.'

'Ruth, haven't you an ounce of self-respect? So you just let yourself be used by a drunken lecher.'

'I suppose it seems like that, but it would have been silly to say no when he was prepared to come, after I'd been so sad not to see him. If you'd rather see someone than not, you don't say no when they do turn up, just because they don't come more often.'

'It's not how often, it's the appalling attitude. It's so bloody selfish and greedy. Oh, Milord mustn't lose one precious minute of his time or attention when *he* has better things to do. He mustn't be expected to make an effort when he doesn't feel like it, he mustn't risk being hemmed in or bored, but everyone has to be ever so careful of his feelings, poor sensitive soul, and when he wants a good fuck he comes to obliging loving little Ruth because he can relieve himself and have his morale boosted without having to do a damned thing about it but get himself into your bed.'

'Oh, Jessie.'

'Well, that's what it is, isn't it? Why are the words more vulgar than the behaviour? I bet he never even brings you anything when he comes.'

'No, he doesn't.'

'And don't you mind?'

'Well, he's not that sort of person. Of course I'd like the other things, but it's just not relevant to the relationship.'

'But you give him presents.'

'Well, I like giving presents.'

'So he gets everything on a plate and you get nothing but insults and disturbance, and upset because you can't help thinking about him for weeks afterwards. Don't forget, I've seen you in some states, Ruth, practically off your rocker wasting away wrapped up in that sod. He's just using you instead of a prostitute. Only he gets it free.'

'It doesn't seem like that when he's here.'

'*When* he's here, once in a blue moon. It's just that I can't bear to see someone like you, Ruth, made miserable so worthlessly, and until you get some feeling of respect for *yourself* you're never going to snap out of it, and you'll go on being used as a doormat. A little bit of anger on your own behalf would be a very positive thing in this case, Ruth. I see you being gnawed away with longing, week after week. It's entirely negative.'

'I know it's feeble, Jess, and silly, but I've never been one to stand up for my rights, so to speak. I *couldn't* say "Why don't you do this for me?" or "I want this or that." If it worked, which it wouldn't, I wouldn't want it that way. I want him to want to be with me and do things. It's not the things themselves. Obviously I wouldn't be happy with someone who is so selfish and so uninterested in me, so I suppose he's doing me a favour, really, making it so clear. It's just that when I see him I forget all that. He seems so full of promise. It's just that I like him and it's silly to pretend I don't for the sake of pride. He is a rude horrible selfish man, I quite see that, but I like him personally, if you can understand that. And it's not true that I don't get anything out of it when I see him. I can't explain. I don't think it's the sort of thing that can be explained unless you can understand it without explanation. For instance, the morning after one night when he'd stayed until about 5, so I'd had very little sleep, I walked around, phased out really, feeling a little bit of an invalid, rather frail and light-headed, but very peaceful, walking carefully so as not to jolt anything, and I felt I was nursing a bit of heaven. And as I came back down this mucky road from the High Street, which, as you know, can be a pretty depressing trek home especially if you're tired, it all seemed bright somehow, and welcoming. The people seemed kindly and one or two nodded or greeted me. And all the babies suddenly looked so nice.'

# 39

They left the hot dance hall, which was a hut at one end of the village, and at once got on to their cycles.

They wanted to be out, away. They would go on and on at great speed. Fragrance of leafage, hyacinth and narcissus, came to them over hedges at certain points like bursts of music as a door opens. They caught it in their onrush. The strong wafts added to the feeling that the lights, the blackness, the vigour in the air, the strength in their limbs, was burning more intensely. The one in front pedalled furiously, head low, and then, head up, let the bike ride, face lifted, up to the sky, the sky that was giving out stars as the earth put on flowers.

'Come on, come on' and then only the buzz of the chain free-wheeling and the rush of the air: and two stars, a red, a white, shooting down the dark tunnel of road between the hedges as the bike sped on. The other caught up round the corner and there were two shadowy forms, skimming silently along together, two waverings of light bouncing and jolting to the fore, and two points of red winking at the same level behind, travelling on.

'Hey, look; look up there!' In the huge sky were myriads of pinpricks, age old stars, tiny eyelets in the velvet. As the bikes bowled down the dark lane, so the circle of the sky seemed to wheel the other way.

And then, across this orderly slow progression where all was held in a great round, three lights moving together pursued their way, little glow-worms busily creeping in a straight line across the dome, one green, one red, in movement, then one white at the same pace; now one winking now the other, as if flashing messages. Strange man-made star-bird among the immortals.

The road levelled out, trees over-arching. Past dark houses they went, on and on, past houses where fires had died, hours since, only ash lifting a little in closed rooms, life breathing low, old bones, slow movements, dying fires. But the fire in them burnt like a bud of blue flame, swelling, growing, until they felt it would flame into a shower of stars, reaching into the velvet darkness, the little frail wobbly lights of their bikes signalling to the lights of the travelling plane, their mounts leaping up over humps, over rises in the road, up and away into the intoxicating night.

# 40

It had been a dark and rainy day. It would be, she thought, on my half-day free from the shop. So she had stayed in and got the dinner prepared early, she could just shove it in the oven and it would look after itself.

As she bent up from the oven, up out of the kitchen, a shaft of watery sun manifested itself on the floor like a dim splash of paint.

She went up to her bedroom and there it was flooded with golden light, the clouds were rapidly drawing away, almost peeling back in the sky and, not yet quite behind the roofs, a dazzling gold was leaking all round the edges of a lilac cloud. But its brightness was dimming quickly and its shafts withdrawing from the near buildings and then further and further away across the roofs, so that she ran out into it to catch some before it should go beyond her reach. She walked further up the hill to where the golden light still came unhindered, following from one patch of sunlight to another as they fell through gaps in the houses, until she was in a little cul-de-sac quite open to it, ending at a railway. She stood against a fence warm to the touch, and out of which the warmth had brought the smell of creosote and basked, her face up to the sky, her eyes nearly shut, letting the fiery sinking ball make red patterns through her flickering lids. Suddenly she was in shadow and only the upper sky was lit with fingers of smoky orange and then an acid burnt lemon from the disappeared orb, but she walked on round unfamiliar roads in what was rapidly becoming dusk. The birds had stopped and then, after a pause, there was a solitary run of song and then no more. She came to a point where she could see far over the town, she had instinctively gone up following the fleeing daylight, and the mist over there under a sky that was greyish and purplish and darkening again, became apparent because it was being lit up from those distant buildings and streets, the points of light vibrating through the moisture. Cars moving over the high track of the flyover began to sweep it with their head-lamps as they travelled on to it and the dusk gathered in patches below. But up here things were still clear.

She had meant only to run up the road for a breath of air when the rain stopped and she had been drawn on into the spring evening until now she had half an hour's brisk walk to get home. She really should go out at unaccustomed times more often, she thought. Dinner half an hour earlier or later was neither here nor there. It was ridiculous to miss such a beautiful exciting time of day for a mark on a clock.

As she came through the side roads to her house she heard a few trial notes on a wind instrument of some sort – a clarinet, was it? a run of notes that seemed to carry on where the last solitary trill of the bird had stopped, and then a beat, beat, beat of a bass and a drum slowly swinging in, and the band, trying out their numbers high up in a house, lilted together into a piece, melancholy at base with gay little twiddles from the clarinet bravely calling that nightfall was not the end of hope, not a closure – a little bit of swing filtering over back gardens to draw people out, out into the spring night, a beat along the channels of their blood suggesting that this hour, as the light dies, as the dusk creeps along the ground, is not an ending but a beginning.

## Demeter

Come, my daughter, we have done our work
The life you bring with you has set in motion
Every urge to the light, that light returned
As you return. Everywhere sap is rising
Siphoned from some source by power, effective,
Your presence gives me.
The lengthening day that pushes back your train
Of clinging shadow, but keeps you here, has woken
The seeds from the sleep they fell to when you went
Down with them to darkness, the dread time
When nothing could reach you, when you were hid away,
And I retreated, sorrowing, hidden also;
And seed cast in the barren furrow rotted
And trees withered and died; and in the womb
Of many a beast the embryo miscarried
And then no germination; and the earth sickened
When in the womb of darkness you were stifled.
All that is over, and we have recovered
And threefold more, for your return, have blessed
These fields and pastures. And food and sacrifice
Of fresh first fruits, crisp bud, green shoot, the corn
Plumping in the ear, waving in harvest
Can be expected.
Come, let us leave these fruiting lovely valleys
Where we have laboured, to the men who till them
And start the journey to our cloud-wreathed home
Where you will live with me among the gods
In joy on lofty Olympus.

*

Someone says 'Summer'
Someone says 'I love'
And more than solstice moves
And more than muscle.
On flattened grass the slumped cow heavy chews.
The corn lies open to the sky above
And larks, a piercing point above the blue
Needle invisibly and the whole bowl fill.
Slowly the great sun through the heaven moves
Taking the day so still and steady with him.
Without hurry Demeter walks through the land.
The thistles bloom on the honeyed hill and the gorse
Pops in the hot noon silence on the moors.
Sitting and stretching his legs, a man at a café
Misting his glass looks deep in the liquor and sighs
To match the hush of the foliage stirring above
Green metal tables, patterns of leaves through sunlight.
He writes his cards and clinks the ice in his glass.
The oil on the road shimmers, and he sees the heat
Haze of distant waters; the wide land
Stretching beyond the town; meadows asleep
Cows, cow parsley, small boys coming to fish
By week-long undisturbed streams. Dangling from bridge
Brown legs, fishing tackle, close eager dusty heads
While out in the meadows the buzz of summer drones
Long after the boys have gone, time
Sleepy, unbroken, day following day
As dawn and evening haul the globe around
In regular breathing like a child asleep
Feeding all the while within its drowsing.
The wave holds its line of foam – then covers the shore,
Above the same small spot the buzzard hovers,
The man on the cliff receives the node of the sky,
The weighted bee lies still within the calyx.

*

188

Slowly the drop collects.
One more ooze of liquid and it will be
Big enough to make a sun of the light.
Slowly the pool fills till the brim is reached
Echo of trickle in basin is gradually dimmed,
Sharp edge of the sound of water dulled in fullness.
Gradually the lake rises and spreads out its silk
An open eye within the secret hills
Fed silently by many secret waters.
Slowly the fish in the lake swells and the skin stretches
Become a bag of eggs when the light touches it.
The peony loosens and the sunflower turns.
The noon swings and stretches, keeping
The dark a long way off at each end of the day
Far, far,
And even at midnight the fishes feed and swim.

Slowly the drop collects and carefully
The spider travels day-long to and fro
All summer building.
We look at the field path near the edge of dream
And pause like someone coming out of a wood.
In a minute the fields will shift into focus
With a path to walk on through the long 'now' of summer.

# 41

The man in the car was making his last call. He usually left this shop to the end because they rarely gave him an order and the road was one he hated. He didn't want to start his day with that. Every time he drove along that narrow strip of tarmac the stupidity, lack of taste, destructiveness, wastefulness, limitedness of human beings when left to their own devices was borne in on him. Here was a most lovely situation, a sandspit which had been built up into a peninsula. On his left – but for the bungaloid eruption – there would have been sand dunes going down to the deep blue sea of the Channel; the stretch of golden sand – had it not been for the litter – making a gentle curve for five miles. The bay was defined by fine trees at the top of cliffs at one side, and at the westward extremity towards the open sea a strange cluster of white rocks split off from the chalk cliff. Because they were of different sizes, people considered the group a family. They called them Harry, Mrs Harry and little Harry. To his right was the stretch of water enclosed, except for a narrow outlet, by the peninsula. It was therefore still affected by the tides, indeed more than usually so. In the harbour you got a secondary ebb and flow between the main tides.

The place he was making for was at the end of the spit of land and he was driving directly into the sun. It blazed naked out of a sky that could not remember what cloud was. He was not spared one concrete-balconied construction, one flat-topped esplanade of shops, one lowly bungalow surrounded by pebbles and called The Palms, one swinging wooden board with "rustic" letters cut in it announcing that the frosted aluminium-framed windows and crazy pavings dotted with fountain bowls and outsize cupids, and pergolas leading nowhere, were part of a residence called Ourranch. On his right in the luminous water of the second flood of the day were dotted little green islands, and the chug of an occasional motor boat echoed from beyond the marshy river mouths on the far side of the stretch of water, rivers full of reeds and duck, up which were villages with stone bridges and beyond which was heathland and peace.

190

Two pairs of feet, black underneath at the bottom of plump dark brown legs, stuck through the railings of a balcony which was boarded on the upper half. Two children were squirting water on to the cars that passed. A head of black silky hair came very slowly over the top of the rail until two dark cherry-like eyes could see over the top. The child obviously thought he was thus invisible. Then a girl said 'Tony, *don't*. I told you just to count them.'

The man proceeded a few jolting feet at a time through the excruciating heat. What a lousy place for children to be stuck in. All the loveliness, all the things they could do, on the shore, in the water, exploring the heathland, and they sit above the road breathing in fumes with a plastic bottle for a plaything. The road was so hot the tarmac was melting. The children were not even at the back of the house away from the road. Poverty of mind, lack of imagination. The car three ahead of him moved three yards. He went into gear. The car in front of him did not budge. So much enrichment to be had and that's all that's offered them. Growing up seeing nothing but these truly ghastly buildings, never using anything that isn't made of shoddy material, how could such children become people who would recognise and choose anything that's beautiful?

As he passed again on the other side of the road on his way back forty minutes later he was caught up in the very worst time of day for traffic.

It was the very best time for the children. Today by some bonus of chance they were being left there to enjoy it and had not been interrupted with a call for tea or to go for a swim with Dad who had just come home. It was the best time because not only were there so many cars, but they went slowly enough for Denise to write down their numbers and makes as Tony shouted them out. Sometimes there were extras. One day just below their balcony a man had got out of his car and gone to the car in front and opened that car's door and started shouting at the man inside, and then the car behind had started hooting and others had joined in.

Everything they had on the balcony got smeared with tar because the floor of it had been macadamed. This was the time of afternoon when they popped the tar. In some extraordinary way it seemed hotter now than at midday when the blistering sun was overhead; such faint breeze as there might be from the water seemed to fall utterly at this turn of the tide. They had erected a little shelter, an old curtain spread across one corner of the balcony and held up by a clothes horse and a chair. One edge of the curtain trailed in the bowl of water Tony filled his squirt from. Denise crouched under the shelter. The other corner was Tony's look-out. They did not sit on the floor. It would have burned them. It was scorching hot to touch. They had two towels they wetted in the by now black water to save the skin of their thighs.

There was a new bubble of tar forming. It was nearly ready to pop. They had a steel knitting needle. At the same time not only was there another G number but it was the same make of car as the last five G numbers had been and it was the same colour as three out of the last ten cars that had passed the other way.

For a moment they were disappointed when Denise realised it was in fact the same car as one already written down. Tony thought the man was coming back for him because he'd squirted water at him so he hid, but the man waved to Denise and she waved back. It was a pity they would have to cross the car off. They never put the same car twice, that was cheating. 'We could have another list, a list for the ones who come again. Perhaps he'll come again tomorrow and then we could put a star for 3, and the one who gets most stars, wins.'

She was in her dream of order, Tony was in his seventh heaven popping the tar bubble. The sun in the end got to the horizon. The road emptied and the tide with a lazy paw had reached up and taken away most of the day's leavings on the beach. It did not of course reach the bowl of scummy water, dirty plastic debris and filthy rags and bits of wood on the balcony.

'Why, Mummy,' the child was asking in the bath, tickling her little bottom moving up and down on the sandy deposit at the bottom of the bath until Tony had nowhere for his legs, 'when the sky is blue very very blue all over and you look at it is it white?' She supposed it was magic, probably it only happened when you swung your head up in a certain way, she would test that tomorrow, and as she dropped asleep it lay alongside the tickets of paper with the numbers she had written, and the tar bubbles and the sun that made red horses and brown splotches when she closed her eyes. It had been the best day yet.

# 42

The farmer got out of his car to open the gate and stood for a moment at the bend in the road. Here the fenceless field spread out to the ditch which was edged with hawthorn, elder and hazel marking its further boundary, a huge stretch of green-gold already lightening. The beards of the barley gave it a restless white ripple like tossed water whenever a breeze ran through the field. The ears were in fine condition. The yield would be maximum if there were no freak storms.

His eye was watching the barley while he was thinking about the outing he had decided to give himself that evening. It was the week his wife took the kids to her sister's caravan at Robin Hood's Bay. The weather had been fine for some days and the mood was right. Perhaps there would be little silvery marks, stretch marks in the skin of her belly, silvery green like the barley field. He thought he saw a movement other than the wind in the distance against the hedge on the far side of the field. Who had the cheek to walk through his corn? There *was* someone in the field, two of them. How on earth had they suddenly appeared there? There had been a path there once but it had been ploughed up and incorporated into the field long ago. Two women, he saw now, one big and heavy, the other slighter. They looked large against the light pouring down over the flat land. He was watching them to see which way they would go. His eyes glazed on the swaying barley and the two figures standing far on the edge.

He leaned against the hot metal of his car that the sun polished and with his mouth slightly open looked at his ripening field. It was quite still for the breeze had dropped and he vaguely registered that the women seemed to have gone. Perhaps they had been on the other side of the ditch all the time and were hidden by it now.

# 43

He lay in bed all afternoon with the light of the summer sky travelling up the walls and slowly across the ceiling. In the morning he had woken with energy racing through him at a pace too uneven to harness. Later he realised he had known even at six on that June morning that the time left would be short before the surge of pain crashed through his head. He did what he could, battling against the discrepancy between the clock's time and the racing migraine. He had managed to collect the lawn-mower from the ironmonger's in the village. It was being sharpened there and he wanted to have the grass mown by the time his wife and children came back. The wait in the ironmonger's and the noises of cars and motor bikes turning and revving in the street worsened the pressure at the back of his neck so that as he finally got the machine into his van and thought of the relief of reaching home and doing the mowing, black tadpoles shot across his vision, zigzagging through all dimensions. By the time he reached home his only aim was to get the van into the garage and find the strength to get up the stairs and to bed.

He resented this interruption of the month with his family. He had taken his boys to the river, they had played tennis with some people they had got to know at the boathouse; he had gone mushrooming in the early morning with the youngest one, whom the lethargy of youth had not yet struck. In the midday heat they had foraged in shady woods for berries and interesting objects, to emerge from shadow to the fields' glaring yellow, heat coming in buffeting waves across the metallic corn. Most of the time it was rigid and still under the hot sky but on the occasions when it swayed, though no one noticed a breeze, there was a tiny ticking noise of brittle head against dry stalk. In the early morning they had got drenched in the grass that waved up to his small son's back, and when the sun struck the dew it was like the silent explosion of a crystal bowl.

By the time he had managed to crawl on to the bed, dragging such scarves as he could find to shield his eyes, for the curtains were only flimsy cotton of a summer rented house, all annoyance, all regret for the wasted day, all intentions, all straining for activity, was gone, absorbed into the panic that connected – as if there was a piston rod – his throbbing head, the lights crossing behind his eyeballs and his churning stomach. He still felt the movement of the van and the racing motion of the imagined mowing as, in his turbulent mind's eye that would not release its trapped images, he let go the clutch on the handle and the motor mower leapt and jolted into movement. As the pain became more intense there was less and less space for his mind to wander over things, undone things that suddenly took on ridiculous and unrealistic urgency, but his thoughts were still churning with his innards and he could not keep out stray fragments of enacted scenes any more than he could stop the brilliant black fish from swimming in the air past his eyes. He considered whether he could tell if they were black or very brightly coloured; and if black, why did they have the brilliance that usually attached to colour? And was there any real difference, if what you saw made the same impression somewhere on the receiving end of sight? He tried to make a connection between this and something he had heard, or read, about the illusion of the face in a looking-glass in that famous picture – by Goya was it, or Velasquez – some Spaniard, no – was Velasquez Spanish, wasn't he making a mistake there, wasn't he Italian? No, that was oh that chap who had painted Venice such a lot, absolutely recognisable, he could see the front-ages of the palaces now, what was the man's name, the sort of name you know so well you couldn't think of it when it wasn't in your mind. Guardi, was it? No. Oh well, let it slip. Anyway, someone pointed out that the face in the mirror was obviously not the face of the woman looking into it, something to do with the angle at which the mirror was held, and what theory they attached to that, whether it had been intended, or a mistake, or even an overpainting at a later date – he did not remember that he had known about that. And he knew there had been something in connection with his wife he was going to think about that picture. Something she had said that had reminded him of it; something she had said about it? The connection slipped. He had thought he was thinking so clearly. Everything was melting into other things. The pressure of pain on his temples let go for a minute to re-arrange itself further back. He heard a pigeon going over and over its announcement with that bounce at the end which sent it always back to the beginning again – coo coooo cou-cou; coo cooo cou-cou. The renewed buzzing of a fly trapped in the corner of the pane ceased to seem quite so near. If he could sleep now . . .

He was jolted back. Had he secured the garage door? He had no memory of doing so. He could see the van rolling down the slope. Its doors shot open and the mower lay smashed on the ground, the effort he had spent himself on, wasted. Then he began to find it impossible to withdraw his mind from a vision of this house empty, and of the rooms he would be returning to. Was the fiction of this bit of family life upsetting the delicate balance of connection he had achieved with his separated wife? Why could they not always live together like this? And if this only worked because it was not "real life" why did it work now? Or – and something came apart in his stomach and turned a revolution and plummeted downwards – were they all politely and patiently waiting with well-controlled longing because it would not be too long now before they could get home and carry on with the lives they preferred without him? Could they only stand it because it was for a short unreal interval, whereas for him it was *the* real bit of his life, this little pocket of otherness, of "unreality", but for him it had been central, the power house, the full granary, the fulcrum. Again he felt himself thinking brilliantly, knowing at the same time that the words he heard in his head would sound ridiculous if used in speech. He probably couldn't even speak clearly enough at this point for anyone to hear him properly. If only he could be sick. If someone would come he could ask them to check the brake on the van. He turned with difficulty and got the keys out of the pocket of his trousers and put them on the chair seat. The effort exhausted him although he could not comfortably lie still and his temples tightened. The light seemed very bright. He longed for thick felt against those dancing panes of fire. There were cars and aeroplanes droning. A door banged and he felt the vibration of footsteps and smelt cigarette smoke. If only his eldest sons wouldn't smoke. Perhaps he had brought it on them by not being there. Then he was violently sick into the bowl he had brought up with him, and retched and shook and thought his head must split and some black spidery demon come out of it, as in pictures of exorcism, dragging its poison with it.

When someone came into the room he realised he had gone out in a sweet unconscious. In the split second he woke he felt wonderfully light and at ease, comfortable in his skin, all his limbs absolutely relaxed in the right order and oh so comfortable where they were. Entire and accessible to the front of his mind was what he had been trying to recall his wife had said about the picture, but it wasn't about the picture. She had told him once as they lay at peace in bed that the sleep after childbirth, an unconsciousness that might only last a split second, was the most complete sleep she had ever known and when you woke from it you felt you had been elsewhere for a hundred years. His head was cleaned of pain and the pain in going had taken away with it all the niggle, the circular gloomy gnawing, all thought. He wasn't thinking at all, just breathing. The evening sun of a perfect day was painting the wall above the chest of drawers in such a pretty soft way. He said to his wife who was in there with the youngest boy – he thought he spoke clearly but she could hardly hear him – 'What a lovely day it's been. Did you get what you wanted?' and a wave of feeling that the day had been good came with the words. He had floated into unknown, and as soon as he was well, unknowable, realms. Where the wings of pain had dropped him, there had miraculously been infinite but unblinding light, a great strenuous joy that was somehow calm, like a crystal bowl that you do not drink out of, and now he had been floated back to the comfortable shore of his cool clean bed. 'I'll stay here for a bit, Jamey,' he said to reassure this youngest child, for children get worried if you don't speak. 'I'll get up soon and we'll have a game of draughts. But I'll stay here for a bit longer. We'll do everything tomorrow.' And the great full summer world, instead of being a throbbing and a weight and a grinding torture, stretched its arms towards him, a lush open welcoming meadow he could never have enough of and was all there, all his, waiting.

'I want to tell you,' he said to his wife but he veered away from the effort which would dim it, tangle, it, and he chose something banal and not what was in his mind. 'Just rest now,' she said. 'I'll bring you some hot water, or can you drink tea yet?' 'Yes, tea. But I want to tell you' – the echo of the chock of a bat against a ball reached him with its moment's delay, and a blackbird ran its first trill through the evening. The sunshaft on the wall was dimming and the sky thickening ever so slightly to an evident blue – 'how beautiful'. Well, she was, but he was not going to make false compliments when he felt so true, so just, so clarified. 'How beautiful the summer is,' he said.

# 44

They lay at the top of the hill. They had just strength to drop their bikes, get over the stile and fall under the hedge. Their hearts were going bang bang bang bang and the younger of the two had an excruciating bursting pain in the middle of the chest that stabbed every time a sobbing gasp came.

Gradually the haze and sweat cleared from their eyes and they focussed over the open valley they had cycled up from. The field stretched in a long oblong down the valley side, filling their eyes. Over on the other side they could make out the chimney of the paper works among rising woods. A glass roof flashed in the sun, far, far.

The bang of the younger one's heart seemed to go right through the earth like thundering horses.

After a bit they sat up and watched the welcome breeze work like an animal through the silver-green barley. This way and that it rippled and shivered and then was still, a great sea.

The older boy thought of the achievement of getting to the top of Glory Hill without getting off. None of the boys he knew had done it.

The younger one cared about nothing now. They were there. The ground supported them. It was done.

# 45

She had been advised that gentle exercise was good. Swimming, for instance. She had given up her job the week before. She had stayed at work up to the proper time to get the full benefits and she had felt important enough, leaving to have a baby, for the loneliness to be kept at bay for the time leading up to her last day. There was no reason to hang on at work. There had been presents and people who had not bothered with her much during the ten years she had worked there became friendly. Because she was going she became much more obviously part of the firm. There were conflabs in the typing pool and that bossy Marianne going importantly round to areas she normally never trespassed in and June had felt it was on account of her. And sure enough, there was a little gathering and some sherry and crisps and olives in Mr Drummond's office, and a very generous cheque and warmth and real kindliness.

But of course all that was because she was leaving. She had worked ten years in the West End and had no friends in the suburb where she and Ron had been lucky to get the second floor of a house when they married two years ago. She was a quick worker and her knitting and sewing, her cleaning of the two rooms and kitchen, her preparing of the evening meal against Ron's return, her visits to the clinic and her regular letters to her mother in Darlington to report thereon, did not fill the day. She had called in at the office once since she left and had been greeted with pleasure. She had a cup of tea and then after half an hour there was nothing for it but to go. She wouldn't try again.

She felt the heat so the idea of swimming appealed to her but she was shy of exposing her swelled body in a bathing costume. She remembered the mocking boys in swimming pools from her childhood. But she had to do something, go somewhere to get through the day. She found out there was a swimming pool on the far side of the common that stretched beyond the railway line. She had not been that way before. There were groves of trees and the fresh green shade dappled with the strong sun outside raised her spirits. They were having a very settled patch of weather. There were not many people at the pool on this weekday morning. It was fairly clean and pleasant and there was a paved bit at one end where the trees from behind the fence cast a bit of shade.

The pool attendant was doing his morning training, up and down he went, thick dark-burnt shoulder heaving in and out of the water like a gleaming seal's head. A woman stood at the shallow end, her hand under the chin of a small child, encouraging it along. Two Indian boys were diving, again and again, from the boards. Apart from the splash of the water, and the squeak and thump of the diving boards, the calls of the Indians to each other and an occasional squeal of delight from the child, it was still, and a thrush, lodged in a tree on the common beyond, dominated for minutes together the air above the sequestered pool. She swam about a bit and felt comfortable. It was a good thing to do. More people began to come in, so that she was no longer alone on the paved bit with her magazine and her sandwiches and her towel. But she didn't mind. She didn't mind that she was obviously alone. She didn't want anyone to talk to her so she could be seen not to be alone. Her pregnancy made it acceptable that she was just there, soaking in the sun, not looking for anything, not seeking, not doing anything. It was not necessary. The great mound and its cargo represented her doing, her being. She was sheltered and hidden behind it. She didn't have to justify herself or explain anything more about herself. She stayed for hours, not worrying, not thinking; not seeing herself doing things, which was her usual way of planning ahead, chopping herbs, washing salad, seeing her hands arranging things on plates, hearing her voice ask for things in shops. This must be, she sleepily considered, what they meant by "living in the present". It meant you weren't there. No, it meant you were there but it was for other people to do something about it – if anything had to be done. You didn't have to bother about it, anyway. It was heavenly.

She must wake herself up. It was really very hot. She hoped she would not get sunstroke. But the baby would have got some benefit. Surely this strong sun would have got through the thin wall of her stretched skin and warmed the baby.

She was glad to get home, to wash the grit from the paths off her feet, to sit down in the cool unglaring indoors. The meal was easy to prepare. She didn't do anything extra. She had done enough.

# 46

He was already thinking of what he would write to her as he turned into the main road:

'Darling,

Darling darling, I feel that I am the luckiest man on earth and I want you to know that I know I am. I am still rather surprised that I had the good sense for once in my life to follow my hunch and come and see you. I must admit I acted with the thought that I could interest you, that some attention would not be unwelcome – I hope I am not so insensitive as to force my company on anyone without some indication on their part – and there was interest, wasn't there? I felt there was when you wrote to me to explain why you wouldn't be at home that day. But I never dared to think we should discover that we both felt the same way.

Oh my darling, I am too happy and excited to be able to write all the things I want to say to you, so much is crowding in, so much has happened in such a short while and I want to pin down some of this marvellous feeling before it all rushes by and becomes more accepted – because, Betty, I do feel that we accept each other, there is a tolerance, a straightness between us that makes it all possible. There is so much I want to say, I feel I can't spare one minute from you when I might be with you telling it all to you.

But it is a good thing that we shall have an interval away from each other. For one thing it gives me the opportunity to write to you, and also I must have time to draw breath and come to terms with this astounding piece of good fortune that has befallen me. I cannot hope to think clearly when you are near me. Good fortune can be as bewildering as a hard blow sometimes. That you should have been there all the while and me not know it all this time! And how easily I might have missed you by not saying anything, but no, you have too much good sense, you would not have stood by and said nothing, would you? You would have helped me, as you did so sweetly yesterday. I cannot believe my luck that nobody else had the sense to carry you off but that you should still be there for me and that – ' Well, that could be taken two ways, on second thoughts that might not be the thing to say, no; 'my luck that you should want me in the same way that I want you. I never thought it would happen to *me*!' Would the right thing be to seem more experienced or less experienced?

Ah, the car was going well. They had done a good job at that garage. He was glad he had assets. She would need to be driven about in a presentable car. She was a woman of class, of taste. He would take her to good restaurants. He hated eating out alone. They would go for weekends to comfortable but not flashy hotels, show her places he knew. There was that very nice place in Keswick where he'd always longed to take a smart woman to stay a day or two. They would go mid-week when he had to go up there for Joskiss's; they need not be vulgar weekend lovers.

The car was going superbly. He glanced to the right. What a view, the squally shower had cleared and the whole of the dale was shot across with beams of sun from behind a strange thunderous purple cloud. Strange light, or was it his eyes? After all, he'd had very little sleep. With a short break in the early evening for a stroll to the pub for a drink and a sandwich, they had spent nearly seventeen hours continuously in bed. She had made him some breakfast about 7.30. They had drunk pots of strong black coffee and he had to leave at 8. His mind had been on the office. He wanted to be there by 10. And so the words welled up. He liked to think of her being pleased at getting a letter. He would enjoy expressing himself to her.

Yes, he must get on now, into the day ahead. He was looking forward to it. All his memoranda had been circulated and should have been digested by now. If he got in early enough he could lunch with George. George had a discreet nature and he knew what was better left unsaid in public. There were one or two points in what he was going to say that he wanted to sound out on George.

He felt full of power. The years of work and attention were bearing fruit now, and suddenly this stroke of luck with Betty. Oh Betty, Betty he thought. He put his foot on the accelerator, he wanted to get there. He thought of the pleasure old man Joskiss would take as his protégé – for he was his protégé – presented their case. Here he was, in this superb humming machine, eating the miles up, with a superb woman of his own. If he went on coming down here, perhaps he'd get a boat. He could keep it in Betty's garage in the winter. It would surely be a directorship within a couple of years, less even if luck went his way and certainly it seemed to be doing so just now. Fortune was smiling on him, it was all coming together, and it was right it should. He looked ahead to where the road curved openly up to the left, free road ahead, that's where he was going up on that open road ahead with this great sense of power behind his eyes, behind his shoulders, in his thighs. He was back in bed with Betty, getting there, getting there, his foot on the accelerator as he shot across the main road that took a steady morning stream of vehicles to the coast. He had a fraction of a second to be surprised at finding himself in the middle of all this traffic, when up there, that was his road, up there, that's where he should have been by now. He had driven straight into a brick lorry, and car and driver coalesced in the final spasm.

# 47

They had found a patch of clean sand half-shaded by the rocks that were heaped on one side of the little cove. They would not have felt at ease if the beach had been entirely unpeopled, and indeed it was not, but over here balls would not bounce nor running youngsters kick sand up on to their towels, and there was the shade essential for Jack, which his wife had still to remind him about.

'Surely you know by now, Jack. Why do you need telling every time?'

'I don't suppose we sit out in the sun above twice a year. I like to hear you tell me things for me own good, anyway.'

'I should've thought you'd be tired of that by now. I've been doing it without you taking much notice for thirty years.'

'Well, I'd feel strange if I didn't hear it, put it that way. Too much peace makes a man feel he isn't at home.'

'Eh, Jack. That's not fair. I've done everything for peace, you know I have.'

'I know. I know. I was only joking. And very well you have done too.'

They lay, their legs getting slightly burnt. It was a very hot still afternoon and May had swathed her head in garments to keep off the glare. From under these came a sleepy: 'Jack!' He lifted one eyelid and the dazzle from the burnished water seemed to prize under it. 'Mm?' 'I do wish Lottie would find herself a nice man and settle down. I'm not happy about her, you know.'

'Oh, you're always worrying about that sister of yours. If you ask me, if she hadn't been so fussed over by you and your Mum she'd have turned round and faced up to things and been a lot happier. It's not that I'm not fond of her, you know that, May, but I daresay her life must suit her. From what I can see I don't think Lottie wants a nice man. A nice man would bore your sister Lottie.'

'She's got a lot of talent, you know Jack, if only she could find an outlet for it. She needs someone to look after her though.'

'Hm. I suppose one reason we've got on so well, May, is that you don't go around resenting things and feeling you're wasted on ordinary mortals. I'd say you're twice as clever as your Mum thinks Lottie is.' He ever so slightly increased the pressure of his hand, which, with hers within it, rested on the sand. And as ever the response was warm and immediate.

In his dozing he wondered if she had been bored with him. She had been too busy looking after people to pay much attention to the way her life was going, but compared with Lottie's life and his brother and sister-in-law's, theirs had been very humdrum. He had kept the same job, they had lived in the same house, they had rented the same seaside bungalow for a summer holiday, year in year out. May had stepped out of routine only if relatives, more needy she thought but in Jack's private opinion more selfish and feckless, had called on her help, or on account of their children, now grown up and living away from home. He knew May was not unhappy, but he didn't like to think he may have bored her. That would be a poor return for all the care she had given him, all the comfort, all the support. All he had wanted was to make her comfortable and look after her.

In her dozing, her mind also wide awake, she thought about her sister. Her mother had always been obsessed with Lottie's wasted opportunities, and that had let May out. She didn't mind the carping too much. Her mother was a very old woman, what could you do? – because she knew there was always Jack, where she was estimated. Jack was extraordinarily straight. He never pretended to feelings he didn't have and if he thought she'd made a fool of herself he'd say so, but never to do her down, never to boost himself at her expense. He had been wonderful about her family whom he did not pretend to like, never made an issue of her going there and he let her run on about them when she got home. Sometimes she fell into their style – endless crisis-discussions and grumbling about how other members of the family had behaved, or should have behaved to each other. The most he'd say would be 'Come on now, ease up. It's not my family you know,' because it was better for her to stop. Oh, he'd had a lot of silly nonsense to put up with, but that was only on the surface, he knew that really, and now that the children were off their hands they could be together more and she'd be less hasty. She felt they were slipping back to their earlier life. They'd never needed to say much. They had both had their fill of talk as children from critical families. It must seem dull from the outside. Her children couldn't understand that she didn't want a different life. She didn't wish to dampen their enthusiasm by explaining that views from windows, various sorts of furniture or food, were much the same to her. She had what she had and the rest didn't affect her that much. If the people she was with were unhappy, that got her down, but you couldn't change that by getting new curtains.

Yes, it was dull. And thank goodness. It came to her very sharply, like an overwhelming odour, the atmosphere she had longed to escape from when she was young, the fearful excitement of her childhood when her father would periodically erupt on to his adoring family, loaded with presents and suggestions for marvellous outings. He had been a mining engineer and away for months at a time. After a few days the household would be creeping around 'not to disturb Dad' who was sulking in his room bored to death with his family, and the children would be trying to comfort a depressed and weeping Mum who had so looked forward to her handsome popular brilliant husband's return and didn't know what she had done wrong. At least May didn't feel boring when she was with Jack.

He wondered if he should tell her how he hankered for nothing outside their life, of how his cup was full enough. Women, they said, liked to be told the obvious. Perhaps they hadn't the confidence they always seemed to have. But you didn't have to keep explaining yourself to May. He thought of the terrible need Lottie had, and the old mother come to that, for praise about the silliest things. Pathetic in a woman of fifty, more so in one of eighty. Lottie and her collection of hangers-on! 'Oh, grow up,' he wanted to say to her. Now May, the fullness of middle age suited someone like May. She was more sure, more relaxed now. She seemed to have settled into herself. Ripe. Yes. Silly of women to try and be young all the while. After all, it was the middle of life that it was all moving towards really. Mature, that was the word. Like cheese. No, of the sun. They used it of the sun, didn't they?

'What you thinking, Jack?'

'I was thinking what's the point you lying in the sun if you swathe yourself up like a woman in purdah. And I was thinking it's about time to go and have our tea.'

'You mustn't mind if the children don't stay very long when they come, Jack. It isn't very exciting here for young people.'

'Yes, I've known for some time that if you want a bit of peace you only have to bore people enough and they'll leave you to it.'

'Jack!'

'Silly, you know I'm looking forward to them coming as much as you are. It's just I don't feel the need to have them round me any more, and I think that suits them and it's silly to make them pretend the contrary.'

'And I was thinking, Jack –'

'You're doing too much thinking. Let's go back to the bungalow in the cool for a bit. Let's go and have a lay down.'

'We're laying down here . . . – that our marriage is rather like the summer, day after day the same, very still, very peaceful. We've done everything we had to do, really, and we can just sit back and watch it all now.' She dozed deeper.

'For another two weeks you can. Come on, May, you've been in the sun long enough. You make it sound as if we're about eighty. Come on, rouse yourself.' She woke, exclaiming that she must have dropped off in the heat. 'Give me the bag then,' he said. 'Let's get back inside now or you'll feel bad tomorrow. A human being isn't like a cornfield, you know. Too much sun's not good for you.'

'Well, no dear, I don't think I would mistake you for a stook of corn. More like a boiled lobster.' They both looked at his legs and laughed. 'But you know what I mean, Jack.'

He didn't bother deciding which of the things she'd said to him she was referring to. 'Of course I know,' he answered. '*And* I know I'm a lucky man. Come on, I'm parched.'

Consider this drop of water and this lilac
The water can be dew on the grass, can be
Pool, or lake or ditch that mirrors sky
Torrent that dashes your arm away, or a quantity
Pumped into a basin – many forms.

And lilac may be standing by the shed
Shaking its head of dew, or swayed in thunder
Or brown-edged mush draggled in puddles, may be
Clean reflection in the lake, sand-bottomed.

And love is a climate, is a way of light
Falling at certain angles (when the earth turns
Bending it into the dark, somewhere day shines)
Which we move in or out of, like a season.
I lie in the meadow, or I kiss your child
I draw on feeling banked up for that time.
The thin red streak shooting in spring through the dark
Has opened to a bowl. It is held, it is still
It receives the sky's distillations. The insects feed.

## Persephone

Every step I take
Somewhere hedges break
Out into myriad leaves;
The soil heaves
With every step I take.

Every breath I draw
Somewhere glaciers thaw
Into a thousand streams;
Sleep is shot with dreams
At every breath I draw.

Every leaf I make
Every babe I wake
I push from dust;
Back to my store must
Come every leaf I make.


## Persephone and Demeter

You come up drenched with sex
Hazy with the sleep that broods the seed.
Everything goes soft at the knees, as if fumed with poppy.
Eyes glaze and glisten, listening to far waters
Trickling and seeping within, beyond the passes
The sweet good streams unbending from the ice
Where iron-cold has lessened its grip, far in the ranges
And blood unblocks, and the knot in the drum is loosened
And all falls in tune on the ear, and the gears mesh.
Everywhere you step – as sperm of horses
Springs a track of mushrooms in a field –
The seed jolts and joins, and somehow a new thing jerks
Out of the honed hard grain that had nothing in it.

You surge upwards, but in this heavy heat
The heat that bakes the clay, that bakes the seed
And from which comes the bread, I come to fullness.
You come up narrow and fresh; but I the fruit
The care, the thickening, maturing of the wheat
The berries in the harvest.
Stay still, my child, stay still and stay with me.
It is enough, earth's richness, why move on?
Why alter, why not hold forever now?

Mother you do not see, I cannot harbour.
Yes, dripping with power I come from the hidden kingdom
From mysteries you do not want to look at.
Harvest is your desire, not mine; for you
To sit with a child in your lap and the sun on the wheat
Is everything there is to aim for. You are done.
But I must move, must travel, must explore
Deeper and deeper, and further, further seeking
And I can only feed your gladsome earth
Because I know, I am, the riches, the terror
That you can never know, or have forgotten
In that blessed sleep that touches the being of those
Who cross
From one world to another, Hades to daylight.
The spirit touches the lip of the babe: 'Be silent'
The spirit touches its eyelid: 'From now be blind;
Only feel and smell the warmth of your mother.'
Mother, Hypnos has given you sun and goodness
And hidden the roots of your power in my knowledge, my being.

*

Blind window flashing from the roof
Looks out towards the unseen sea
(Beneficence of iodine
Carried inland on the southern breeze)
As a face is tilted (eyes elsewhere)
Up to the sun, up for the grace of love.
Heavy with summer's apogée
The trees are hanging in distant squares;
Petrol and tarmac shimmer there.
There is no hope, but no more need to hope.
The long note is held quavering
Stick on a drumskin is still.

# 48

It had been a pearl of a day at five, and fine since, for the last day of the fair. The forecast thunderous cloud seemed to be keeping off. There were going to be fireworks to finish, 'at dusk' according to the poster on the park gates.

All through the hot week people crept along the streets, hugging the edge of shade that buildings provided, half a foot and one side of an arm at least out of the burning sun, though still sweating. Office workers who on the first day possible in the early year had rushed out in their lunch hour to cover any patch of grass with bare legs and arms, floral patterns and jackets, as if some strange immediate growth had been brought out by the sun, to die back in the early afternoon, had by now got the habit of staying in the dark bowels of buildings when they could. They would be trapped in sun and light enough crossing the great unwinking glare and oven breath on their journey home.

But by the time strands of sounds of the fair floated up from the park, people were beginning to get home, wash, relax and pick up again. As the great ball of fire sent shafts of heat more obtusely across the town they began to turn their energies outwards again. The glare dimmed and outlines of roofs and trees and angles at street junctions, lampposts, signs, doorways, scaffolding and cranes – too molten to look up at at two in the afternoon – calmed into focus, became distinct against the astounding pure clarity of the sky, and later became so sharp and clear that looking at them was like a note you could not hear but only sense within the ear by some change in vibration. And though not a leaf or outline moved, there seemed more air, and a fresh little welcome breath from time to time near one's skin.

The woman had promised the youngest child that she should go to the fair, but she must go when it suited her mother. She would not agree to her going on her own. The woman was tired. She had spent the day nonstop before and after work preparing for the weekend. At last the grease and stickiness from the meal was cleared, the whole house was straight and cleaned and orderly. Blinds drawn down in the heat of the day had made an oasis of quiet shadow, a source of energy that could be drawn on now like a pool of pure water guarded from the dust of the track. She would have liked to sit down and enjoy it, or at least take the child early so she had some evening left when they got back. 'It's no good till later, Mum. Honestly, there are hardly any people there.'

Her husband was away visiting his ailing mother, and the rest of the family was out. The peace of the evening stretched before her, enough of light and sun left for her not to feel cheated of her daytime. That was what she liked about the summer. The day was not impatient. It waited for you. You did not have to rush and worry that it would have disappeared by the time you caught up with it. You could start another, different, private day all over again when normal work was done.

She thought fairs dangerous, though. It wasn't just that machinery might burst apart causing disasters, but the things they sold to eat were risky, especially in this heat. She had seen the little plastic bowls of grey water at the back of the hot-dog stall in which the woman rinsed her horrible cloth; she knew what the lavatories in the park were like. God knows what they made the candy-floss out of – the colours alone looked poisonous.

And it could be such a disappointment. A child clutching its small amount of pocket-money was so rooked, so palmed off with rubbish. The rides were short, the games rigged.

But there were other things, things she remembered hearing had happened, although she did not want to alarm her daughter by warning her against them. Fairgrounds attracted strange people. Unsavoury characters lurked at fairs and with the crowds jostling, and the dark, there was cover for more than pick-pocketing. So she could not let her go alone but must stand in the crowds being shoved, the smell of greasy food and litter breathed over her in this hot air, and the constant blare of noise grinding at her.

Well, but the child had been good and she would not deprive her of saying to her friends on Monday 'I went to the fair'. One or two turns would probably suffice and anyway the money would not go far at this year's prices.

When they went down the road the air was getting pleasant. Groups of people were drifting leisurely towards the park.

Clusters with prams on pavements stopped to talk to groups coming the other way. Two boys were fondling a large panting dog they had on a lead. The big fat greengrocer sat under the canopy that covered his produce. His bulk bulged over the invisible box he perched on. He sat among his piles of fruit mopping his brow with a clean tea towel and pushed a piece of melon at the face of his grandson, a babe in arms. Catching sight of Catherine he insisted on giving her a piece. The shy ten-year-old did not want to take it because she had her new skirt on and a clean blouse and was intent on the fair. A large-limbed young man got up from one of the tables outside a pub, and, like a policeman, stood in the middle of the road, his palm held up high above his head towards the cars while a very slow old lady got across the road. He then swept the car forward with an extravagant gesture of a bow and rejoined his mates who were laughing and calling out to him.

The same leisured friendly atmosphere prevailed among the crowds in the park. The paths were thickening as people slowly converged on that part where the machinery was getting into motion, but plenty else was going on far over by the tennis courts, by the children's playground. Couples were strolling around, or sitting on seats rocking prams. There was a slow setting across, a perpetual ripple of movement, not restless, not disturbing. Here was this summer evening, their forms seemed to say, to be enjoyed by all, going on for a long time yet, with more ahead, and the fair when they felt like it, and the fireworks.

As the light withdrew from the grass and the dips in the turf and those paths that were beneath overhanging branches, and collected higher in the sky, the flashing and the music of the fairground became more prominent. Catherine agreed that now was the right time to go there. She gravely tried the things she liked, and sat solemnly in a bumping car with one of a family who lived in the road at the back of their house. He said she could come with him if she didn't want to go on her own and she didn't know how to say no. He let her hold the steering wheel, but she didn't want to go again. She didn't like the bumps.

What she did like was a roundabout where you went up and down gradually as over waves, in a car that swung slightly but didn't turn. It went faster and with more noise than the roundabouts for little children with engines and ducks and bicycles fixed on. But it did not take your breath quite away and you were not turned upside down, which she hated. Round and round she went, just scared enough to hold on tight to the pole, the wind blowing back her spread of straight golden hair. It fluttered up and down on her shoulders when the machine slowed. Round she went, mouth slightly parted, eyes seeing who knew what in that circle of lights running into a liquid line as the machine quickened; in the faces, all one blur below her as she was swung out to them and back away from them again; in the dark caverns of leaves away above in the trees which seemed so distant, so other, lit in strange patches by the wandering spotlights, strange shadows feeling their way over branches as the lighted islands in the gathering dark turned and twirled, swayed, shuddered, slowed and came to rest.

Catherine had spent her pound. Her mother bought her a double ice-cream to lick while they walked away. The child was full of gratitude to her mother for having left the peace of the house so she could come, but of course she wanted to stay among the people. Everyone else was going to stay for hours yet. Just as they were leaving she did at last catch sight of some friends from school. Her mother waited while she pushed her way through the crowds jammed round the booths.

'She'll be all right with us.' They all came over to talk, friendly, polite children. 'We're not going on the big dipper. Our Dad's here too, and he won't let us go on anything dangerous. We'll stay together. We'll look after her.' 'Mum, please, I'll be all right. I won't go on any more things. I don't want to. I'll just be with my friends.' 'All right then, be sensible. I tell you what, I might come back in an hour when the fireworks start. If I do I'll go to the bit of railing by the drinking fountain. But if we don't find each other, don't worry, come home straight after the fireworks. I think they'll have them up there by the café. I'll go and do something for an hour. I might stay in. I'll see how I feel.'

'You don't have to come if you don't want to, Mum. I'll be all right.'

'Of course you will, darling, enjoy yourselves.'

'Oh we will.' She took a step or two, and then turned back. Catherine's heart sank. Her mother had thought of some new worry. Some fresh picture of danger had sprung into her mind.

Perhaps she was only going to warn her yet again not to trip over the electric cables. The woman looked in her purse. There were two pound notes. Something jolted under her diaphragm. Hadn't there been a fiver? Then she remembered she'd put the children's money for Monday on one side already, and Rory had collected his shoes from the menders. She fingered the notes, casting her mind forward. She could leave the blanket another week at the cleaners. That wouldn't hurt. She took out one of the pounds and gave it to her daughter. 'Don't buy any of that candy-floss, mind. If you're hungry have something to eat when you get home.'

It was worth more than £1 to her to see the child's face; and again as she watched from beyond the crowd – for she waited a little once she got free of the press. Catherine was right. It *was* lovely at the fair. 'Let me never forget' – her anxiety relaxed into a peaceful seriousness – 'the beauty of that sight'. There was her daughter going round in that car, clean hair flying, her good face not alarmed but alert, perhaps a hint of scare, a rather solemn smile when she caught sight of her friends – every time she came round she smiled at them, so proud – soaring up there, graceful, absorbed in the movement, not moving herself.

As she walked the woman breathed a great breath of warm night air and syringa, a waft of lime trees came with a burst of music as the big dipper swung into action; smells of beer, cigar, shampoo, sweat through clean clothes, intermingled with the night exhalations of leaves and grass.

The sexuality in the air was like a gauze backdrop in a theatre. If a light is shone you see a whole background, and then it sinks into invisibility as if there were no wood, lake, palace among rocks, and winding paths. She had reached the edge of the park and looked down the slopes to the fair in the dell on the far side. There was litter, shoddiness, people here were no less commercial (the contrary, they were trying to get in three days enough to balance out the winter), no less hasty. They had no more taste or imagination, they were no more honest; but there was a feeling of celebration, of cohesion, of festival. It was a peak everyone had worked up to all week, in a way through all the dark dreary closed early part of the year. They were open, ready, belonging, pausing at the fulcrum. There wouldn't be anyone, she thought, who could get hold of someone tonight, who wouldn't be in some blotto clinch later; but it would be mutual, a tenderness of lust, like the balmy air, not rough. The intertwined limbs against a dark tree she passed as she left the park seemed beautiful to her. A pity Derek wasn't home, but only in a way. It left her free to be moved by the whole range of feeling, which was fragmented by personal action: the enmeshed lovers, the pleasure of the children, the beauty of her daughter, the fondling of the gentle night air, the great sky deepening gradually but surely, as it was being veiled in film on film of darker blues and velvets, it was all for her. She didn't any longer need Derek absolutely here and now for her to feel the throb in her blood of full summer throwing its haze of satisfaction over everything that came to her senses.

She passed on up the street liking and not being detained by the people there and reached her house. It was so still, so quiet. At the back occasional noises of activity from the park broke across the air; she sat in the front room cool enough now to sew. She had some soft material she was making into a blouse. It lay on her bare knee soothing to her skin. She was embroidering the collar with poppies. The thread was clean, her hands were not sweating. She saw her hand, brown, veined, slender, as if a separate thing from her. It had done a lot, that hand. It seemed to have a life of its own as the needle ate up the cloth. Cotton smelled so nice. This heavenly bit of peace. Nothing stirred in the clean house. The doors of the rooms were open and patterns of light slid imperceptibly down the landing walls, feeling their way, as if on tiptoe across the threshold. She would not go down for the fireworks. She had had enough of being out among the crowd, enough excitement. She had seen plenty of fireworks in her life. She would let be.

But after an hour she had sewed enough and she felt a shift in the air. She heard a sudden tap tap. A little breeze had got up and the bottom of a blind over an open window was being knocked on the sill. Catherine might need a cardigan. She would go down after all. She had had her timeless hour. The child might prefer not to come home alone.

They started the fireworks when there was still rather too much light in the sky, although it was dark under the trees over in the dell. Then suddenly the stars began to show up and people gathered round the ropes and paid attention. And 'oh' they went as their heads tipped back, and 'oo-oo-oh' as the slow rain of fireflies sank through the air to invisibility against the earth. Something in the blood adjusted to the expectation of the flight, the whoosh, the pause while it hung silent and concentrated in the air, and then the burst, first upon the ear and then the scattering upon the sky; and then the relief of the fall as it died down, back again, done with, on the ground. It is a visual equivalent of flowering, she thought, as the last petal jerks back and the calyx lies open, defenceless, the pollen blown, come to its end; and of the flowering of the body as it lets go, and offers up its clenched treasure, in the rush through narrow flight, in the relief of its settling, falling, dying, coming to its end. And perhaps real death would be like that for the body, the final sinking and rest home of a pulsing star.

High red serpents swayed up to hang for a lingering minute and fade; busy green heads with white tails thrashed hither and thither and then dived to death. Some were sudden and burst out in a blaze, some were gradual and soundless and floated about in bits like tinsel blown and scattered, extinguishing one neither knew nor cared where.

The sky was quite dark now, with remote insignificant stars above the trees away from where the fireworks were, and the air was full of the smell of gunpowder. The noise from the fair had lulled. There was a really wonderful rocket. A terrific whoosh rushed up that surprised even those waiting for it. High, high it went, travelling at speed. It would escape, it would burst, if at all, if ever, only beyond their sight up among the undiscernible stars. And then, when it had vanished, it appeared suddenly above their heads, an astounding burst hanging there, myriads of bits of light yet together, a unity. And then, slowly, arbitrarily, in wandering divagations, every thousand fleck of light, myriads of tadpoles of fire dispersing floated down through the summer night and somewhere came to rest, black specks, on the earth again.

# PART III

In those days in autumn when it is fine
The brick of the old church is such a red
The house next to it white, such a white
Ultimate, and the paint extreme of black.
The essence of all substance stands and declares.

Babies turn and look at their mothers
Boys lie on turf with dogs on no restless business,
Traffic waits without swearing, with open hand
As if to say 'Pass by, pass by you all
I, only guardian to wait and hold.
The beautiful girl, a joy – she is not searching,
The ugly old, relaxed, are not bitter.
Nobody barges into any other;
Day's fulcrum at the point before the year plunges.'

We have not thought to expect anything further
Yet as we unbend from looking at the grass
Moving too quickly, slightly giddy from the blades
There is a luminosity, world of light – gentle:
We catch it as we straighten.
Though some of the grass is brown, it is rooted
And the mud it is rooted in gives off this light
That swells out from the patch of herbage, and shines
Up at the red brick walls, the paint, the washed sky,
And the eye that looks stores up the life for it –
Part of it
Grass become flesh and flesh exhaling light –
As the seed
Which keeps the tree entire within its thought
Holds the strength for the plant against the season
We all know is coming after this day dies.

Nearer the wall she swings, nearer, nearer
Each time slowing the circle, each time hearkening
Pausing to catch the stillness in the earth.

## Hades

Waiting
Waiting for one last drop that will be the berry
Waiting for the drop to colour, and darken the plum
Waiting for pin-pricks of mercury to run together
The last one received and all within the round

Listening
Listening for the knock that chinks on the place that is hollow
Listening for the foot to halt and the steps to end there
The stopping of sound telling the ear she is here now.


## Persephone

Nearer the wall these days lingering, faltering,
In her walk in the meadow taking a wider sweep;
Halting near this tumble of old bricks
Nettled, unsavoury,
She seems to examine the tufts, the ruined embrasures
If anyone comes that way. And when they have gone
Relaxes into her musing; drawn it seems,
Pulled more and more to this unkempt edge of the field.


\*

On the bush touched by autumn one fiery leaf
Blazes a clarion, calling across the sunshine;
On the bush by the wall one fiery leaf and one bird
Calling; announcing an approach, slowly from a distance.

Messages go out like an arrow over the wood;
Gather your strengths now, harbour them together
For soon a busyness, a stir, a progress
Will arrive at these portals, collecting from all directions
To pause before the tunnel wind absorbs them
Mustering for the journey to Hades' halls.

# 49

The mother had taken a house by the sea for a month for her daughter's health and it turned out to be an Indian summer that year.

When they came up the grassy track that led to the headland, out of the wood that clothed the side of the valley where the village was, the girl was delighted and her mother relieved that she liked it. She had been listless for some time and the woman could only hope that moving her right away from the influence of the people she went around with into these beautiful surroundings might bring her back to herself. She had been surprised in the end that her daughter had agreed to come, she had been so arbitrary and changeable lately, and there had been no way of knowing what would please her, and what bring out her bitter scornful sneer.

It was a two-storey white house nestling just within the last gentle curve up to the headland. The back rooms looked into the soil of the hill, but the front over the richly clad valley and shining estuary on each arm of which were clusters of houses that thinned to scattered dwellings dotted among trees on the promontories. If you walked up the brow at the back of the house you were in two minutes up on a great closely cropped bare turfy expanse, looking down at the sea; and to the left all the indentations of the coastline, the bays, the beaches and coves within them, the tumble of rocks at the bottom of some sheer cliff, far west to lonely and uninhabitable shores, was visible. If you looked up to the right there was just a green shoulder and endless sky, day after day blue.

The house itself had one big comfortable room taking up the front with a glassed-in porch that caught the sun, and would have been called a conservatory in a grander house. The rooms at the back were of course dark and pokey and the cupboards had a strange sickening shut-up smell that remained however much they aired them. They stayed mainly in the front room where there were rugs on a black-flagged floor that made it wonderfully cool to come into from the burning heat of the headland. In a cupboard the girl had found a string bundle which turned out to be a hammock, and she spent hours lying in it. Her mother would have been happier if she had seen her walking or going off swimming, but after all, she was resting and that's what she had brought her here for, and perhaps she was turning things over in her mind. After one or two walks over the hills together the girl preferred to stay at home so the mother went on her own; on one of these occasions Peony had actually tidied up and got tea ready and gone a little way along the track to meet her mother when she saw her coming up the hill. And she was quite like her old self again for the rest of that day, her mother thought, showing her a great clump of Mont Bretia she had found behind an old stone wall that went up out of sight across the turf. 'Perhaps it was built as a wind break,' she said, 'there doesn't seem to be anything to keep in or out except the wind here.' The idea of the futile brave attempt to soften the life up here – for it would have been hard and isolated when the house was built and savage in the winter – trying to set a garden on this soil, in this salt air, appealed to her. It was what was in her immediate life she was fed up with – anything distant or in the past could bring out her interest.

Another thing that drew her was what was called the "power house". This was a wooden hut in which there was some old machinery that generated electricity for the house. Its working was rather fitful and it failed in a couple of astounding thunderstorms they had. Mother and daughter were glad of each other's company then, while the electric storm boomed and crashed around them in the black night, as if aiming for this one exposed place. It was difficult to keep the flickering candles alight, even, because of the draughts sweeping across the floors, lifting the rugs up as if there was an animal under them. The next day was fair and washed with a spent air about it and strangely there seemed no damage to the house and none of the crumbling-looking old stones on the outer wall had fallen. 'They knew their job when they built this,' the woman said. They were both slightly embarrassed at how they had clung to each other when the thunder crashed and how the daughter had nestled in, practically under, her mother's nightgown when the sheeting rain slashed down around them, beating on the windows, just as when she was a little girl. Peony went off to the power house and got the machine turning again. She was good with her hands and was rather pleased to be more competent than her mother in this.

But after the first explorations and when they had absorbed the impact of the delight of the situation, the girl began to be restless. The village was four miles away, the walk back a long climb in the sun.

Her mother of course was aware that fifteen does not relish the solitude that fifty does, and came back from the village one day when Peony had been particularly silent and lumpish, with the news that Mrs Price who kept an antique shop had her grand-children staying with her, and she was invited to go round and play tennis with them and have tea.

'Tennis! I suppose they're very good and all in white and very "county" like those awful people you got to ask me over and it turned out they weren't expecting me at all and there were four of them anyway. No thanks. I'll make my own friends if I want to. But I might as well wait till we go home.'

'As you wish. But if you do feel like it, you only have to call in at the shop. Why not, Peony? They might be nice.'

'Oh, I expect they'll be *nice*, ever so nice. I just don't want. If you're so keen, why don't you go?'

'I'm quite happy here,' and she would have been if only Peony could be pleased.

Next day Peony said she was going to post a letter, did her mother want anything from the village? In The Beehive the woman said 'You must be Mrs Dummett's daughter. I'd recognise you as her daughter anywhere. What a likeness!' Peony preferred to be regarded for herself and not just as a stamp of her mother's, for her mother was beautiful, but Peony knew that although she did look the pattern of her mother, she had not her beauty or her presence. Her mother was the one who was always at the centre of any gathering, it was her attention, never Peony's they wanted. To people who went on about their likeness the girl was assiduous in pointing out that every feature when compared was different, but they were recognisable instantly as mother and daughter, as the woman in the shop said, they were from the same mould.

She accepted the invitation. She bought plimsolls in the morning and washed her hair and sat in the conservatory drying it. She said to her mother not to worry about when she got back. She imagined that after playing tennis and having tea, they would go on somewhere and she would like to be available to go with them. Perhaps they would go down to the harbour in the evening and watch the yachts coming in to the anchorage, and sit with other groups at the chairs and tables outside the Bell Inn. Perhaps these young people went sailing themselves. They would walk in the dusk by the water, listening to the lapping of the tide against the boats, and there would be someone there, perhaps, whom she would understand, appeal to more than his usual friends, for she could do things like deal with electricity and mend things, and she had not always lived in England, that was interesting, and she did not just giggle and think about clothes, and he would find her a relief to talk to, this rather exceptional, different person, someone with imagination.

She was back at 6, her plimsolls still very white. 'Did you have a good game?' her mother asked. 'Quite nice, but I didn't want to stay. I wanted to come home when we finished playing, but it would have seemed rude not to stay to tea when the granny had made it. I talked to her mostly – about Georgian furniture. Anyway, I thought I'd come back and be with you for the evening in case you were lonely.' Her mother had made some scones and pies in her afternoon leisure and picked some flowers in case the child came back in need of cheering up, so they ate some supper and then went out to the headland. The sun still shed a great sparkle on the sea but the heat had gone from it and the dusk was gathering back in the valley. Little lights were springing up in the woods as if the houses thus made apparent had been magicked into position on that instant. 'They were quite nice really,' she told her mother as they strolled and paused and looked and mused, 'but they were really good tennis players. It was nice of them to let me join in, they were very patient, but you could see they were itching for a good game and I'm just hopeless. I suppose the most annoying thing was that I couldn't stop saying "sorry" all the time. They play every day, you see, this girl and her cousin and the two boys they know. It was a beautiful place with an orchard and then the tennis court, but I'm not their sort really. I – I don't think I'm anyone's sort.' 'Well, you're my sort, darling.' Peony was grateful but the fact that it was true didn't help. If she was her mother's sort then she would never never get among the life that everybody else seemed to get. 'I'm sure you're too sensitive. You say they asked you to go again, I'm sure they meant it.' 'Well, they did say was I going to the Swimming Gala on Monday and if I wanted to go along with them to go round before, at least the granny said to go round, but I said I wasn't sure what I was doing.' 'Oh, Peony.' 'I don't want just to tag along, Mum, and anyway, I told you, I'm not their sort. Anyway, I like it up here. It's beautiful here.' And she was her mother's sort.

On Monday the endless time to fill suddenly collapsed, for Mrs Dummett developed a violent bilious attack. She had not her usual antidote with her. Peony set off to the chemist urgently. If she could get there before the long closure for lunch-hour he would make her up a preparation, and Peony could get it back to her mother and possibly get back again to the harbour for the Swimming Gala. Earlier her plan had been to go down to the village a little before the gala on the pretext of shopping and finding out the times of the events and perhaps look in at the antique shop (for Mrs Price was on the Gala committee) and let it be known she would join the young people, but now that her mother was ill that was out of the question, she pushed it on one side, the urgent thing was to get to the chemist's and get the stuff up to her mother. She went very rapidly indeed but she knew what a long morning it would seem to her mother lying there alone unable to move. It was a long distance down the great side of the hill, through the woods down to the estuary. She could then either wait for the ferry, which was sporadic, or go back up to the head of the estuary and up to where the river was narrow enough for a bridge. If the ferry boat was there it would be quicker, if not she would have lost precious time by not taking the direct path to the bridge. She tried to make out from the hill, as she jogged down the track, whether the ferryboat was plying among the craft in the harbour. There was a lot of activity, surely someone would take her across. But when she got there the ferryman was not around. All the boats were getting ready for the regatta that afternoon, bailing out dinghies, coiling ropes, and smells of food frying wafted across the smell of the estuary. She preferred the additional wearisome walk, half an hour up and half an hour back down on the other side, to bothering one of these absorbed people. One man in a clean white polo-necked pullover unbent from the cockpit as she passed. 'Nice day,' he said as she measured distances with her eyes. 'Yes,' she said and hurried on. The girl in the chemist's shop said the chemist would make up the prescription the minute he got back from the bank. She supposed he had been held up because it was Regatta day. Peony felt that she and her urgency were out of place in the holiday mood of bustly leisure that had settled over the drowsy little place. It was very hot and her head was beginning to ache. By the time the medicine was ready the ferryman had materialised and she slumped with great relief on to the cross seat, wishing the crossing was a little longer. It had taken her so long to walk round, it took hardly more than three minutes in the boat. The instant she set foot on the land she must set off, all uphill, to the point. She should have got something to drink while she waited for the chemist but she hadn't thought of it then. Her throat stung with dryness. The man who had greeted her was on the deck of his boat cleaning something. 'You're in an awful hurry,' he said. 'You won't have any breath left for the races.' 'Races?' 'Aren't you going in for the Swimming Gala?' 'Oh, well, I don't think I'll be able to.' 'You look worn out. Rest a bit. Here –' he shoved some gear off the wooden slats of the cockpit, 'sit down for a bit.' She hesitated, but not for the reason he imagined. 'It's quite safe and so am I.' He laughed. He was indeed not what Mrs Price's grandchildren and their friends would have thought prepossessing. He had a tooth missing which showed because he grinned a lot, and the rest were stained, and he was not reticent. 'Oh, it's not that,' she said. 'It's just that I haven't time. Now she had to sit in his boat or he would be insulted and she was glad to rest. She'd get·a move on once she was up from the harbour. At least she hadn't had to wait over the lunch-hour. He wanted to show her his boat which he was very proud of; and it, and he, were immensely attractive to her. She liked the way the compass sat in its wooden box but swung free and the cleats and little pegs and everything secured with little wood or brass polished and shined fitments, and the charts in their rack behind wooden clips, smooth and varnished. He seemed to think she would be capable on a boat. He thought it a great feat that she had got in from the Point in an hour and a quarter. He said he had a daughter about her age but she didn't really like sailing. 'When my wife comes back with the shopping we're going to try out this new jib; she'll be back any minute. Why don't you come with us and

I'll show you how she sails?' 'Oh, but I can't. I've got to get back.' 'It wouldn't take more than half an hour. You'll go faster for a rest.' She definitely couldn't, though she thanked him and looked longingly at the boat. Would he think her very rude and stand-offish now? Perhaps he thought she was refusing because of his broken tooth. She wished more than anything that she could say yes, or at least explain that if it had been left to her she would have come with all the will in the world, but there was her mother. Hours seemed to pass. He would think it funny when she had said she had to hurry if she just went on sitting there, so she got up to go. 'I've got the kettle on for a cup of tea.' Oh, tea, lovely tea down her sore prickly throat. But she felt she couldn't stay and drink tea and then just go off, it wouldn't be right to be slaking her thirst and sitting here chatting with her mother lying ill wondering what had happened. 'I really don't think I can,' she said, 'my mother's ill.' 'Oh well, as you like – you just looked a bit whacked – off you go then. She could wait ten minutes though without dying, you know. Perhaps you'll get back for the Gala.'

When she reached the house, in record time, full of worry, her mother seemed calmer. 'I don't know if it will do any good,' she said as she looked at the medicine, 'but it might. I'll try it.' She seemed totally unaware of the difficulties Peony had overcome to bring her the medicine so soon. She welcomed the tea she made and said, when her daughter could no longer contain the fact of her marathon, 'Oh there was no need to hurry like that, darling. It was sweet of you to go; I just thought I better get something but once these attacks start it's a bit too late to take anything really. You shouldn't worry so. I probably looked worse than I was. It will wear itself out.'

The girl spent a long time wondering whether she could pluck up courage to mention she'd thought of going to the Swimming Gala if her mother really felt there was nothing she could do. Of course, if she had been going to get there in time for the beginning, she should have rushed back straight away, but upset at such times was the very worst thing for her mother and it would upset her to think that Peony wanted to go out immediately she'd got in. What should she want to go out for? She had been out and the mother left alone and ill, all morning.

By three o'clock she had asked her several times if there was anything she wanted, brought her biscuits and tea and watched the clock for an hour. She wouldn't be able to join in the races now, but she could get there for the prize-giving at the end of them, and for the diving display, and this time, if the yacht was there, she would stop.

'I wouldn't have thought you'd want to go all down there again, dear, haven't you had enough walking for one day? It's up to you. But I'd rather you weren't late, if you don't mind. I don't feel up to coming and looking for you and it's quite worrying alone up here when one can't move around. Enjoy yourself.'

'I'm sure I shall *now*,' Peony thought, the more bitterly because she had been repressing her disappointment. Soon, however, the swing of her downhill striding left her mind free for an image of the yacht and the clean white pullover and the laughing interested face of the yachtsman.

She watched the last races and the diving display. She was very tired. She watched groups of people come round the winners, groups of friends going into the two pubs on the harbour street, people hailing each other, saving places of vantage on the wall for their friends. No one spoke to her except the woman at the public toilets. She did see the yachtsman as she trekked back to start on the long walk home, and she went towards him. 'Oh, you made it to the Gala then?' 'Yes,' she said and stopped. 'Mother all right?' 'Yes, thank you. She is better now.' As he said no more there was nothing for it but to walk on.

The next time she came down to the village was after a day or two. She looked for the yacht but another boat was on the mooring it had used. As she stood on the quayside looking, a little yappy dog scuttered up from the cabin snarling at her bare toes a few inches from the deck, and a woman in maroon trousers and a yellow and orange flowered bikini top bulged over with fiery red flesh looked crossly at Peony. 'Never mind, Tiddy dear, was you fwighted den?' she said to the dog. Tears, partly of fright at the sudden yap, had sprung into Peony's eyes. 'If only . . .' she thought, 'if only I had . . .' and returned to the house on the headland.

Draw the curtain on their room
So that the moon's long fingers, broken
By thin cotton, shall not harm
These beautiful beings of the sun,

Warm and soft and animal
Almost fragrant to the mouth.
Let a little moonlight in
So the night air comes and goes
Not shut up, not spirit sealed,
But protected, made at home.

Heat of day and year, has passed
Dreaded dark is yet ahead.
Cold but fruitful harvest moon
I dim a little of your light
Lest too soon you make my children
Creatures of your glittering night.

## Persephone

She looked back on the whole expanse of land
That she had walked towards, pale, seeking, joyful,
Months before, bringing back life to the earth.
Golden and brown and dried and harvested
Shone on by the temperate sun, it stretched
And nothing she could think could raise her arm
To set things going, nor no raise of head
To look into another's eyes, and smile.
She walked, as half in dream, under sycamores
Thinned from the luxury of summer now.
Their floppy yellow leaves batted the sunlight
Reflection to reflection, and the warm wind
Lifted the light covering, so that dappled blue
Splashed on the path she walked beneath the trees.
She went out to the dykes on the edge by the water
Where flat brown ploughland met the darkening sea,
Tide at low flood held still by a spent moon,
Brown of the shore-mud colouring the green.
Far inland her fellows played and sang
Locked in a lush valley, weary to her now.
She sat among coarse dune-grass and fixed on the distant
Pale horizon that vaporised into sky,
Incredibly far, utterly swept and empty.
After some time she roused and took her way
Back inland to gardens, to town parks
Deserted in this quiet noon but for the sweepers
Leaning on rakes and watching the slow leaves sinking.
She found a soft mound of them behind a shed
And in the afternoon warmth she sank and slept.


## Hades

Nearer she comes to the wall, nearer
Longer lingering each time, shorter
The periods of time out in the open meadow,
Drawn by the taint of what she tasted

Nearer to the ground droops her head
Slower she walks away and sooner, sooner
Returns each time to listen.
                              And I wait
For she is coming, coming. She is mine.


## Persephone

Now when the sun strokes my face
And the leaves fall
They are soft and soothing as they cover my body
Not brittle on my arms and neck, not dry yet
They are like the silk petal
Of some left poppy in an autumn jar
Black stamen all revealed, red dropped away
Like an eye open.

Why do I need this sleep that covers me
As these leaves do, nothing complete, nothing heavy
But masking, blurring, changing?
Is there memory in dreams? for I had a sense
Of another sleep, a different arousal, a time when I breathed
And woke to rain falling on houses, on gardens,
Where I live now
That do not know my past as my sleep does.
But these hold, perhaps, a life that some time else
Waking elsewhere, I'll be struck and sad to have lost.

So, as the year turns, wherever I am
The stirrings of the shadows come towards me
And I must give them quittance. In the sunlight
I sense the drum that beats beneath the roots
And in the black world sometimes through my trance
Drifts conflict, longing, birdsong, to remind
Me, as through yards of water, that up there,
Somewhere up there I cannot see or hear,
The earth and and my mother and the great day waits
Waits and gathers strength for my return.

## 50

The Way We Were

**PERSEPHONE PHOTO STORY**

*They didn't see me at first . . .*

*They always met in the coffee bar. Nothing seemed to change for them.*

235

OH COME ON OVER LUCY, GREAT TO SEE YOU!

Of the bunch of one-time class-mates, Tom was the one who would soonest be a man, in a man's world.

How like children they were.

WE'VE KEPT EVERYTHING BACK TILL YOU CAME, PICNICS AND THE RIVER RACE . . .

AND YOU'RE IN TIME FOR THE FAIR, IT'S COMING NEXT WEEK.

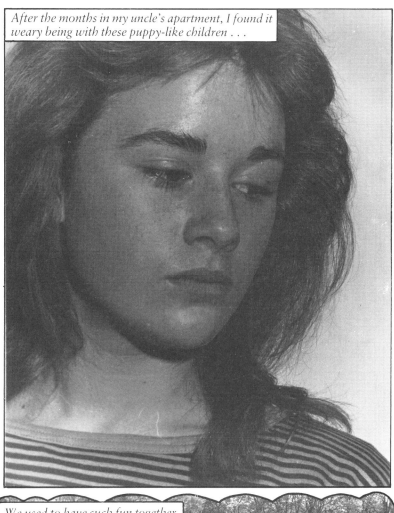

After the months in my uncle's apartment, I found it weary being with these puppy-like children . . .

We used to have such fun together.

237

238

239

DO COME LUCY.

*As he spoke I could see the glistening hard painted pool — white sheaves of water breaking over our heads.*

FRIENDS AGAIN!

*Then other memories flooded over me.*

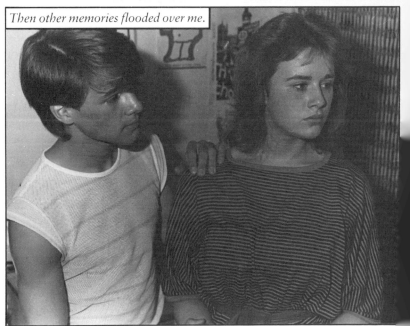

A bar in the city.

241

Waiting for Uncle — past two in the morning. The snow settling then drifting then muddying on the black oily streets outside.

I caught a glimpse of a sad face in the mirror . . .

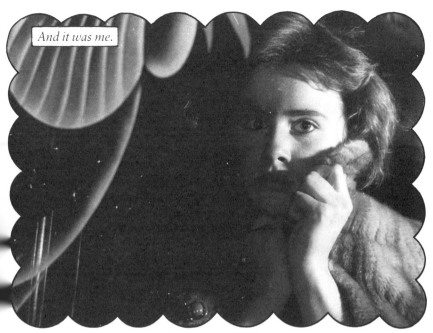

And it was me.

WHY, LUCY, WHAT'S THE MATTER? DON'T YOU LOVE ME ANY MORE?

OH JOHN, I WISH I COULD COME SWIMMING WITH YOU. I WOULD HAVE LIKED TO, I REALLY WOULD!

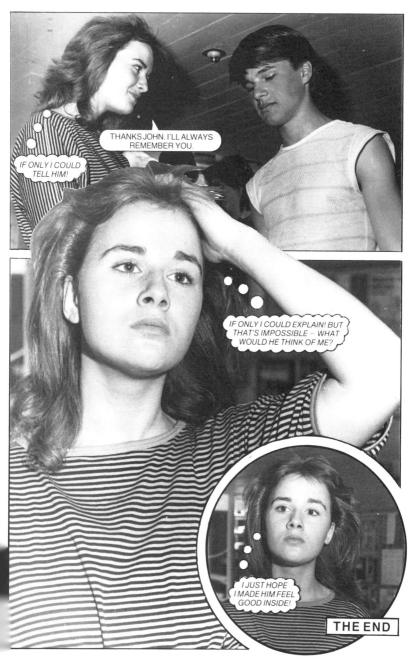

245

# 51

*Wednesday.* You suggested that while you were away I should continue with my diary and record anything I would wish to talk to you about. I shall try to do so and also follow your suggestion of writing down my dreams at the time of waking. As you know, I have great faith that I shall receive help from you. I feel I am at last in the hands of someone who will bring me back to health, to life.

I have set down the following experience as one that has haunted me for many years. I could not write anything here yesterday because I was too desolate at the thought that I could not come and talk to you. There are long stretches when I forget this experience totally, so much so that when it suddenly comes into my mind again it is each time with the shock of newness. It concerns a place. As you suggested, I have set down what significance I think this experience has for me.

On the occasions I have returned it has usually been late afternoon. As far as I can remember it has always been a hot one, in that season beloved of medieval lyricists. As I linger in the grassy cart tracks joining two fields that sleep in afternoon idleness, the smell of Rayless Mayweed crushed underfoot overcomes the other pleasant hay and pasture odours. The bleached shafts of a cart of a design current for centuries stick up very high against the flawless blue sky. It is country, but populated. Knowing that the village is close at hand, that the inn and the villagers will be awake for hours yet of summer light to welcome me, I linger, enjoying that expectancy of pleasure that is perhaps the most pleasurable part of a journey home.

Later, in a company of people whose paths have crossed throughout the day, promising each other further meetings as they prepare, with a sort of leisured bustle which is its own end, for some special occasion, I stroll down the hard stamped dirt roads from which the heat of day is withdrawing. Everywhere people are sitting or standing outside, some on wooden benches outside their houses. I walk unhurried but purposefully and, with gratified surprise but with recognition, I come across the house I have been seeking. It is secluded but not shut off. Inside the two women who keep the inn serve through the hatch that opens on to the one room. It is all of wood. I have never elsewhere come across the style of this interior, although I recognise it as in a very common tradition. We sit talking, the door wide to the humming summer air. After a short while we go off, saying we'll be back in an hour or two, to stay; the night is long, the people are gathering. I am excited and absorbed in my purpose to return to the inn but I never find my way there again.

After a long searching, entangled in other happenings, detained by pointless encounters far from the village, I wake, and that place whose spirit so often but always so briefly has been within my reach, is once more lost forever.

The sureness with which I carry out all motions on this return journey, the knowledge that is part of the recognition, overwhelmingly convinces me, in the dream and on waking, that I have often, often been there, although, as you know, I never lived in the country as a child, and all the lore that I needed for my little articles on Nature was garnered later from various sources. The only outings I remember being taken on as a child were once with the school to the zoo and once by my mother to a seaside promenade. There was nothing green there, only a high concrete wall, and beyond it a huge stretch of agitated grey water that frightened me. It was freezing cold and we didn't go inside anywhere.

What I mourned – even in the dream I feel the sadness coming – is what I never had, the unattainable. Fulfilled happiness, like the circle, leaves no ends dangling to sway in our dreams, waking or night-time. The pain lies in the reminder how far, how irrevocably, hopelessly far we are from what we might once have had, from what was so nearly within the grasp. Between waking and full consciousness I see clearly that I should never have so casually left the inn once I had got there, taking it for granted I could get back quite simply. Even awake I feel that if I had sat on there, I might have kept it forever. Whatever has gone wrong, it was all our fault, but we are trapped in helplessness, and as we contemplate the dull ruins of the fabric of our lives in the light that shines from our visions of what might have been, our "real" life seems messier and drabber, and we weep in self-pity for the golden afternoons that never were ours.

For everyone, I suppose, there is such a place, a place that is not, for it is a country of the mind – the medieval city, the 'fertile land between the two rivers', my village of the heart's desire. I think you would say that the details, important to the sufferer are immaterial to the state of mind. They merely mirror a greed, a longing to achieve what we have no will to work for. I can see that now.

And this is what I think the dream is trying to tell me, a message so clear now you have shown me the way to understand these voices speaking to us from the hinterland, so to speak. It is this: the pain of loss corrupts our waking hours, what we think is a beautiful light from the imagination is the gleam of poison cast over the furnishings of our minds. It is hopeless beauty that brings the tears to the eyes, a beauty we give to the dead hopes of our past. No one has loved us as we did ourselves, and nostalgia extends self-love through time. It is the knowledge of our grossness that causes us, like Caliban, to cry to sleep again. The longing for home embodies the feeling of loss not of a place, but of time, and, if I understand your teaching aright, we must not cling to it, but turn outward to the real world. So it was something in my subconscious trying to push me from infantile dependency to maturation that brought it about that, in the dream, I could not find the inn again.

*Thursday.* This morning rang up my sister and said I would visit her tomorrow. Cannot write much here today. I am finding it difficult to keep up this diary knowing you are away. I could do it when I thought of you in your house waiting to hear it all at my next visit. But have tried to follow your instructions and arrange to see people. Mrs Pitt was rude to me again today when I came out of the bathroom. She is the one who needs treatment.

*Friday.* Rang up Doreen and told her I cannot come after all.

Evening. Turned on the radio to listen to a play, but it was stupid, so went to bed.

*Saturday.* v. depressed yesterday, Friday. Had the dream again last night. At least it was recognisably the same track and the same inn I came to. But when I was there it was all different. I looked out of the window and it was the back garden of Dr Jane's house, and when Mrs Pitt came up to serve me and I complained Dr Jane laughed, and it was really Dr Jane all the time and the whole place was horrible and dark and dirty and when I got outside to follow my friends the ones who were usually in the dream there weren't any people and we were in a sort of studio and the village and the inn it was so obvious now I felt a fool for going in and sitting down and expecting to be served was the crudest sort of cardboard stage set like a model for a child's history lesson and the colours were horrible and it smelt of a sort of horrible glue and –

Dear Dr Jane,                                              *Tuesday.*
          As you will be expecting me for a visit on your return tomorrow I am writing to let you know I shall not be attending your sessions again.

          Yours sincerely,    V. Hynes.

P.S. I would rather be "disturbed" that "normal" like you. I don't suppose you're even capable of having dreams like the ones I used to have before they sent me to you. And I'd rather have the things I used to see than your phoney talk any day.          V.H.

Dear Dr Miller,                                          *Wednesday.*
          I was very pleased to hear that you will be leading the sessions I am to attend. I think you will find me co-operative as I have taken pains to become informed on my condition and related states. Indeed, this was what caused the split between Dr Jane and myself. He did not seem able to deal with anyone who wished to work from understanding, or able to think for himself. I suppose he felt threatened.
          I have great faith that I shall receive help from you. I feel I shall at last be in the hands of someone who will bring me back to health, to life. It might help you to know that I have been writing down my dreams on waking, an accepted practice, I believe, in some circles, and perhaps of more use in my case than

in some as I am by profession a writer. You will let me know of course if you think it better to discontinue this when I start the new treatment. Whatever you advise I shall do my humble best to concur.

Yours sincerely,
V. Hynes.

P.S. Dr Jane was kind enough to give me a time early in the day. As I do not sleep well I find I am very tired in the afternoon.        V.H.

Look through the pane
What do you see?
A person moving
Away from me.

Look on the hill
What do you see?
The sap retreating
Down in the tree.

Look on the meadow
What is there?
The grass shrivelling
Dead like hair.

And on the road
That leads to the farm?
The place is shut up
The people are gone.

# 52

The man had her address and was going to write, but by the time he'd got home had decided not to. 'Let it lapse,' he thought. They'd had a good time, it had given him a good holiday, her too. Silly to have bother of it when he needn't.

Enough to do picking up the threads of his own life. Julia – should he? He tried to imagine her crossing to the phone, sitting down on the chair, legs slightly apart. The image didn't really spring into life, rather vague, figure behind glass, partly Julia, partly the girl he'd met on holiday. Time enough. She'd probably ring him tomorrow. Leave it to her. Give him a free evening.

He unpacked and put everything away immediately and strolled down to the canal. Nice excuse not to cook – no food in the fridge, too late to shop.

The trees were heavy with full foliage and here and there some were beginning to dry and turn. There was a rather thundery purple-grey sky and the big trees were swaying about, like restless tied animals. There will be no more growth now till next year, he thought. They have reached their peak. They can only go down now.

In a small pub by a bridge he had a drink and a salad. He could not think clearly at all of any women he knew or had known. Immense relief not to be accompanied – man or woman. He settled, spread on the seat, smiled. There was a group of three at the bar, two men and a woman. The one with his arm round her calling her darling was much older than she was and rather older than the thin other man. The vociferous one had a cape and a velvet waistcoat and was either more than a little tipsy, or had been so so often he could behave no other way. He spoke so that you could not avoid hearing his conversation. At the moment it was the traditional tale of going up to Jackson's at 10 in the morning after an all-night session at Dobell's – *wine* we drank in those days, Poppet, wine that was *wine* not this filthy MUCK – and demanding double portions of oysters all round and when it came to pay no one had a penny, so Dobell, who even then still had the charm of a boy of twenty, and a slim waist to go with it, said he would bring in one of the engravings from his collection, and Gaston, who always recognised a gentleman – not like the CLODS who run hosteleries nowadays – with tears in his eyes said it was an honour, an honour to serve Mr Dobell and his friends. 'I think Dobell did take him in something, later. Lucky Dobell isn't around now to see what the place has come to.' It was *some*thing then, to be an artist, and there were people like Gaston around to recognise it, whereas the English, ba, what did the English know of the art of LIVING? The woman was in a white dress with thin bronzed arms, and thin goldened hair in a page-boy cut with a white band round it to match the dress, and good legs and shoes. They would have included him very willingly, he could sense that. The theatrical man occasionally glanced towards him looking for an opening; but he didn't let himself be drawn in. He was quite comfortable as he was. There was nothing new. In the past two weeks he had had enough of being outgoing, talking to strangers, spending time money and love of a sort. He wasn't interested now. Back to work on Monday, back to his own life now.

He smiled at them as he went out. Nice the air was outside. Quite a few leaves underfoot here and there autumn almost upon us, next thing you knew when you looked round the trees were bare, the people hurrying home of an evening, winter upon you. He went the long way home, but did not go down the little gang plank to the barge of a friend of his – a woman who kept ten or so cats on board and brewed some awful drink out of peaches. Not going into his local, not going anywhere near the street Julia lived in. No. Hoarding possibilities, he would just go home by himself.

The squirrel has nothing on this:
Bags and bundles, bags within bags, each labelled,
Jars, in order of size, scalded, sealed
Each summer thing as it's finished with, laid mended
Washed and wrapped, away in its proper drawer,
Drawers cleaned and sweetened with mothball and lavender.

Stage by stage the whole place is turned over
You almost think they want the winter to come
They eye the toys of summer thinking 'surely
I could get that put away, I could get that seen to'.
Coal-holes rendered, cupboards whitewashed, pans
Scoured or replaced; gutters scraped, brickwork pointed
Boxes of things from hardware shops, pickling spice
Sugar massed in the kitchen, storage jars
Stacks of wood for the saw and always some job
Waiting for men in the evening; and then some days
A secret bustle that they cannot share:
'Hurry up and get done – I've got so-and-so coming.'

You say: 'By spring the nails and tools will be rusty
Cobwebs covering the jars, things going mouldy
The door swinging on a hinge you could put your fist through
The spirit flown from the hearth.
You cannot stop it, the decay in time
You cannot keep all safe against the winter.
One little puff, and your feeble defences go down
In the face of what they're up against:
The long bare shelf, the dark ooze through the wall.
Black tide of time will wash above your house.
When the waters sink in the spring, what will be there?
The wind kills action, however full your shed,
Furnishings rot and crumble into dust
Of no more strength and substance against inertia
Than a black rag left by a tramp in a derelict ditch
Keeps off the cold.
There is no need to do this scraping and sorting.'

They look past you as you speak and it seems they see
Morning and afternoon encircled in one light
And the wind, high up, making a parabola
Of all the daylight hours until a dimming
Near tea-time brings a sudden night, surprise
After the harmless blue day when the sky
Tossed beyond the trees
And grey little vapours crept along the ground.
They look past you and smile, but not at you;
And when they have cleared go round to see some neighbour.

The women have seen the horizon drawing nearer
Hurry hurry, they say, we must get done
Now is the time, while there is light, while yet we can.
While the wind waits we must ensure the harvest
While the earth waits we must prepare the season
Gather gather in a short frenzy of effort –
A few days left alone would do it –
We do this for the future to grow out of:
A concentration of thought, a hidden communing
Stowing in the dark, filling, sealing, storing,
Assuring the stock, planting next year in this year.
One last reach to direct the good powers to us

And then we can sleep.

# 53

The night of the wedding party had been clear and beautiful. The happy voices, the beat of the band, had drifted out of the open window to the street, including the neighbourhood in the festivities. People going out of the crush for a breather and intimate talk away from the throng could linger without the girls needing the pretty shawls they had brought out to cover their bare arms.

But the next morning was cloudy. It was still warm, but close, and very quiet, muffled.

They had the wedding in the big upper room that occupied the whole of the second floor of their Auntie's pub. It wasn't really their Auntie's pub, but she worked there and it had been convenient to make all the arrangements on a friendly family footing. The landlord was glad to leave preparing the room to Auntie Hetty and Philippa, and it meant they could pop in and out during the week bringing now the cake stand, now extra vases for flowers. They were a large family, much married in the neighbourhood, and certain members of it spent quite a lot of money in his pub. He found it worth while to put himself to the trouble of finishing touches. The drink order would be a large one. They were people who really let themselves go on high days and holidays, not likely to fuss about anything left over.

When Philippa arrived outside the pub she almost felt ashamed of her approval and excitement and admiration of the evening before. It was as if she had come to the wrong place, as if the magic that shrivelled Cinderella's full satins to limp rag had breathed over this place, enchantment vanished in the wood, only the old dank trees still and always there.

Shut, the place looked very shabby. She did not wish to have any connection with it now. The pavement outside and the walls round the side of the building were stained with spilt drink, vomit and dried runnels of urine. Through the early hours the close air had kept in the smell of grease and vinegar from fish papers littering the street in both directions from the fish and chip shop two or three doors down. There was plenty of broken glass and several glasses left on the window sills and the pavement, and of course, little piles of fag ends that barmen, saving themselves journeys to the dustbins, had tipped out of the doors after everyone had gone. Philippa had come early because she wanted to get in in the hope of finding an earring she had lost, before the cleaner started on the room. She had hardly been able to sleep, anyway. This was to have been a double wedding, her twin sister, Corrie's and hers, celebrated on the day of their grandparents' Golden Wedding anniversary. But her own engagement had been broken off. By the time Corrie's wedding took place Philippa was over the worst of her sadness and in a good position to enjoy it to the full – the closest to the centre of the ceremonies, yet fancy free; and she had had a very good time – much affectionate sympathy from aunts and cousins, and husbands of aunts and cousins, and admiration and flirtation and kissing enough. Everyone was relaxed and happy at that wedding, everyone included in the goodwill, genial and unconstricted.

She and the cleaner stood a good while before the blear-eyed landlord stumbled to unbolt the door. He said nothing, merely walked away leaving them to push it open and then shut it after them, and on Philippa explaining to his departing back that she wanted to look for her earring and take back the vases and one or two things 'out of his way', he said as ungraciously as he could 'I suppose so'. Thank goodness, she thought, she had not taken up his hinting last night. She blushed at the thought that she had half considered it, that the pressure on her hand and admiration had added something to her pleasure, that it had made her feel successful. As she went upstairs she saw him toss something in a little glass down his throat in one gulp and she saw the swollen nicotine-stained fingers and the watery bad-tempered eyes. Oh, she was glad she was going away. Last night she had rather regretted that she was, so many possible associations burgeoned, seemed to welcome, so much activity with aunts and uncles, cousins and children of these connected families, a really pleasant time opening up. And of course, when Corrie left, changed into her new suit, her mother, emotional after the ceremony, had had another little upset at the fact that she was going away too, just when she needed some comfort for one daughter's departure.

But this morning it had all gone. Her sister Corrie had gone. Everyone had gone except this boorish man and his sleazy dirty place, and the poor old decrepit cleaner, who didn't seem particularly dismayed at the sight that greeted their eyes when they went into the room where the reception had been held.

There were long streaks of stickiness on the floor to which ash had stuck, glasses with remnants of drink, some with cigarette stubs disintegrating in them, some tipped over in puddles of booze, plates with remnants of food and cigarettes that had smouldered out among them. And a sickening stench of stale alcohol and stale smoke and an awful smell from the lavatories. The whole corridor had a black patina that stuck to the soles of her shoes as she walked on it, cigarettes smeared in spilt liquor with the occasional squashed sandwich mashed in.

The cleaner wasn't surprised. 'People are pigs when they enjoy themselves.' 'But it wasn't that sort of wedding,' Philippa said. 'It was really nice and the room looked lovely and I didn't notice anyone getting very drunk or anything. It was all family and friends, you know. Of course, we had a good time and there was plenty to drink but nobody got silly as far as I can remember.'

'I expect it was after you left. It usually starts after the bride's gone.' She was collecting glasses and plates from all over, slinging the contents in a vile bucket, and Philippa noticed that she wasn't particularly careful where she stubbed out the cigarette that dropped a little trail of ash wherever she went.

Philippa didn't find her earring. She hadn't really expected to, she realised. She got two of the vases. The third she found broken, knocked over on to its side, the water dripping from a puddle on the windowsill on to a seat below and through that on to the floor, and the flowers scattered and brown-edged, as if they'd been picked for their beauty and freshness by a little girl and then loosed regardlessly on the path from her sticky hands as she ran off to do something else.

It wasn't really the earring she'd come for, then. Perhaps she sought some prolongation of that feeling of joy and unity and excitement, the festival holiday feeling, the warm inclusion, yes, even being embraced by those formidable satiny bosoms and kissing the soft powdery cheeks of the old women, had made her feel part of it all. At one point she had joined a group of these elderly relatives, women either widowed, de-childed or, their men at the bar talking men's talk, temporarily joined in huddle with sisters. They were sitting on a bench waiting for the toilets and wanted Philippa to sit with them. 'Don't you want to go then? I suppose you don't need to like us old people,' and entered into detailed descriptions of the state of their bladders and allied organs, and operations; and then the jokes and the guffaws and laughter and the pokings and teasing turned to sexual matters, and Philippa felt ashamed for them, these shrivelled old dames, with dazzling movable white teeth, among them some whom surgery permitted to continue without wombs, without breasts, so gloating on the idea of dicks and holes and hairy entrances and moist lips, and cheeks and cracks, and their skinny stiff twisted hands, the thought of them pawing and patting revolted her, but of course they wanted to touch her, her shining hair, her firm face, her lovely arms. 'It'll be your turn soon, Philly,' one of them, who didn't know of her broken engagement, said. 'Someone's going to be a lucky man. Ah, if I had my time again . . . ' 'You'd do the same, Teresa.' 'Yes, I daresay, but twice as *hard*.' This was regarded as a great joke. One put her hand on Philippa's leg, and patted and gripped so it quite hurt her, up on her thigh. 'You take it while you can get it, my love, you take my advice. There's nothing like it. Nothing. I took everything I could get when I was young and I don't regret it. I was married young, of course, and he was well pleased. 'Course, we didn't have telly in those days, and couldn't afford holidays or anything like that. So we concentrated on the pleasure we could get for nothing. I still think of him, though I lost him before we was fifty – that's more than thirty years ago now dear. Oh, he had a lovely lump of flesh. No, I don't regret it.' 'Yes, and look at you now,' thought Philippa, 'woe betide anything in trousers that came your way, you filthy old hag.' Another said mournfully, 'Don't you let them impose on you, dear. Time enough. You keep your freedom as long as you can. You young girls can call the tune nowadays. Of course it wasn't so in my day. I've had nine, so I ought to know. And it's the first one that traps you. Once a man's lumbered you with one, he's got you where he wants you – in the kitchen and in the bed. You lead your own life as long as you can. It's a long time at the sink.'

As Phillippa disentangled herself she heard them on some well-worn tale. 'And when she fell for her thirteenth I said, "Can't you get him to leave you alone" (not that that's what she wanted, knowing her), and she said, "Well, what can I do? He's a big man and if I say I'm not well he says he'll have it up the back then and . . ." and I said "Well, you'll just have to put a stopper in it then, won't you?" Haw, haw, haw.'

But they had made her feel restless with their talk and it was in that mood that she'd let the landlord get close to her by the open landing window as he was bringing up some more beer. She had been rather grateful to him at the time. But now she was glad she would have nothing more to do with this place. 'But why must you go away, just when Corrie's leaving me?' her mother had asked when she'd told her she had fixed up a job as a nanny with a family in the north which would give her a better chance of training as nursery nurse. 'Mother, it's best for me to go, really. And it's not so far. I'll get time off. I'll be coming back to see you.' And much as she had disliked the old women when they were grasping at her and joking about her, she did notice that they comforted her mother, talking about her two lovely clever daughters, and made her join in a bit of a singsong and made her laugh. After all, they were family, friends from long ago. Anyway, she seemed to cheer up a bit listening to their trite old remarks about it coming to everybody, and after that her mother had been all right and seemed to accept it. She probably just had to have her little weep as part of the whole business.

As she went out she caught sight of herself in the mirror at the back of the counter. She looked tired pale and dispirited. As well as the two vases and the cake stand, she was clutching the remnants of the shrivelled flowers. She stopped and looked full face into the mirror, as if, among the distorted outlines of the bar she was standing in as it stretched far into the mirror-room that swallowed it up and pulled it into strange shapes, she was looking for something not apparent in the real room. She picked up her things again and made for the dim daylight outside, rather relieved it wasn't a bright day. She was longing to go somewhere away from all this, among people who didn't know her, quiet and dark where nothing happened.

As the door clicked to behind her she had an image of the bunch of flowers on the counter, their stained reflection gleaming in the glass. 'Let them lie there,' she thought. They were finished anyway.

## Persephone

A warm wet evening she takes her last look at the earth,
Off towards the town as the lights start up,
Sets off one tea-time dusk to the end of streets
Through a drizzle that comes in from enclosing air.
You cannot see the cloud from which it falls
It is a warm damp veil in the lower sky
Soft on her face and soaking through her hair
Deadening sound and making a privacy
With the drape of dusk, a veiling not a blocking:
Beyond the damps occasional lights emerge
Winking and then receding in the wet.
She goes to dead-ends that give upon a hill
No lights on these unmade roads, only great space
Felt spreading beyond the rain. She turns back
Among the market lamps that hiss above fruit
And shine on skin, black pavement, crates, fresh faces
Hands reaching and paying, bustle in the evening.

As the dark comes the air clears; a sharp breath
Of more astringent stuff pushes away
The warm damp wrap, and now by the railway cutting
Sound is clarified; trees drip, but on the hill
The sky thins, beckoning, drawing
And vapours from the ground begin to rise.
She stands down the platform when the train has gone,
Puddles on the wooden boards, the benches wet
A solitary porter 'No train for at least an hour.'
Light still lays on the cutting where the track curves
Out beyond the trees, arrow over the town
Into deep vales, wide meadows, and then the sea
Far, far.

Saying goodbye to the earth she wanders home.

Next morning the sunlight lay cool over the berries
And later, arrows of rain slashed from cloud rags
Tossing and whisking across the turbulent air.

Then it ceased and all the black had gone,
Clearing back from an empty and steady sky
Pale almond and burnt umber
With a sliver of untroubled moon hung high above.
We had just time to look at the immense clarity
Before the dark came and we turned from our window.

The next day she had gone.

# 54

She was in the full sun by the river for half an hour, and had gone through all the possibilities for her friend's non-arrival. You couldn't expect anyone to control time exactly in this traffic but for a casually arranged meeting like this, to wait more than half an hour would seem foolish. To fill time in earlier she had had a drink in a pub, a mistake for her in the heat of midday. The hot still days came up one after another. It was three weeks now since the start of it. How they would pay for this Indian summer, she thought, as physical discomfort began to take up her attention.

She suddenly sensed that it was the glitter on the river that was numbing her. She had watched it at first enchanted, then mesmerised, not realising the effect it was having on her. When she had crossed the river in the morning her step had been brisk, her hopes ahead, her eye glancing around taking it all in, the flags sending colour in waves across the city as they stirred, the sparkle on the water, the pleasure boats crowded sending back a waft of band music. People smiled and waved and so did she. Foreigners asked her for directions, she took pleasure in fulfilling a role of guide and welcomer, felt the history of the place, its greatness. By the time she was due to meet her friend – but for which arrangement she would not have been in the town – she had rather used up her social energy and flights of fancies. Anyway, he didn't come, so she crossed back, dragging and sticky now in the heat, head beginning to throb, feet hurting, gritty dusty sweaty. All the things that had so delighted her on the way were still there as she came across them in reverse, but this time without attraction. She had gone out to her world which included the sun and the river, and now it didn't belong to her at all. The sights floated like a parody, a chocolate box picture with no light, no relevance to it. She was exhausted.

She found her way to a large store and made for the ladies but they were rebuilding and she walked through deserted acres where rolls of carpeting lay piled. She followed a scruffy little arrow that said 'Ladies' through a gap in some boarding, through the labyrinth of the old building. She walked miles over floors that stretched into dim corners without coming across a soul. After giving up and trying to get to the ground floor again and then going up again when she once more saw an arrow, she finally found a little box with a lavatory in it. It was so quiet here, so peaceful, only dim light filtering round the plasterboard and hardboard stacked against whatever window gave on to whatever street. What a place for someone who wanted to disappear, she thought. She had no idea, except by an effort of memory, what part of what town she was in, and she was sure no one knew she was here. She could stay for days, lying down to sleep on the mounds of soft rugs, and no one would come to disturb her, but there was no tap and it was stifling and her head was throbbing.

What a way to spend her day out – all that money and preparation to get into town only to sit in a daze on the edge of a lavatory five storeys up in the corner of a warehouse of a run-down antediluvian store. She had nothing to show for all her earlier activity. The responding to everything, the noticing, the running here and there to look, to lap up, to take in the life of this city on a full crowded blazing noon, all that had evaporated. She hadn't even done any shopping or gone to an exhibition. All she now wanted to do was to get away from it all, home, but she had hardly the energy to propel her to an intention.

After a bit she left the store, grateful for its refuge but hardly able to breathe. Up there under the roof with all that dark stuff it had been very airless. She would get home somehow, and then she would stay there. She would not try again.

Autumn, the time for going up into lofts
And from the tiny window, look! one last
Trumpet of honeysuckle, out of place, beautiful, flowers,
Reminding us by its life more than the dead plants do
Where we have come to:
                                    these hours
So present (as clear in outline as leaves that hang
From the top of that climber I see, framed by this window)
Are not late, or last, or "last chance" before the winter:
They are not one among a number of steps
For there is nothing after them – not a slab
Leading into the water, the next one covered, the next to your
            knee –
After this there is nothing, match out at a puff
And the dark has come.

On the bush emptied by autumn, one fiery leaf
Hanging, embalmed, bare dead branches else
On the bush by the wall, one leaf and one bird
Who now for the last time calls his cry
Telling, who hears, of the approaching departure,
Telling of closure, of sinking, of even that leaf
Fading to a listless earth
Dun-coloured, dimming; see, the last colour is going
Yellow leaves in the bush, sparse, sapless
Like the hair of a fading girl.

## Demeter

If she had listened to the birds, Demeter,
If she had noticed that they gathered
With strange activity, about the branches
Rustling by her yard door
If she had noticed
But her eye was as a backed mirror, gazing
And in the dreaming days of glut let through
No registration of this busyness:
Whirling of insects, the up and down
Of gnats under trees, scurryings
To get all in
Pattering of all the little animals
Tweaking and hauling and rolling, ubiquitous fever
Before sleep fall on them, before one morning
They poke their nose out on a blotted world
No leaf, no herbage, no movable soft morsel;
Hard-clamped winter globe, and white harsh air
Sweeping sterility from pole to pole.

If she had only taken notice, Demeter,
Taken notice of the birds, how they fell silent
No mark of their presence in the long hot days
The time she thought the world was back, returned –
And forever to stay with her, Persephone.
If she had noticed and then heard the warning
Chkk Chkk (not opening into song) after the silence
Chkk Chkk of alarm that tells us, woken, how
Absent they have been . . .

Early one morning there was a thunderstorm.
Demeter woke, had heard birds in her sleep
In the rain that followed. She called Persephone.

She came to Hecate's cave, not angry, not restless:
Bowed and weary, sad and weary and silent.

# 55

Twenty of the holiday group who were returning home the next day sat in the places they had taken on each fine morning. They occupied the five wooden seats spaced at intervals on the Lower Cliff Walk overlooking the Corporation Car Park. The tending of the flowers in these gardens was a feature of the town, and it was clean here.

'I've got a plastic bag. I'll put it in and a heavy white bag. I'll put the cheese in and what matter if it goes a bit soft, it won't leak on me because Lurpak's got a tin foil wrapping and I've got a little cellophane bag and then I can wrap that in newspaper and that can go in a white plastic bag with handles. The cheese and butter can go in the bottom of that. The cheese goes in a square box, I've got butter in my green earthenware dish at home, but I'll bring some Lurpak home because I don't know if it will have gone bad. I've left butter in it before and it hasn't gone bad. Because I've got a cool cupboard and it's got white tiles on the outside. I shall have my breakfast at half past eight. I shall have finished by nine, because I don't like to hurry my meal. I've ordered the car for ten past nine. I think that's all I've –'

'It's surprising what you see when you've the time to look around. How I best described it to the people at the hotel was "a thin skinny rabbit". Yes, I thought I was right in thinking it a stoat.'


*Demeter*

I hope it is well set down
I hope it is somewhere marked
The curve of the track up the hill
The crisp of the waves on the shore
Once I and this sweet earth go
It will never come again.

The cartload's swing to the barn
The sigh of the harvest done
The stately shade of the elms
Along the drive to the house
I hope it is well remembered
I hope it is somewhere held
Once I and this sweet earth go
It will never come again.

I hope it is recorded
In some safe treasury
The laugh of a child in a meadow
Watching a butterfly
The breath of the plants at evening
Rising to a room that sleeps.
Once I and this sweet earth go
It will never come again.

The quietness gathering in the valley
Full of far sounds from the hills
The rustle of waves on the shore
The tick of stone in the heat
The bell of the icicle's thaw
The great bare rock which we called from
And which gave back, booming, no name
The glade opening in the forest
To the fingers of sun through the gloom
The secret babble in mosses
As the spring becomes the stream
Travelling over clean stones
Through tunnels of oak and hazel
I hope it is somewhere recorded
I hope it is well set down
For I and the whole earth are going
And we shall not ever return.

# Demeter and Hecate

'But surely you knew, Demeter, she would go?
Surely you knew that he would come to claim her?'

'How when I look at the land can I think of death?
The wolds waving with golden corn, the blue
Arch of air on grass, sparkle on sea
The haunches of the down thick-clothed in pasture
Everything fruiting, and my Persephone
Standing in it all, and laughing with joy
How could I think of death at such a time?
I cannot bargain or plot or deny my nature.
She was there and earth's delight returned.
She was there and I opened out my hand.
Surely when they saw this, they would let her stay?

'Oh yes, I knew, and lately found her strange
And lately shivered when the evening came
But the long warmth of autumn distracted me
And leaves me defenceless now that it is gone.
I thought my enemy had gone, relinquished,
Gone over the hill, another way – found another.
The nip in the air and wind relaxed their attention;
At the time I thought he would come
Soft air somehow found a passage through them
Crept over the roofs again, sidled up rivers
Wafted from fields of azalea, from fields of no season
Ever to hold –

'Hecate, perhaps we still could keep her
See, Hyperion's still in his tracks, triumphant.
These soft little breezes lap the iron king.
I thought if the day passed with you still here
I could therefore keep you. Oh my daughter
You cannot be far. Hecate, she came back;
After that loss, that grim time, she came back.
If we could reach her she need not go again.

'Did I not know, did I not think, you say?
Hecate, you think of death, and live,
You brood on dark and hidden things, and thrive.
Do you think if for one instant I thought of that
All through the summer and the shooting corn
I could go on? Could bring the rose from the cup –
Slowly slowly filling through dews of dawns –
If I thought of canker and mould and spotted black leaves?
Get the sturdy lamb to butt its mother
Thinking of foot-rot and foaming at the mouth
And vultures poking its eyes out, and the mother bleating
Far in some snowy impasse? Get a babe
Rosy and breathing, a pleasure to its mother,
Little hand resting on flesh that succours it,
And think of it old and sotten, a stinking carcase
Its sense blotted by fear before its death?
Do you think I could make one little blade of grass grow
Thinking of death?
                              I do know
But if I act I must be blind to it.
That is what life is – total impulsion
Towards the light, no knowledge checking it
Of where it comes from or is destined for;
Only to move and thrive, only to flourish.
With Persephone gone I cannot move
Or speak in any person I could say is real.
You may see me in the daylight, running about
On ordinary errands, but my actual self
Is buried numb and silent in despair
Blackness and death my daughter's going to.


'It is so cold here, Hecate. I feel
Gravity winning, pulling my head back
Down on the earth, like a split pig, lids closing on sight,
My legs becoming rigid and the grey
Slow wraiths gathering around like the cold
Breath of the slow creeping fog along the ground.'

# 56

"MY MUM JUST DOESN'T UNDERSTAND!"

Dear 'Teenage Heart'

My Mum and I used to be such pals and suddenly we don't seem to get on any more. She criticises everything I do, my clothes and my make-up and everything and she doesn't like my friends. Nothing I do seems to be right in her eyes. Don't get me wrong, I love my Mum and do not go against her "just to be different", but she doesn't seem to understand that young people these days do things differently to when she was young. When I tell her the world has changed since her day, she says I don't know what I'm talking about!

All my friends go to discos and stay out late and dress modern, and they've all got boys. They laugh at me because my Mum won't let me. It's not that we want to do anything wrong – we're not vandals or anything, but we like clothes and music and we don't want to lead dull boring lives like them.

I'm writing to you now to ask your help because all this has come up again because there is a boy I like who wants to take me out, but my Mum just said she didn't like the look of him at all, and he was much too old for me. I think that's just prejudice.

How can I get my Mum to see that it isn't the end of the world if I go out with a boy like everyone else? I don't like seeing her unhappy but feel I have a right to my own life too now I am fourteen. Please help

"Depressed and Worried."

Dear "Depressed and Worried"

You are obviously not a vandal because you mind about upsetting your Mum, and I am glad to see you still want to discuss things openly with her, which is a very good sign. Do go on taking her into your confidence.

However, there are, unfortunately, things that with the best will in the world we cannot always understand about our parents and your mother may have a very good reason for feeling worried about your boyfriend and for not liking him as much as you do! Although you feel your world is different, remember you mother *is* more experienced than you and she has your best interests at heart. It is not easy to know when to leave young people to learn for themselves, and of course there are some things you must listen to her about. At your age you can easily make mistakes that affect the whole of your life. So however upsetting it is for you, do remember she is doing what she thinks will protect you.

However, I do think it is a little bit old-fashioned to expect a girl of fourteen not to go to discos and hear the latest music and have new clothes and want to enjoy herself, and she should not stop you from having friends of your own age. After all, we're only young once, and I expect your Mum liked going out when she was your age.

Perhaps you could explain to her that there is nothing wrong in the discos you go to or in meeting boys when you are with your friends. Perhaps it would help convince her that it does not "lead on" to other things, if you agreed on your part to be in by a certain time – and stick to it! Then she can see you are the responsible girl I'm sure she knows in her heart you are. You could try bringing your fella home with your girlfriend and her fella and having an evening in with your Mum – organise a friendly little "at home" evening and make a point of showing your Mum that you all want her to be there with you. If she sits down and watches a favourite TV programme with you and you all have coffee together, she will soon feel your friends are not the ogres her love for you makes them in her eyes, and if your fella is polite and considerate to her I'm sure she will be won over.

When mothers criticise daughters it is not easy to keep cheerful, I know, but see if you can do just that! I'm sure this difficult patch will pass if you can be patient. You never know, your Mum may be going through a difficult time herself in her own life and need just that extra bit of love and understanding that makes all the difference. Parents need that too, you know!

The ragged wind
Pulling the skin off the clouds, stripping
The seed heads from the stalk, emptying
The blue mirroring gutters full of water;
Hauling-down wind
That broadcasts and let fall handfuls of sorrel
Dry-pulling with a rough finger
Scattering on to the soft earth that even under this cloud
Shows colour from its moisture, that reflects
Not high blue heavens, but leaves and seeds and shoots –
Loot that the wind has dropped –
Little green spears like fuzzy mist on the ground,
Mirror of spring.

# 57

'Take another sandwich, Dottie. Maritza always makes such a pile on her day off and I feel she thinks it's a slur on her efforts if too many are left.'

Mrs Castle and her friend sat on the fresh striped fabric of a swinging seat in her beautifully kept garden. Never once did night fall without the cover being put back on the hammock. Never once was it forgotten to open and shut the greenhouse at the proper hours. Mr and Mrs Castle were indefatigable in the maintenance of their house, garden and appurtenances and thus, at much less cost than was supposed, their house was extremely comfortable and their garden a delight. Woe betide the child who in forgetfulness left its tricycle and, later, its bike, outside in the dew, or tools on the grass. So they had everything and all their things were in good condition and lasted, but they were not "spoilt children".

'It's difficult to know what the young people do want these days. You know Bobby's getting married? A very nice girl. Now, his father and I would be quite prepared to help them. After all, that's what Alec's worked so hard for – so his children don't have the struggle we had. And there's a nice little house on the market on the other side of the Green – yes, down Pond Road, that's the one. It would have suited them down to the ground. Not too big a garden – young people don't want to slave all their free time in a garden – but a pretty one, and if the rooms are a bit small, well, they could have made one lovely big room downstairs, with a nice little second bedroom upstairs Bobby could have used as a study until they needed it. But would they consider it? Not a bit of it. Wouldn't even go and see it. They want to go and live in a basement, a pokey little flat in one of these dreary parts of London – not even Chelsea or Highgate, somewhere in West London I think where there's never anything on.

'I mean, it's not as if there's any necessity. All right if we were poor and not in a position to help; I admire people who get on with it and don't depend on others, you know that, Dottie, I can't bear a limpet. But there are enough people who have to live in damp basements with no outlook; I said to Bobby, why put yourself in a position other people are doing their best to get out of? Alec was all for the house too, and he's no fool about property. And, Dotty, he's the easiest man to accept things from – he's never made the children feel they owe him what he's given them. It's his main pleasure. I think it was very wrong of Bobby to refuse, misplaced pride, I'd call that. "We want to make our own way, Mumpit" – he still calls me that silly name! – "in fair competition with other people." I didn't tell him competition's never fair! They so don't know, these clever young people. Of course, his father's put down the deposit and enough for the first year's rent in his account, but I'd have liked them to have a proper house to start with. I really don't know what they're after.'

'But Millie, they want the same thing as we did, I suppose. Didn't you fret to be on your own away from your mother's eye? And I think of the places we lived in and the jobs we did!'

'Why yes, Dottie, we had no alternative. Times were different. Don't tell me that you wouldn't have been glad of help with buying a house when Abie lost his job. You didn't exactly choose to live with Edie, did you?'

'Oh, what I would have done . . .'

'We'd have been only too pleased to have things made a bit easy, which it never was. All we wanted was to be able to get married and find somewhere to live.'

'But you knocked around a good bit first, didn't you? You saw the world. These youngsters have led very sheltered lives. They want to look around a bit before they settle down. You can't blame them.'

'We had no choice. And we've worked to save them having to go through what we went through. Besides, Bobby's had an education; there's no need for him to go slumming and he's not used to it. Do you realise there's never been a day in that boy's life when if he's wanted a hot bath up to his chin and a thick clean towel and clean clothes, all he had to do was put out his hand and turn the tap?'

'Ah, you've spoilt him, Millie.'

'Not really, Dot. And I suppose it is the way he's been brought up that's made him want to be self-sufficient. Although he and the girls have always had everything they've wanted, he's never seen money thrown away. He's seen that money should be made to do things. No, he's a good boy and I must say I'm rather pleased he isn't just out for all he can get. But, Dottie, your heart would sink if you saw the place. All right they don't want to live in a house like this, but why go to such extremes? Why rub your nose in filth when you don't have to?'

'I seem to remember you going off once or twice and doing things your family didn't altogether approve of.'

'Oh, that hospital, you mean? Well, there weren't so many alternatives for women then, were there? And if I'd known what I was in for! Still, it did me no harm. But I was tough, Dottie, had to be, we'd had a different upbringing, but today the youngsters don't know what it is to say no – they want something: they go and get it; it never occurs to them that it isn't the end of the world if they have to wait. And this looking for hardship when you – why it's false, it's indecent when everyone's struggled to get out of the mire.'

'You'll never stop young people thinking they're going to change the world, Millie. We wanted to, didn't we, and what good did it do?'

'I think it did something.' Mrs Castle looked at the clean welcoming well-kept façade with the open French window flashing in the sun like a message and the cool cavern of the house within. 'You know, this was a dump when we bought it. It's something to have made it into what it is now. And Alec, look what he's achieved – three hundred well-paid men, everyone with a decent house of their own and an interest in the business, all from him and me sewing up blouses, sewing, sewing, and taking round the parcels ourselves to save the carriage. I remember, he'd say at first his delivery boy was off sick and he wanted personally to make sure his customer got the order straight away, but of course, there wasn't a delivery boy, or a work force or an order clerk. There was just him and me! And you've seen the works? Well, that was all just a piece of waste ground that nobody else would have touched with a barge-pole – rats, broken glass, leaking pipes, worse. And when he'd shown what could be done others followed suit. I laugh sometimes when I hear the people in the Town Hall up there boast about their model industrial site – as if it was something they'd done. Because I remember the obstacles everyone put in Alec's way, and the scorn and the pompous way they brushed him off. I sometimes say when the architects depart-ment bring guests to show over the factory "You could have done with a bit of encouragement then, when you needed it, not now when you can provide it for yourself." And there are those silly children, offered help at the time they need it, and they turn their back on it! What good will our money be to them later? They'll have made their lives by then.'

'You'd have done the same, Millie,' said her friend, thinking 'if anyone had only made *me* such an offer!'

'I suppose so.'

'They'll be all right. The apple never falls far from the tree.'

'Alec was disappointed, you know, that Bobby didn't want to go into the business. But I can understand that. I'm not sorry, in a way. You want your children to do something different, don't you?

'Shall we go into the house for a bit?

'With all the children leaving, this place will really be a bit of an anachronism for Alec and me. We'll be like two dull peas rattling in a pod. There'll be no point in all this just for the two of us. The children will be too busy with their own lives to come often, and we don't do the entertaining we used since Alec's heart attack. Ah well, I suppose it's served its turn. No good being sentimental about bricks and mortar. It's the people in them that matter. You've got to move with the times. I suppose Bobby and Ann will make a nice place for themselves in the end. Come along, Dot. Can you take the teapot, if I carry the tray?'

On the bush emptied by autumn one sapless leaf
Hanging, forgotten, bare dead branches else
On the bush by the wall one leaf – or perhaps a bird
Silent and still, as dusk thickens to dark.

## Demeter and Hecate

'If I had taken no delight
There would be no grief
If there had not been pleasure in her
Then this horror
Would not be stifling now
If she had not been so pretty
Then less the loss
If I had not had her love
If she had not been
Benison and laughter and sunlight, and her opening eyes
Orbs of day for me
Then not this choking and dark and eternal closure
The heart that shuts in shock and does not
Start up again.'


'You sorrow because you had such great delight
You shake with loss because you once were clothed
In the fabric of love and company and cheer.
You have breathed the sparkling air of summer
With your little maid's nimble fingers plaiting
Rushes for your hair
You have seen dawn and watched her wake from sleep
And heard her laugh and shout beside the streams
And had her come home when the evening came.
If you had had no delight you would not sorrow.
To wish away your sorrow now is to say
"I did not want her in the glorious day."'


'Hecate, I know. And I accept.
I cannot fight against the pull of the earth.
But as I told you I am fast and bound
Until Persephone returns. I will travel
To some far cursed bleak place and no one
Shall know who dwells among them, sorrow-eyed.
Hecate, I leave her in your care
Who strangely resembles in some bent way
The pale and awe-ful presence she becomes

In those grim halls; and now I plainly see
I made her solemn as I made her laughing,
Her silence, as her chatter of spring waters,
The power of silent forces and the terror
As well as the love, the joy, the great relief
Men feel when they see her smile, and the earth is softened.

'Child, you have brought the peach tree from the stone
We could not crack with rocks from lofty Olympus;
At your vapour it eases and opens and gives
This thick strong stem, this headful of cool blossom
Puffed in the sky against an upper window
And from the petals pushes the forming fruit
As, from the depths I do not visit, your power.
You with Hecate preserve the source.
But I made you in sunshine, and once you were mine.'

She drew herself to her height and covered her head
And no one saw her go.

# 58

Dear Di,

It was so nice to see you last week. Many thanks for the meal – marvellous. You *are* a good cook. And *I* thought the garden was looking very nice. I know the other man's grass is always greener (and yours is certainly greener than mine!) but I honestly don't see why you should worry that you don't do more to the house and garden. It all looked fine to me, and very comfortable to spend the day in. But I know it's easy to say that when one just sees the result and not the labour that's gone into it.

I want to write now before the tracks of our conversation get covered over with boring domestic concerns, and even so may be interrupted as I'm waiting in for the central heating people (ominous drip drip through the kitchen light! – something in the radiator in the bathroom – or something *not* in the radiator that ought to be); and because you did seem rather depressed.

Your stories of the behaviour your poor visiting students have to cope with were horrifying – and even more, almost, the feebleness of the theories at the back of their training. No wonder they can't cope when they're fed all that pie-in-the-sky – the old pie-in-the-sky was at least effective in giving growing minds something strenuous to combat. One is tempted to believe that the people who write books about education do so because they couldn't hold down a job in the classroom with real live children. (Grossly unfair generalisation, of course!)

I can understand someone wanting something and stealing it – awful as it is to live in perpetual anxiety about one's things (did I tell you of one school I visited where I noticed all the children struggling under enormous piles of stuff as they went about, and asked didn't they have anywhere to leave their things and was told they (the teachers) advised them not to leave anything in the lockers provided (presumably at considerable cost to the local authorities) because it would be taken, and went on to blame 'them' for not building strong enough lockers – no question of trying to tell the children not to steal!) but what possible gain can they get by smashing up their own equipment?

*However*, I don't want to go on about that really, but as I was going home in the tube (and although I was tired the wheels of the old mind had got turning again thanks to you, and I felt immensely much better for seeing you again) I suddenly thought I did understand – not the destruction and the stupidity. It was just one of those flashes and I wish I could have written to you as soon as I got in while the experience was still fresh. It seemed so conclusive and clear, and now it just seems obvious and true.

We had waited a long time for the train so by the time it came there were crowds, but as we'd all given up getting home quickly most people were quite good humoured. I was rather exhausted and just let the swaying of the train push me up and back against the side of the carriage and it was all rather blurred and all the heads moving and bobbing about down the length of the train made it all rather strange and unreal. There were lots of anoraks and plimsolls and skinny girls in flimsy little vests and great shadows painted round their eyes and bare feet with leather thongs, and others in great huge sheepskins and beards and jingle-jangles, and one or two alert and interesting faces and people talking to each other, and all sorts of bundles and bags – a real motley. And I thought of the sort of comments two old gentlemen in waistcoats and polished shoes with briefcases and bowlers – the lot – sitting straight and silent among it all would make, indeed the sort of reaction Geoffrey, had he been there, would have made at this munching unawed untidy crowd. They would have thought them utterly lost, hopeless, deprived and threatening. And I suddenly realised that it not only happens that the old disapprove of the young, and feel that the good things of their world are being destroyed, feel unhappy in the places and with the ways of the next generation, but that it is inevitable; and then not just that it is inevitable that it is so, but that it would be bad, in a way, if it wasn't so. (I'm not talking about young and old not getting on personally). Because if each generation is to thrive and use its energy and *like* life and feel hopeful about creating some sort of life for itself, it's *got* to break the mould of the one it finds, and that is always painful – it cannot just take what is O.K. and patch. It must go on, it may not want to, but it must move; and I felt somehow relieved that the young people liked the sort of world they live in, and relieved of responsibility for doing anything about it (and of course thankful that there still are some corners I can creep into and turn off the noise!). It doesn't mean we personally are going to like it any more, but that is only an individual matter, and I don't think all this general doom-feeling is quite relevant – the young seem to like life and are perfectly energetic in getting the things they think they need for it – they may be wiser than we know when they say what's the point of working if you don't like it; and being able to read and write and have sensitive tastes may not now be what they need to survive. I think the young – each new generation – have inbuilt in them some instinct about what they need for survival – programmed into them like muscle reaction, if you like – and that is the adaptability of the human race. And it is strongest at the point of growth, those few years when they are battling up, before all the old things naturally take them over. Perhaps we were just lucky (and perhaps the last generation to be so in that way) that we didn't have to give up so much just to survive without going mad,

281

as in the Middle Ages people had to give up the luxury of sensitive feelings sometimes for their society to survive.

Well, as I say, this carefree feeling in the face of the ghastly mess people seem to be creating round them was maybe a flight of fancy borne on the fumes of your delicious wine and excellent conversation (and you would say that no one will be able to afford wine, or travel to their friends to talk, if the mismanagement of the economy continues); or the fact that the curse has finally come so I don't feel quite so "jammed" in my mind – you can bring it all down to a subjective physical state – the condition of the light when you take the picture etc. The actual things don't change. And perhaps it's just my basic frivolity and irresponsibility – I don't want to spend my life worrying about not being able to do anything about the state of the world – so I find some justification for finding it tolerable as it is – well, no, there is a lot I would say is not tolerable – the cruelty, what we do to ourselves as well as to others, the waste, the destruction. But that's not really different to what it ever was.

Well, dear Di, that's quite enough from me for now. It seems that once again those blasted central heating men are not going to appear, so I better dash out and get to the shops before they close, or there will be a bit of "younger generation reaction" when there is nothing to eat for tea.

Keep well, and thanks for the lovely day, and let's meet again before too long.

Love,   Heather.

Through the wall of glass, wall of solid water
Figures of people. People talking? Not hearing.
Figures turning away, gesturing weakly
To others who do not see; drowning
Open-mouthed in horror – but no sound.
Glass or water or ice, clouds. The people are gone.

I went back up to bed on that dark morning
As the fog rolled in, and under heavy chill covers
Curled up in misery, my face to the wall
In a room in one side of a crumbling house, in a corner
Jammed up against the side of an empty building.

Nothing stirred within, without; no hours
Moved, and nothing happened to tell me
Of any life or stir, or that there ever would be.
Perhaps I dozed or merely, blanked with numbness,
Let time fall.

Then suddenly I heard him, a blackbird
Showing, I suppose, quite natural next to me
On the other side of the wall, then, there was air,
Space, movement, and a blackbird calling somewhere;
Telling Demeter, if she could have heard:
Do not, O mourner, look in the summer fields
`They can be nothing but symbols of barrenness now;
Life's attributes are shifted to the grey wall
A little green lump of moss and flirting of wings:
The herald sings above the gaping hole
Opening to a black tunnel through the wall.
Do not you wait in a barren field that the sun
Once touched but has no power with now.
Here is the power
And here the new life harbours.

## Hades

A brown interruption flashes past the eye
Mother bird, mother bird,
A brown leaf on an empty bush,
Quick-moving clod among the dead brown leaves –
A flash and the bush is empty

And somewhere calling from a pole by the wall
The black male bird, calling, telling, announcing
Down the dark tunnels that the time is ripe
That soon a busyness, a stir, a progress
Will be arriving at these portals, that Hades' dark halls –
Empty inactive waiting –
Will soon be flushed through every spore of darkness
With a strange activeness, blue flash
That gives no heat or light but sets a-thrumming
The wires within earth's fibres, and brings to fruition
The inert power of Hades
Blue electric gleam
Darting here and there through earth's chambers, earth's antres.

Somewhere she's on her way, her progress started
Far distant
Across the plains, sea shores and river-banks
And mountain pastures
She is skeining in the filaments and will soon withdraw
The net of her influence from every field and pathway
From ever ditch and wood, from every hedgerow
And she is bringing it down here to me.
Here is her rest, her feeding, her fulfilment
My apogée and the kernel of her power.

*

Ah, once again I hear you, Hades' bird
Unmarked these many months while the young girls played.
Now he calls, beginning his new time
Suddenly quite near after long absence,
The bush that holds him bare of any cover
And yet I do not see him for the dark.
There again, quite natural next to me,
The blackbird sings, staying close to the wall
Summoning, drawing, so that I turn again –
Herald, harbinger of real adventure
Calling all together for procession
But he stays near the cleft in the wall, the hidden tunnel
Stays and declares, calling beyond the dusk
Calling to the flocking ghosts, and the wraiths that dissolve
In the short dim day, singing that the earth may mourn
And all on earth may shrivel and be sad
But not for her, for she has escaped earth's death.
Leaving, she fades into power, wrapped in Hades.
Mourn, he calls, mourn for Demeter, mourn
For your poor cold hearth, your loss, your diminishment

But as for Persephone, as for Hades' bride
Why, she goes down to riches.

# 59

'Will Uncle Harry be coming soon?'

'Not just yet, Pearl, but let me get on with the dinner now, there's a good girl, so it's ready when he does come.'

'Will he take me to the park this time? Last time when we couldn't go he said he would when he came again. Do you think he's forgotten?'

'We'll have to wait and see, won't we? Go and play with something for a bit, there's a good girl, and the time will go quicker.'

The husband came in with some bottles of beer. 'What time did Harry say he'd be here?'

'Oh, I said come for Sunday dinner and told him we eat about two but I shan't be surprised if he doesn't get here till after three. You can't time a journey exactly on that particular route at this time of year, there's always some hold-up at Uttoxeter or Andover or somewhere.'

'Or, in the case of Harry, the King's Head or the Andover Arms, or somewhere.'

'Oh Brian! Anyway, I've done a meal that won't spoil waiting. Now, do be nice to him. You won't change him and he doesn't come very often. To tell the truth I don't think he goes anywhere much these days. His depressions seem to be getting more frequent.'

'What relation of yours is he exactly, Mary? Your family were never very forthcoming about him and yet I always seem to remember him at weddings and funerals being made a great fuss of.'

'He's the child of a cousin of my mother's actually, but not, according to gossip, the child of the man that cousin married soon after my parents met in Canada. I'm really not in the mood for family history today, Brian dear. You'd need a genius to unravel it. It'll be enough to have Harry for the afternoon. Now, would you put that bowl of potato salad on the table and put a plate over it and – oh good, you got some lime.'

Harry in fact did arrive a little after two, and as the meal went on with Mary and Brian's kindly attentions and Pearl's chatter he seemed to find his attempt at brightness less of an effort.

Brian and Pearl did the washing-up while Mary and Harry sat and talked and Harry then suggested he should take his niece to the park.

'Are you sure you feel like it Harry? She was out quite a lot yesterday, if you'd rather rest.'

'Nonsense. What have I been doing but sitting in the car? And after that excellent meal, Mary, it would do me good to move about a bit. It's not very often I have the company of a charming young lady. Wouldn't you like to go to the park, Pearl?'

'Yes, please, Uncle Harry, and they've put a new roundabout thing that goes up and down and round at the same time. It's great. And it's quite strong and safe,' she said, glancing at her mother, 'even grown-ups can sit on it.'

'I am a little scared of these things, Harry. There've been one or two nasty accidents lately.'

'Well, we won't go on anything that isn't safe, will we Pearl? I thought you and Brian might like a bit of a rest.' Mary blushed as she saw him wink at Brian. They had never pushed the child out so they could have a cuddle on Sunday afternoon and anyway, Mary thought, given the opportunity of an hour or two's peace Brian would probably disappear to his greenhouse or his carpentry shelf in the garage.

'Well, that's nice of you Harry, if you're sure you wouldn't rather sit down with the papers. Pearl would understand I'm sure, wouldn't you Pearl?'

'Yes, Dad. But there are benches there and Uncle Harry could sit down if he gets tired.'

'What's all this about being tired? I don't suppose you two get a lot of time to yourselves. Come along, Pearl.'

And Brian to Mary when they had gone: 'There's nothing to worry about, Mary, he's plainly enjoying being with Pearl. And even if he was – well, you know, didn't quite toe the line as much as the rest of your family, today he obviously took the trouble to keep off the bottle before he came. He seems quite responsible.'

'Oh, quite. It's just that he's unpredictable. With Harry you never can tell which side of him has come to visit you. Somehow when he's around . . . Oh, of course she'll be all right, but she is so easily over-excited. Well, *shall* we put our feet up for an hour while they're out?'

At the corner shop Harry stopped to buy cigarettes and a luxury double ice-cream for Pearl.

'I don't usually have ice-cream just after dinner,' she pondered, 'or just before tea.'

'Are you too full, then?'

'I am quite full, Uncle, but ice-cream's the sort of thing you can eat when you are full, if you know what I mean.'

'That's all right then,' he said and slid some rolls of fruit pastilles and peppermints into her pocket.

'I don't really need sweets and ice-cream.'

'Keep them till later then.'

'Thank you, Uncle Harry. Like a lick?'

When she'd finished he wiped her face with his handkerchief. She would normally have resented being treated like a baby, but she liked Uncle Harry to look after her and his hanky was clean and his hands smelt nice. She knew he wasn't used to children and probably thought she still couldn't do things for herself.

'The swings are really quite safe, Uncle Harry, you know. It's only Mum that doesn't like them. The child who fell off was being stupid and showing off. I mean, I'm sorry he got hurt – he's still in hospital – but it wasn't the swing's fault. I mean, the swing didn't break or anything. I like the swings best.'

So after a go or two on the slide, and being twirled round like a starfish held by one arm and one leg by Harry, and being shoved round on the roundabout that went up and down and round and round at the same time, she made for the swings. He leant against a tree and saw her firm brown legs go up together, white ankle socks, brown sandals, pointed upwards, and as she got it going back went her head, silky golden hair falling straight like water to the muddy patch of earth between the iron struts. Then up she heaved, legs tucked under the seat, arms curled round the chains, straining forward, head down, and a slight pull of the flowered cotton bodice of her dress where a shadow of roundness was beginning to be apparent. She stood up, she twisted round and accomplished various feats and then couldn't see the person she was demonstrating all this to. She got off and ran across the green calling Uncle Harry, Uncle Harry. 'I'm here,' he called, stepping from behind the trèe by the swings, and as she ran toward him he caught her by the arms and twirled her round at the height of his shoulder.

'You must be very strong, Uncle Harry,' she said when she got her breath back. 'Daddy says I'm too big for him to do that now.'

'Well, I am quite strong. He's right, you are getting big. How old are you now?

'I'm eleven and two months and three weeks.'

'My, no wonder you're too big to be pushed on the swings.'

'Oh, but I like being pushed as well,' she said. Perhaps he had been bored just watching her and had really wanted to push her all the time. 'You can push me if you like.'

She got back on to the swing and settled her dress and smiled back at him with a demure little smile. 'You're not really my uncle, are you, Uncle Harry? I mean, like Uncle John and Aunty Charmian, who are my Daddy's brother and sister?'

'Not quite as much as they are. But, well, sort of. Ready?'

'Ready.'

'Let's go then' and he gave gentle firm pushes so that she went evenly and each time the straight neat back in the fresh cotton, and the little firm bottom sitting still in the middle of the seat, and the shapely warm-looking neck where the hair fell away from it, was very near to him, but only for a moment as it swung away, then back to within his reach, then out again.

'Do you want to go higher? Shall I push harder?'

She woke from her trance of pleasure. 'Yes, harder. Hard as you like' and this time joined in, bending forward and back. She was going very high now so that the seat came up almost on a level with the top. It hung up there for a moment before it dashed down, twisting slightly. So he thought he ought to stop and let it go slower. But she was caught up in the excitement now and when she realised he had stood back to let it sink called

'No, don't stop, Uncle Harry. I'm not frigh-tened. Go on. Don't stop. Higher, Uncle Harry; swing me higher. *High*er.'

# Author's Note

At first glance this book might seem unconventional in its use of verse and prose. Mixing forms, however, is an old practice. Opinions change about what is suitable for verse presentation, what for prose. We are quite used to Shakespeare bringing in a funny man to do a bit of prose rambling among the verse-speaking characters, and to protagonists in an opera or musical breaking from recitative into a duet and then into a dance. Music hall and its modern TV descendant depends on the variety of a succession of acts.

In my poetry I have been interested in using the voices of characters to tell their own stories, but in this book I wanted to extend the range. I have reversed the more usual choice of prose for the argument and verse for heightening of atmosphere (as seen, for instance, in Boethius' *Consolation of Philosophy*). In my account of Demeter's loss and retrieval of her daughter the story-line goes through the verse. At certain points in the verse account there are groups of short prose pieces apparently set in modern times. These do not so much tell separate stories as reinforce the stage the narrative has got to, so that when Demeter is in despair at her brother Hades taking Persephone to his kingdom, the prose descriptions are of death, desertion and darkness. But when it is known that Persephone will after all be released and will return to us for part of the year, the same sorts of events are related with a good outcome: the woman does not miscarry, the sick person gets better, the child survives.

The suggestion is not only that every disaster has its counter-part in its due season but the more fatalistic one that without the time in the Underworld, without surrender to the powers of darkness, without loss, there can be no birth or fruition: no winter – no summer. This is obvious agriculturally and the very ancient story of the two Goddesses developed from the primitive Greek attempt to explain the workings of good and evil in the world, and to some extent to direct them.

For the early Greeks the dark powers of the spirit world were part of the same force as the helpful Goddesses of Spring and

Harvest. Who has power over death has power over life. They were not separate humanised characters as they became later in the Homeric presentations of the Olympian deities. Hecate, Demeter, Persephone were different aspects, different functions, of the one power. They are all one in the way that the ear of golden corn at harvest *is* the green spear of barley breaking the cold clod, and again *is* the new seed to be put into the ground. Persephone rules the Kingdom of the Dead and she is the frail new birth. She was one of the most powerful figures whose aid humans invoked in their actions to propitiate the wronged ghosts who might otherwise throw their baleful influence on human life.

J.J.

# ⌐CHALLENGING FICTION⌐

### Angela Carter
## Come unto these Yellow Sands

Four radio plays by novelist Angela Carter, one to pictures by the mad painter Richard Dadd.

### B.S. Johnson
## House Mother Normal

Anthony Burgess called B.S. Johnson 'the only British author with the guts to reassess the novel form, extend its scope and still work in a recognisable fictional tradition'. *House Mother Normal* was his fifth and finest novel.

### Shena Mackay
## An Advent Calendar

'Shena Mackay's talent is to put the ruth back into ruthless rhymes. Her novels are visions of universal anguish . . . Funny, terrifying, and written by an angel'
– BRIGID BROPHY

### Eva Figes
## Days

'*Days* has a kind of violent stillness, great turbulence beneath a surface calm . . .It's extraordinary how much this gifted writer manages to pack into her austere frame' – *Guardian*

### David Constantine
## Davies

Davies was famous for a moment in 1911 when Home Secretary Winston Churchill raised his case in the House of Commons. But who was Davies? In this fictionalised account of a lifelong petty criminal, Constantine unravels the mystery of a shadowy loner caught in a vicious circle of self-perpetuating crime.

*For a complete list of Bloodaxe publications write to: Bloodaxe Books Ltd, P.O. Box 1SN, Newcastle upon Tyne NE99 1SN.*

# BLOODAXE BOOKS

# BLOODAXE BOOKS

POETRY WITH AN EDGE

## HART CRANE
## Complete Poems

One of America's most important poets. Lowell called Crane 'the Shelley of my age' and 'the great poet of that generation'. This new *Complete Poems*, based on Brom Weber's definitive 1966 edition, has 22 additional poems. *Sunday Times* Paperback of the Year.

## JENI COUZYN (editor)
## The Bloodaxe Book of Contemporary Women Poets*

Large selections – with essays on their work – by eleven leading British poets: Sylvia Plath, Stevie Smith, Kathleen Raine, Fleur Adcock, Anne Stevenson, Elaine Feinstein, Elizabeth Jennings, Jenny Joseph, Denise Levertov, Ruth Fainlight and Jeni Couzyn. Illustrated with photographs of the writers.

## FRANCES HOROVITZ
## Collected Poems*

'She has perfect rhythm, great delicacy and a rather Chinese yet very locally British sense of landscape . . . her poetry does seem to me to approach greatness' – PETER LEVI

## MIROSLAV HOLUB
## On the Contrary and Other Poems*
### *Translated by Ewald Osers*

Miroslav Holub is Czechoslovakia's most important poet, and also one of her leading scientists. He was first introduced to English readers with a Penguin *Selected Poems* in 1967. This book presents a decade of new work. 'One of the half dozen most important poets writing anywhere' – TED HUGHES. 'One of the sanest voices of our time' – A. ALVAREZ

## PETER DIDSBURY
## The Butchers of Hull

'Peter Didsbury is a clever and original poet . . . He can be simultaneously knowing and naive, wittily deflationary yet alive to every leap of the post-Romantic eye . . . a soaring, playful imagination . . . I suspect that he is the best new poet that the excellent Bloodaxe Books have yet published' – William Scammell, TIMES LITERARY SUPPLEMENT

## KEN SMITH
## The Poet Reclining*

Ken Smith is a major British poet. *The Poet Reclining* was internationally acclaimed: 'A poet of formidable range and strength' (CHICAGO SUN-TIMES) . . . 'With Ken Smith we expect excellence . . . his achievement is remarkable' (SCOTSMAN) . . . 'Formidable, brilliant' (CITY LIMITS) . . . 'Compulsive, impressive' (LITERARY REVIEW) . . . 'Brilliant, impressive' (TLS).

## SEAN O'BRIEN
## The Indoor Park

Sean O'Brien won a Somerset Maugham Award and a Poetry Book
Society Recommendation for *The Indoor Park*, his first collection of poems.
'I would back O'Brien as one of our brightest poetic hopes for the Eighties'
— Peter Porter, OBSERVER

## DAVID CONSTANTINE
## Watching for Dolphins

Constantine's second book won him the Alice Hunt Bartlett Prize in 1984,
and with it the judges' praise for 'a generous, self-aware sensuality which
he can express in a dazzling variety of tones on a wide range of themes'.
'His imagination moves gracefully within the classical precincts of the pure
lyric . . . There are some very beautiful poems in this collection'
— George Szirtes, LITERARY REVIEW

## PAUL HYLAND
## The Stubborn Forest

'Paul Hyland has never written much like anyone else' (THE CUT). 'His is a
rugged, hewn, earthbound poetry' (ENCOUNTER). 'Hyland's work has the
character of primitive sculpture . . . an impressive, memorable and
powerful talent' (NORTH). 'This is work of power and subtlety . . . *The
Stubborn Forest* is a strikingly impressive achievement' (ANGLO-WELSH
REVIEW). Winner of the 1985 Alice Hunt Bartlett Prize.

## MARIN SORESCU
## Selected Poems
### *Translated by Michael Hamburger*

'Sorescu is already being tipped as a future Nobel prizewinner. His poems,
however, have crowned him with the only distinction that matters. If you
don't read any other new book of poetry this year, read this one'
— William Scammell, SUNDAY TIMES

## JOHN CASSIDY
## Night Cries

'John Cassidy has produced a strong, delicate volume of nature poetry in
*Night Cries*, sensitively alert to the mysterious unpredictability of natural
things, lucid and tenaciously detailed . . . A kind of *Lyrical Ballads* of our
time' — Terry Eagleton, STAND. Poetry Book Society Recommendation.

*Asterisked titles are available in hardback and paperback. Other books are in
paperback only.

*For a complete list of Bloodaxe publications, write to:*
**Bloodaxe Books Ltd, P.O. Box 1SN,
Newcastle upon Tyne NE99 1SN.**

Writers published by

# BLOODAXE BOOKS

FLEUR ADCOCK
MARTIN BOOTH
BASIL BUNTING
ANGELA CARTER
JOHN CASSIDY
EILÉAN NÍ CHUILLEANÁIN
DAVID CONSTANTINE
JENI COUZYN
HART CRANE
PETER DIDSBURY
MAURA DOOLEY
JOHN DREW
HELEN DUNMORE
DOUGLAS DUNN
STEPHEN DUNSTAN
G.F. DUTTON
STEVE ELLIS
RUTH FAINLIGHT
EVA FIGES
TONY FLYNN
PAMELA GILLILAN
ANDREW GREIG
TONY HARRISON
MIROSLAV HOLUB
FRANCES HOROVITZ
DOUGLAS HOUSTON
PAUL HYLAND

KATHLEEN JAMIE
B.S. JOHNSON
JENNY JOSEPH
BRENDAN KENNELLY
DENISE LEVERTOV
S.J. LITHERLAND
EDNA LONGLEY
SHENA MACKAY
JILL MAUGHAN
VINCENT MORRISON
SEAN O'BRIEN
JOHN OLDHAM
TOM PAULIN
IRINA RATUSHINSKAYA
CAROL RUMENS
DAVID SCOTT
JAMES SIMMONS
MATT SIMPSON
KEN SMITH
EDITH SÖDERGRAN
MARIN SORESCU
LEOPOLD STAFF
R.S. THOMAS
TOMAS TRANSTRÖMER
MARINA TSVETAYEVA
ALAN WEARNE
NIGEL WELLS

*For a complete list of poetry, fiction, literature, drama and photography books
published by Bloodaxe, please write to:*
**Bloodaxe Books Ltd, P.O. Box 1SN,
Newcastle upon Tyne NE99 1SN.**